From Start-up to Success:
The Xiecheng Management Story

Xiecheng Management Team

SPM
南方出版传媒
广东经济出版社

Paths International Ltd

Preface

"What are the primary conditions for deciding the success of a start-up enterprise?" Once, Shi Yuzhu was asked about this question.

He answered, "There are three preconditions—a good team, a good product and a good plan."

Master Shi thinks that a good team is the primary condition to start up an enterprise. Coincidentally, Bill Gates has a similar saying which goes like "This is no perfect man, but only a perfect team." Great minds think alike.

There are around 2.5 million private-owned enterprises in China, many of which are formed with partnerships. Among so many entrepreneurial teams, one particularly stands out like the Seven Northern Stars in the cosmos that areso bright, so clear, and so prominent.

It is the "Shanghai Ctrip".

We can't deny that this entrepreneurial team is a powerful one because the four partners are all postgraduate students from top-ranking universities—three of them are from Shanghai Jiaotong University, and one from Yale.

We can't deny that this entrepreneurial team is a powerful one because it started with the seed money of merely one million, and then it coaxed its investors into investing additional capital to the amount of 18 million USD.

We can't deny that this entrepreneurial team is a powerful one because it made two companies go public within seven years, both of which have brought in enviable profits.

......

It is not that there lacks entrepreneurial teams in China, but that there lacks invincible ones like the "Shanghai Ctrip Four". Some of the teams become dismermbered and collapse even before getting on the right track.

It has a lot to do with the team-work consciousness of the Chinese people that make those teams collapse right after their births. There goes a saying that best fits this situation, "One Chinese makes a dragon, while three Chinese make a worm." Another saying goes like, "The way a nation's people entertain themselves reflects the way they cooperate with each other." For example, the Japanese like playing Weiqi, which says that they are willing to make partial sacrifices for the overall interests and the ultimate triumph; the Americans like playing bridge, which means that they can work closely with their partners to defeat the other two competitors; the Chinese like playing Majiang, which represents that they like to fight as a loner—they keep a close eye on their previous, next and opponent players, and if they can't win, neither can any of the rest of co-players.

What would it take to make a great team? A British team expert Dr. Belbin makes a conclusion that it is the team's goal and the self-identification of the team members that are important. That is to say, only with a clear goal and a precise orientation could a team solve its conflicts and execute its plan.

There is always a way to success and a reason for failure. There is got to be some points that others can learn from "Shanghai Ctrip" now that it is so excellent. Is this team really so powerful? Now let's take up a microscope and scalpel to dissect and analyze the following questions about it

How did they meet each other among the sea of people? Was it a geographic reason, a relationship reason, a business reason, or another reason that prompted their gathering together and this splendid and inspiring career later?

For what reason did they enter this business? Was it just a moment of over heat in the head, or had they done specific market researches in the first place?

Did they have a clear direction when the company first started? How did they make the company successfully transformed when they met with obstructions along the road, or when they realized that they were far away from their goal?

Since money is always a pain in the heart of entrepreneurial teams, how did they manage to win compassion from the capital market? Was it because of the perfect teamwork and the business model, or the brilliantly persuasive and bluffing quality of one of the team members?

In order to make their own company grow rapidly, did they feel around in the market all by themselves, or through merger and acquisition of other people's mature businesses?

The Ctrip team has finally succeeded. The question is: does this case represent the generality or the particularity? Does this case tell us that life can be predesigned, and that the success of a career can be a complete reservation?

Let's read the following stories in the first place!

Contents

Chapter I   A Reverie Team / 1

Quotations / 1
Reflections on the business market 1-5   / 1

A fable / 1
V-shaped wild geese fleet   / 1

Text / 2
Section I   The enthusiastic entrepreneur Ji Qi   / 3
  The boy from a poor family who ventured into Shanghai   / 3
  Growing-up with confusion as a new bird in the workplace   / 5
  Pursuit of an American dream across the Atlantic Ocean   / 8
  The choice of entrepreneuring and meeting new partners   / 10
Section II   The computer genius Liang Jianzhang   / 12
  The genius who was special   / 12
  A transformation from technology to marketing   / 14
  The plan for making a travel website specifically   / 15
Section III   The master of capital Shen Nanpeng   / 17
  The prodigy from Zhejiang   / 17
  The job in an investment bank upon graduation   / 18
  Agreement on the golden value of website   / 20
Section IV   The authority of travelling—Wang Zhenghua   / 22
  The leader of travelling business—Chunqiu   / 22
  The relationship not meant to be   / 23
Section V   The expert of management Fan Min   / 25
  The bitter-sweet years   / 25
  The career in a state-owned enterprise   / 26
  The new home Ctrip   / 27

Summary / 28

Ⅰ. The elements in an entrepreneur's development / 29

Ⅱ. A common model of an efficient organization / 30

Ⅲ. 5P elements of a team / 31

Application / 33

    Ⅰ. Is he an ideal partner? / 33

    Ⅱ. Who would you choose? / 33

Test / 34

Choices for the answer / 34

Chapter Ⅱ   Enterprising and Financing / 35

Quotations / 35

    Reflections on the business market 1-5 / 35

A fable / 35

    The hare and the tortoise / 35

Text / 37

    Section Ⅰ   Positioning of the website / 37

        Fan Min's and Shen Nanpeng's viewpoints / 37

        The decision made by Liang Jianzhang / 38

    Section Ⅱ   The first round of financing / 39

        Ji Qi's pioneering / 39

        Making the first acquaintance of a venture capital investor Zhang Suyang / 41

        The second meeting with Zhang Suyang / 44

        The failure of the road show / 46

    Section Ⅲ   The second round of financing / 48

        Success of the second round of financing / 48

        The start of the "money-burning" competition / 51

        The continuance not to earn profits / 53

Summary / 54

    Ⅰ. How can a team get through an unrest period? / 54

    Ⅱ. Discovery of the opportunities in the market / 55

    Ⅲ. How to negotiate on financing with venture investors? / 58

Application / 60

    Ⅰ. Should I enter the market of cactus drinks? / 60

    Ⅱ. How much shares should an one-hundred-million RMB investment take up? / 61

Chapter Ⅲ Transformation and Purchase / 62

Quotations / 62
Reflections on the business market 1-5 / 62

A fable / 62
The bees and flies fleeing for their lives / 62

Text / 63
Section Ⅰ The trend in websites / 63
The first one to try tomato—Info Highway / 63
The two models of making money / 65
One example of a business model—Sina. com / 66
Section Ⅱ Decision on transformation / 68
Which product is promising? / 68
The most profitable service-hotel reservation / 69
The shortcut of purchasing / 71
The companies which were the not bad / 72
Section Ⅲ Start of the purchasing / 76
The real difficulty in negotiation / 76
Wu Hai's being moved / 78
Wang Shengli's hesitation / 79
The real number one Ctrip / 81

Summary / 83
Ⅰ. The formation of the team spirit / 83
Ⅱ. The importance of market research / 85
Ⅲ. The benefit of market positioning / 87
Ⅳ. The rapid growth brought about by purchasing / 88
Ⅴ. Serious consideration on share holdings / 90

Application / 92
Ⅰ. Which one should be the leading product? / 92
Ⅱ. How to build the selling-point of the goat milk? / 92

Chapter Ⅳ Growth by leaps and bounds / 94

Quotations / 94
Reflections on the business market 1-5 / 94

A fable / 94

The chuck of the hen   / 94

Text / 95

Section Ⅰ   What have the rivals done wrong?   / 95

The cause of the leading   / 95

Tourism websites' unawareness of how to make money   / 96

The detours Elong had taken   / 100

Failure of travel agencies to break the bottleneck   / 103

The aborted Landlord Card   / 104

The failure to follow the time of the room reservation centers   / 107

Section Ⅱ   What had Ctrip done right?   / 108

The competition on tour tracks.   / 108

Ctrip's focus on room reservation   / 109

A good stuff-the Ctrip Card   / 111

The mad card dispatcher   / 113

The miracle   / 114

The further success of purchasing Coast Ticket   / 115

Summary / 117

Ⅰ. The four principles of founding a team   / 117

Ⅱ. The important of sales promotion   / 121

Application / 129

Ⅰ. Where and how to hand them out?   / 129

Ⅱ. Which distribution and promotion method to choose?   / 129

Chapter Ⅴ   Listing and Monetizing / 130

Quotations / 130

Reflections on the business market 1-5   / 130

A fable / 130

The ideal of the eagle   / 130

Text / 131

Section Ⅰ   Liang Jianzhang's efforts on internal improvement / 131

The work sharing scheme for the leaders   / 131

The leading of technology   / 133

The top-ranking service   / 137

Striving for perfection   / 141

Section Ⅱ   The recovery of the Internet   / 144

The Internet company saved by text messages / 144

The popularity of online games / 146

Section Ⅲ   Ctrip's successful listing / 148

Which company gets listed first? / 148

Who could tell the best story? / 149

The wave of listing brought by Ctrip / 152

Summary / 153

Ⅰ. Roles of the team / 153

Ⅱ. The wings on creation by technology / 158

Applications / 159

Ⅰ. Why wasn't Huawei listed? / 159

Ⅱ. How to achieve seamless joints? / 160

Appendix Ⅰ   Teaching Materials of team management / 160

Appendix Ⅱ   Answers to application questions / 179

Appendix Ⅲ   Development History of Ctrip(milestones) / 198

Bibliography / 200

Chapter I
A Reverie Team

Three people gathered together when Ctrip was initially founded—the businessowner Ji Qi, the technician guy Liang Jianzhang, and the investment guy Shen Nanpeng. Still, a person familiar with tourism was absent, who was regarded as "a page missing from an encyclopedia". Finally, with every painstaking effort he made, Ji Qi found Fan Min who knew well about the tourism business. The four of them got together and named themselves "A Reverie Team".

Quotations
Reflections on the business market 1-5
To make a fortune, one should obtain business. But how to obtain business? One should go and secure big clients-the first step: find the right path; the second step: hold on to it.

— reflection on Ji Qi's first temporary working experience

If you've got talent, show it to me; if you have no talent, then work harder; if you've got no talent and yet don't work hard, piss off!

— reflection on Ji Qi's second temporary working experience

Start with working for successful people, then cope with soon-to-be-successful people, and finally make those who will succeed in the future work for you.

— reflection on Liang Jianzhang's business stories

Everything begins with thinking; every change is made in a jiffy; every road has been designed; and every goal can be realized.

— reflection on Shen Nanpeng's business stories

Only when a seed is willing to be buried under the earth, could it burst out; only when one is willing to start from the lowly, could he reach the peak.

— reflection on Fan Min's business stories

A fable
V-shaped wild geese fleet
Flocks of wild geese fly from the North to the South always in a V shape. Why?

After many years' research, scientists have discovered that it has something to do with the habits of geese.

When the leading goose flips its wings, it produces an upward force for the following geese. When the whole fleet is flying in a V shape, they can fly extra 71% of the distance compared to that when each one of them is flying alone.

When one goose is falling behind, it meets the resistance so instantly that it will fly right back to the fleet to borrow the upward force from companions.

When the leading goose is exhausted, another one will replace it in the V-shaped fleet. Geese flying behind will whistle to encourage those in the front to maintain the shape.

If one goose is sick or shot down, another two geese will leave the fleet and follow the former leader to provide help and protection. They will keep company with it until it can fly again or dies. Then they will start over again all on their own or join another goose fleet to catch up with to their original fleet.

This story tells us,

(1) People heading to the same direction and having group awareness success more easily.

(2) You will grow up faster in a team.

(3) Team members can take turns to lead, but not necessarily every one of them will have a chance to do so.

(4) Team spirit is shown in neither giving up on dreams nor abandoning partners.

Text

It is still vaguely remembered that on the night of February 22nd, 1999, a group of young man gathered for dinner in a large room inside a private residential house, when it was shortly after the Spring Festival. Among them, several were postgraduate students from Shanghai Jiaotong University. They were enjoying the meal whilst chatting to their heart's content. Though it was still winterish, and heavy wind blew outside the window, they were excited and discussing with each other enthusiastically. They talked about the Internet, Internet economy, IT companies in the U. S. , to the current situation for IT in China, NASDAQ and IPO, and then to the entrepreneurship. It was already three o'clock in the morning, but they had no intention to sleep and became more and more excited chatting to one another.

One young man among them with a slightly bigger head and a baby face said, "If we could found an Internet company now, it would definitely become promising. "

To follow him, another young man with closely cropped hair and glasses said, "Sure! I have been having this idea for four years. I just couldn't find a better point to get in. "

"Yes! It seems a good idea to make a website. But what kind of website are we talking about?" A slim young man, whose hair all combed to the back, interrupted.

Thereupon, they listed dozens of ideas and discussed about every choices from portal websites to professional websites and e-commerce websites. As soon as they sensed no promise in a choice, they'd stop it and turn to another one. In the end, all of them focused on tourism websites. The young man with closely cropped hair, the owner of this house, concluded, "Let's make a tourism website. It does not only fit the current economic level, but also has everything to do with the lives of ordinary people. Besides, it's easier to realize e-commerce."

The next day when they woke up, some had already forgotten about their discussion the former night. Only three of the dozen of young men truly worked together on their idea they finalized that night. They were Ji Qi with closely cropped hair, Liang Jianzhang with a slightly bigger head and Shen Nanpeng with his hair all combed to the back.

Section Ⅰ The enthusiastic entrepreneur Ji Qi

The boy from a poor family who ventured into Shanghai

The story begins with Ji Qi because it was him who gathered those young men that night for the "IT Entrepreneurial Seminar".

Ji Qi was born in a poor rural family in Nantong, Jaingsu Province in 1966. The past several generations of this family were all farmers, so few of them received proper education. The biggest wish from Ji Qi's parents was for him to finish high school. They never expected him to go to college, not to mention starting his own business. But it was not what was on Ji Qi's mind. Something happened to him when he was in junior school and had such a big influence on him that he could still remember it many years later. It was a stormy noon with heavy snow. Ji walked more than one hour home for lunch, only to be told by his mother that they forgot to leave anything for him because they did not have enough food. Ji had to walk back to school with an empty stomach. On the way back to school, Ji Qi wiped off the tears on his face and swore to himself, "I must study hard to change my own fate and not to live like my forefathers anymore as farmers who could only work in the field under scorching sun."

The result was worth the efforts. In the year 1985, Ji Qi entered Shanghai Jiaotong University with the second best grade in the examination in the whole town. The day they heard about the news, Ji's mother asked, "Does it mean you don't have to pay for trains if you go to Shanghai Jiaotong University (Jiaotong literally translates to transportation,)?" Ji Qi answered, "Pretty much like that." In fact, when he was enrolled by this university, he didn't know much about it. And it was only because he saw the brochure about it before his college entrance exam.

To choose a major, Ji Qi asked his head teacher for advice, "What do you think of the two majors, automation or computer science? I think they are trendy." His head teacher replied, "Don't apply for those unpromising majors. Engineering mechanics is good for you. Earthworks would bring you lots of benefits from the labor contractors if you are good at it."

"Oh! Then this one is a good major! A very good one! " Ji Qi followed his head teacher's advice all because that money was everything for a young man coming from a poor family who was eager to change the situation.

Ji Qi took a steamship from Nantong Port to Shanghai, beginning his trip of seeking knowledge.

He could not sleep at all that night, especially before daybreak of the next day. Ji Qi was astounded to see the bright neon lights at the Shanghai beach when he got up at the Sixteen Pu Wharf. Ji Qi felt confused and lost. He shuffled with his three suitcases along the bustling streets all by himself, not knowing where to go at that moment. He could vaguely remember hearing a song from a shop on the street, a familiar song named "I am a wolf from the north" by the famous singer Qi Qin.

Having lived in Shanghai Jiaotong University for a while, Ji Qi, a country boy, realized a gap between him and the city. Before going to the public shower, he asked his classmates, "Should I take a shower by myself, or that we do it together?" His classmates answered, "All together, including our teachers. "

Another example of the gap was about the raining weather. Whenever it rained, he would be wearing a pair of high-cut rain boots, whereas people in Shanghai either wore fashionable rain boots or did not wear them at all.

Later, Ji Qi came to know that his major, engineering mechanics, required a lower score in Shanghai Jiaotong University than other majors, while automation and computer science was the hottest and highest requiring majors. What disappointed him the most was that engineering mechanics had nothing to do with earthworks because it was about force on submarines and the take-off speed of missiles.

Bored by his major in addition to his self-abasement, he felt more inspired to seek for knowledge. During his four years in the university, he spent most of his time in the library reading about philosophy, history, and biography of Mao Zedong. He had not only learned knowledge from his major, but also thought through a question-

One's life is too short compared to the whole world. Some lives are dull and ordinary, while others are great and magnificent. One cannot extend the length of his life but can broaden its width.

In 1989, Ji Qi was graduated from his university. This year's political crisis affected job assignment of all university students. In addition, his major was not in wide application, so it was very hard for him to find a job. Failed to secure a job in Shanghai, Ji Qi had to go back to his hometown Nantong. After begging and bribing decision makers with wines and cigarettes, he, as a recent graduate for the current year, was finally accepted by Nantong No. 2 Designing Institute.

However, Ji Qi hesitated the day before going to work. He whispered to himself, "I spared no effort to go from the village to Shanghai, and now I can't stay in the big city. Didn't all my efforts end up in vain?" After balancing, he decided to go back to his university and applied for the postgraduate examination. This time, he applied for another major-robot in the Mechanical Engineering Department of Shanghai Jiaotong University.

In 1992, Deng Xiaoping made a speech after his South Tour, "The planned economy does not necessarily equal to Socialism, as Capitalism has plans too; the market economy does not equal to Capitalism, as Socialism has markets too."

The South Tour Speech greatly inspired the Chinese's enthusiasm for doing business, and Ji Qi was one of them. He opened a computer company together with his classmates.

As a major in robots, Ji Qi was among the earliest to know about computers, so he knew the huge profits from selling computers-thousands, or even tens of thousands RMB can be earned from selling one single computer. He could not wait to learn how to assemble computers. When first started, he did not even know how to initialize a computer. But he had a determined mind not to lose faith until reaching the goal, and quickly got command of the computer hardware and software, and even the networking. Because of the good timing, and his solid knowledge of computer science, his company soon started to make profits. Over a few months, Ji Qi and his girlfriend had already had tens of thousands RMB saved up. He became a "rich man" in his university.

That same year, Ji Qi was about to become a postgraduate student. One day, his dean had a conversation with him and tried to persuade him into staying in the school. This elder man was sitting in between two wooden tables, laid on which were all kinds of papers and notebooks. The tables were especially dirty with numerous ink stains-red, blue, black inks, which looked very unpleasant to eyes. Ji Qi though, "If I stay, how many years would it take for me to become someone in his position? What if I would still be like him thirty or forty years later? Would that kind of life be meaningful?"

Growing-up with confusion as a new bird in the workplace

Ji Qi thought it would be interesting to work in a foreign company. But it was not easy. When the household chemicals giant P&G was offering jobs in Shanghai, more than a hundred students were competing fiercely with each other for a few vacancies. P&G was offering a very tempting salary—3000 RMB per month for new employees.

Only four people survived the competition rounds after another, and Ji Qi was one of them.

Unfortunately, P&G did not have personnel quota, which meant if Ji Qi wanted to work in P&G, he would have to change his registered residence from Shanghai to Nanhai, Guangdong.

Between a job offer from P&G and the registered residence in Shanghai, Ji Qi chose the latter. He was thinking about settling his registered residence in any Shanghai company by chance.

Therefore, randomly he found a company named Shanghai Computer Service Company. This company came with a splendid background—its mother company was Changjiang Computer Corporation. Ji Qi looked at the shabby office and felt very uncomfortable. He never even considered staying in the company in the long run. He just planned to use it as a means to solve his registered residence problem and then would walk away.

On his first day at work, he had himself coolly styled-he held a cell phone as big as a brick in his hand, and pinned a wal*km*an round his waist. He patted his boss Hu Bangyi on the shoulder and said in an arrogant tone, "Boss Hu, I won't be working here for long. The salary offered here means nothing to me. But, it's OK. We can make friends with each other. Just a tip in ahead, I'll muddle along for a few days before I leave."

In a state-owned enterprise, few leaders could put up with a new comer speaking in such a tone. Hu Yibang had great tolerance. He did not get angry at all, instead, he said to Ji QI seriously, "Son, you are just like a younger version of me, vigorous and capable. But I have to warn you that you need to qualify for being a person before doing things. Personal quality always comes first before your personal product. What you've just said won't work, which could only make you a trival person. And you can never make a big difference."

Ji Qi did not hear a single word of what his boss had just said. When he first entered this company in March, 1992, he could have never expected himself to have spent two and a half year in here, not to mention remembering these words Hu Bangyi had told him many years later.

What changed Ji Qi's idea of "muddling along for a few days before leaving"? On one hand, Ji Qi realized that he was lacking of so many things; on the other, the reform in the company offered a platform for Ji Qi and his genius.

The so called service company actually was inclining towards technology while it didn't show power in marketing and selling. In 1992, Changjiang Computer Company was taking a reform-all the subsidiary companies were to take responsibilities for their own profits and losses. On hearing the news, some employees jumped to other subsidiary companies. There were only seven or eight technicians and three or four salesmen left over.

On a regular meeting, all were discussing about what to do next and everybody showed very low morale. Only one was not destructed by this and believed they were not meant to fail, and it was Ji Qi. He thought, "A few months ago, I could make money by selling computers riding a bike. How come that so many people gathering together could not make any money?"

Thus, Ji Qi suggested on the meeting, "Now that we are already stuck in this situation, why don't we put up a fight? We are strong in technology and that is why we should take advantage of it to do bigger and better projects instead of competing with other companies on selling computers. "

Hu Yibang was very glad to hear this and promoted Ji Qi as a project manager immediately in the meeting. Actually, it was a position with no real power and leads not a single employee.

Having no idea that it was harder than reaching the sky to lead a big project, Ji Qi set off by bike towards his big project on the street all by himself.

He wandered and wandered along the streets. Suddenly he realized something —securities companies would probably be a potential target of his "big project". It was a time when securities companies were booming in Shanghai, and many of these companies needed computers and networks after settling down in this metropolis.

The best way to win over these companies was to win over the Shanghai Stock Exchange in the first place. Back then, China Securities Regulatory Commission had not been founded yet, and most of its work was done by Shanghai Stock Exchange back then. Any company must go through Shanghai Stock Exchange to enter the securities market in Shanghai.

However, the door didn't easily open for him in Shanghai Stock Exchange. Its office was located at 19th, Huangpu Road. It was a building with a neoclassical Victorian Baroque style. Everyone worked in the building sent out a noble scent. In their eyes, only people from big international companies such as HP and IBM were qualified to enter this building. Changjiang Computer Service Company dared to send such an inexperienced child to them! It must be kidding!

Having made several direct contacts with the exchange and being rejected again and again, Ji Qi had no choice but to "save the nation through a curve". After inquiring about, he finally met a former schoolmate from Shanghai Jiaotong University who was working in Shanghai Stock Exchange through whom he enter the gate of Shanghai Stock Exchange in the end.

Two months later, Ji Qi successfully expanded his business in the securities market in Shanghai. Following this, he signed contracts with influential companies and organizations such as the Head Office of Bank of Communications, National People's Congress of Shanghai. He even got the dealership qualification for large corporations like Oracle. Later, Boss Hu assigned an assistant to him, who completed the department which consisted of only two employees with Ji Qi. However, they gained quite considerable achievements that took up 80% of the company's total sales volume and profits. Ji Qi alone could make profits as high as several millions RMB in a year.

Ji Qi was unable to leave the company once his business had started to grow. Two years had passed before he realized that his business got bigger, business-expansion wilder, and job-position higher.

Ji Qi considered these two years as his first experience of entrepreneurship, during which he had learnt about three things,

1. Entrepreneurship required making do with whatever is available-cook with whatever material there was in the basket;

2. Friends made in business would come in handy when he needed help during the beginning of his business;

3. He began to understand the things his boss said to him before. When he finished his postgraduate education, he thought he knew everything, whereas he gradually realized that he actually knew nothing, especially nothing about how to be a nice person. He might have been stronger at the technical stuff, English, and sales than his boss, but he had neither clue of how to lead people nor how to update business relationships to friendly relationships.

Pursuit of the American dream across the Atlantic Ocean

With his position getting higher, Ji Qi sensed that there was no more room of development for him in the company any more-he was already the second in command in the company and the only way for him to get a higher position was to replace Hu Yibang, which could never happen to someone like him who respect the mentoring relationship too much to damage it.

Therefore, he decided that it was time to leave the company.

At that time, it was not easy for an employee working in a state-owned enterprise to leave at his free will, let alone that Ji Qi was already the core of the company and had got an apartment distributed to him by the company as welfare housing.

Still, Ji Qi thought up of an excuse that no one could reject-his wife was living in the U. S. and he had to visit her.

Finally, Ji Qi left the company. In September 1994, Ji Qi left for America and had 10, 000 American USD in his pocket.

The first thing he did when he arrived in America was looking for a schoolmate of his who was working in Oracle. It was on an ordinary weekend day that Ji Qi met his schoolmate at the Oracle Headquarter whom he had not seen for a long time. They were chatting happily before his schoolmate suddenly said excitedly that he had something to show to Ji Qi. Hence, he brought Ji Qi in front of a computer and connected it to the Internet. Back then, they used the early version of Mosaic browser and browsed Yahoo. Yahoo was still in its infancy stage and reacted very slowly, so they had to have some coffee while waiting for the webpage to open up. They referred to a picture of Mona Lisa that showed itself on the screen line by line. Ji Qi thought this was incredible. He looked at the computer screen in a trance and roughly came to realize that there was coming a chance to change many people's fate and probably to change more people's lives. That day, he spent the entire afternoon in front of his schoolmate's computer until dinner, and then he left reluctantly.

This trip to America was an eye-opener for him. It was not only the first time he made an acquaintance with the Internet, but also the first time when he truly understood the luxury life people were living in western countries.

Ji Qi had stayed in America for a while until he came to realize that he could no long live on there. First, he had no money to do any business; secondly, nobody in America would recognize his post-graduation diploma issued by Shanghai Jiaotong University. Thanks to his computer knowledge, he got a job opportunity in a computer company offered by a businessman from Taiwan.

Ji Qi met a bunch of people from Taiwan in his work and most of them suggested that he should go back to Mainland China because they thought Mainland China tomorrow could become as prosperous as Taiwan at that time. According to their experiences in Taiwan, at that time, people who had education background in America would be very popular in both business and political fields. On the contrary, most of those people from Taiwan who had chosen to stay in the US could only work as obscure clerks.

Ji Qi also realized that in America, most opportunities there had already been taken a-way. He had no chance to succeed unless he had some innovative skills.

Ji Qi decided to go back to China after living in America for one year. This really con-fused his schoolmate who was working in Oracle, and he asked, "It was not easy for you to come to America, nor to have had a stable life here. Why are you going back to China?"

Ji Qi responded, "I can already see where the road you are taking leads to-you would make 100,000 USD this year and 120,000 USD next year, and then you would buy a house and car, and hang out with your wife and children on weekends. But I could no longer be in-terested once I get to see where my future is. I want to live a more affluent and challenging life. "

In 1995, he went back to China.

After he had returned to Shanghai from the America, Ji Qi was full of passion and ready to fight for his own business.

Just at that time, he received a call from the manager of Beijing Zhonghua Yinghua Smart System Company. This manager used to be a client of Ji Qi's when he was working in Shanghai Computer Service Company. He was in Shanghai on a business trip and called Ji Qi to company him in Shanghai that night.

They hung out in a compartment in the New Huaihai Entertainment Center on Fuxing Middle Road. This manager said to Ji Qi, "Ji Qi, you have just been back from America and currently don't have a job. Why don't you come and work with me?"

"OK! Let's work together!" Ji Qi answered without any hesitation. Ji Qi made his de-cision so quickly because he had already come into contact with the manager long time ago and considered him a decent man. Besides, Zhonghua Yinghua was already famous in the field because it had already had a smart system built up. Most importantly, the manager made an invitation and offered him with partnership, which meant that he treated Ji Qi seriously. Thus, Ji Qi felt obligated to join Zhonghua Yinghua without even knowing about his future position and salary.

Zhonghua Yinghua offered Ji Qi general manager for its Eastern China business region and 100,000 RMB as initial capital. Thereupon, Ji Qi rented a 40-square-meter office in the Brain Research Institute of the Chinese Academy of Siences which was located in 320 Yueyang Road. There, he started hiring people and expanding his business.

There were only a small number of salesmen working with Ji Qi at the beginning, but he had personally trained each one of them into top persuaders. From December 1995 when Shanghai branch was founded to the latter half year of 1997, their contract value had increased from 100,000 RMB to more than 30 million RMB.

Just at that moment, Ji Qi heard a news that the general manager of Zhonghua Yinghua was planning on entering the pharmaceutical industry and selling Zhonghua Yinghua (Zhonghua Yinghua was a joint venture of Zhonghua Company and Yinghua Company) to Sinochem. Ji Qi felt so frustrated to watch the branch company he had personally founded to be sold.

"Don't they just want money? I can afford the money!" Ji Qi went everywhere he could to raise money and even got some from the venture capital firm IDG. To his disappointment, though he wanted to buy Anglo-Smart Systems, Sinochem didn't want to sell it to him.

Ji Qi had to leave there with his team.

He had learnt two things from this experience,

1. Capital was a really powerful thing. A company's owner didn't need to notice you in ahead that he was going to sell his company. Your talent, loyalty, ambition, and ability to make money would become useless compared with a piece of contract of capital transaction.

2. Buying a company was in fact buying its people. Zhonghua Yinghua's Shanghai branch was making profits worthy of millions a year. Ji Qi and his team went away from the company, leaving it no longer able to make such profits.

The choice of entrepreneurship and meeting new partners

Recalling the painful experiences and reflecting upon that, Ji Qi understood one thing-he had to be on his own. In September of 1997, he opened his own company and named it Xiecheng, which was also a smart building business.

Everything went on smoothly of the company's development. There were few clients when it was first started. But Ji Qi called one of his former clients to tell him that he was doing his own business on system integration. This client had a conversation with him face to face. And without a second thought, he had sealed a deal worth more than one million RMB with Ji Qi. After the deal, Ji Qi had a thorough retrospect.

A salesman's moral quality was mostly valued by his clients. A client could refuse to listen to you because he didn't like you; he could also refuse to buy your products because he didn't trust you. If you could gain trust from your clients, they would trust your products.

When he left Zhonghua Yinghua, Ji Qi didn't take any of his business clients from there. He didn't want to leave no room for Zhonghua Yinghua. Instead, he wanted to compete with his former employer in bids fair and square. Once, Xiecheng and Zhonghua Yinghua were both bidding for a comprehensive wiring project of Hualun Mansion in Xu Jiahui. The outcome was that Xiecheng beated Zhonghua Yinghua over specialists' judge and got the project for Hualun Mansion. At that time, comprehensive wiring projects brought great profitability. Out of such a project of one million RMB lump sum, Ji Qi could make profits of 300,000 RMB.

Ji Qi got his other business through friends he met when he was expanding the securities market working in Shanghai Computer Service Company. Those friends brought him quite lots of business contracts as soon as they knew Ji Qi was running his own company company now.

Why were those friends so loyal to him? It was all due to the small convenience Ji Qi brought to them in the past years. Generally, when doing business, few people were willing to do more than what was written in the contracts. Ji Qi had, on his own behalf, helped many securities companies that had bought computers from him to solve some small problems such as a computer crash. Those small favors Ji Qi had done turned into big contracts for him later.

The Shanghai Xiecheng Technology Lt. Company founded in September 1997 had already gained profits of more than one million RMB by the end of that same year. Ji Qi had dug his first bucket of gold.

To make his company more profitable, Ji Qi had tried to do as much business as possible ever since his company was founded. He had done comprehensive wiring, system integration, software development, and even ERP corporate management system projects. In 1998, Xiecheng was appointed as the High and Innovative Technology Company by Shanghai Municipality. Back then, there weren't many private owned high-tech companies granted with such title.

Still, Ji Qi didn't forget about the Internet. While managing Xiecheng, he was also observing the development of the Internet industry in the domestic market. He was pondering on how to realize his Internet dream in China. Ever since he had got to know of the Internet in Oracle, he couldn't get the idea off his mind. And the idea had become stronger and clearer as time went by.

Ji Qi's dream of diving in the Internet had become stronger and stronger especially when there emerged many portal websites in the domestic market in 1998 and Internet was about to reach its highest peak.

However, Ji Qi didn't make any actual move before carefully observing the entire landscape because he hadn't found a good point to cut in yet. He knew very clearly that in the Internet industry, the only choice for him was to make it to the top and ranking second was out of the question. If he had to do it, he had to do it best. So he had to wait for his time patiently.

Later on, once when he was doing ERP consultative subcontracting for Oracle, he met Liang Jianzhang, the Consultative Inspector General of China Region of Oracle. They had a lot in common-they had both studied and lived in Shanghai and America for a while, and they were doing similar business. Hence, they became good friends very soon and used to drink together.

In March, 1999, Liang Jianzhang and Ji Qi were in a restaurant serving Shanghai Cuisine in Xu Jiahui, Shanghai. Liang said to Ji, "Internet is very popular in America these days. What do you think of us setting up a website?" Ji Qi answered, "What? You want to set up a website too? This idea has been in my head for a long time. But I have never been able to find a suitable partner to work with. Ah! Speaking of website technology, you must be an expert!"

Section II   The computer genius Liang Jianzhang
The genius who was special
Speaking of website technology, Liang Jianzhang was undoubtedly the best guy.

Liang Jianzhang was from Shanghai, and he was born in 1969. Since he was very young, Liang had got a nickname as "the big-headed child prodigy". There was another person that had the same esteemed nickname who later became the owner of Eachnet, and his name was Shao Yibo.

Liang Jianzhang was named "a child prodigy", but the question remained how high exactly his IQ was. He answered to a journalist, "I have never had my IQ tested, but it ought to be very high."

Liang was brought into contact with computers in his very early age. When he was 13 years old, primary and middle schools in Shanghai were attempting on introducing computer courses. It was held by China Welfare Youth Centre and lectured by Professor Zhu Hong'e from Shanghai Normal Universtiy. Around 200 students all from some local middle and high schools attended and learned computer programming.

In the computer interest group, Liang Jianzhang had come across with quite a number of problems that he considered profound, to which he would seek answers from his father after he returned home. His father would help him solve these problems using advanced mathematics. To a middle school student like Liang, these mathematic solutions were far beyond his understanding.

He asked his father with his head inclining to one side, "How long would it take for me to understand these things?"

His father answered, "Probably five or six years. That's until when you enter college."

"No! That's too long and painful for me to wait. I must learn these right now."

At Liang Jianzhang's request, his father introduced him some books on mathematics from the easier ones to the more difficult ones. Soon, Liang had mastered mathematical courses supposed to be learned in high schools and colleges.

With the mathematics problems conquered, it had become unobstructed for Liang to master computer programming.

Unexpectedly, half a year later, Liang Jianzhang developed a program in aid of poetry writing. He had thus won the golden award in the 1st National Computer Programming Competition. On the stage to receive the award, the self-assured 14-year-old Liang Jianzhang came into acquaintance with another golden award winner Shen Nanpeng, a gifted 15-year-old child from Haining, Zhejiang. These two could have never dreamt that 17 years later their lives would be tied together again to accomplish a spectaculars cause.

Liang Jianzhang was very outstanding among teenagers of his age in this aspect. Of course, he had become a target for all media to chase after. In a news interview done by Shanghai TV in 1984, Liang Jianzhang demonstrated his powerful poetry writing program. All viewers could see that on the screen of the monotonous DOS system, only by inputting the title, format, and the first character and thyme of each line, you could have a poetry written by a computer.

According to Liang, to finish his poetry writing program, he had finished reading professional books such as *300 Tang Poetries*, *Notes on One Thousand Poetries*, and *One Hundred Ways to Study Poetry*, and tools books like *A Dictionary on Tang Poetry Appreciation* and *Rhymes of Chinese Poetry* all within half a year. He had also studies books on computers such as *The Theory of Artificial Intelligence* and *The Theory of Database*, and other books on logic and linguistics.

Liang Jianzhang must have had a self-study ability that no one could ever compare so that he could have finished studying so much within half a year. It was said that he rarely listened to the teachers in class since primary school, but still, he could manage the knowledge by browsing the new books that were just handed out to him. This was especially true after he had entered middle school and joined the computer interest group. He had learnt mathematics and physics courses for high school and college students all by himself. Since then, he was taking giant leaps on his journey of seeking knowledge.

When Liang was 15 years old, he jumped from middle school to the Youth Class of Under-Graduation of Computer in Fudan University. One year later, without even finishing the under graduate study in Fudan, he got admitted by Georgia Institute of Technology in the United States.

A transformation from technology to marketing

It took only one year for Liang Jianzhang to finish his study in the United States which could take other people two years. By 1989, the 20-year-old Liang Jianzhang had successfully got his master's degree and went on directly for his doctor's degree. One may wonder how he could have finished so much learning so quickly. For one thing, Liang was especially great at studying. And for another, he was under so much great financial pressure that he had to do it fast. Besides, Liang was living in a strange land where he was embraced by another language and life style. When he was pursuing his doctor's degree, however, he realized that the most advanced knowledge could not be learnt from schools but from corporations. Therefore, he dropped out without graduating and joined Oracle, a corporation lead by the world's second wealthiest man Ellison.

It is needless to mention that Oracle is one of the world top 500 companies. Here, I want to insert a story about Ellison, a business prodigy known as "the Silicon Valley Madman" who once dropped out from school and started his own business.

Allegedly, Ellison was invited to give a speech on the graduation ceremony of Yale University. He opened his mouth and said some daring words, "Look around you. Look to your left, and look to your right. Please imagine what the future would be like-the man on your left would turn out to be a loser five, or ten, or thirty years from now on, so would the man on your right. How about you—the man standing in the middle? Also, a loser! So, no matter however superior you were before, you would turn out becoming a loser. Then, how to not become a loser? Let me tell you. You must drop out immediately like me and Bill Gates, or..." Ellison was driven off the stage by securities and unable to finish his speech.

To a regular research member like Liang Jianzhang, Ellison's arrogance in the public was not effective at all. What had truly changed his plan of the career path was a trip back to China to visit his family.

Upon that visit, he was greatly shocked by the thriving entrepreneurship and humongous business opportunities hidden there in the domestic market. He felt that the chance for him was still in China in the long term. So he made a decision to make a transformation.

Back to the United States, Liang Jianzhang applied for a position in the Customer Service Department to carry out ERP projects. It didn't matter to him though the status, payment and options were worse than in the Research Department. He was looking for a chance to go back to China, whereas he could never get such one in the Research Department.

In 1997, Liang finally got the chance he had been expecting for a long time. Through an internal job application, he got the position of Technology Supervisor in China Business Region of Oracle and went back to Shanghai. On his term, he took over many big projects-the Financial Management System of the whole domestic aviation industry, the Information Management System of China Telecommunications, and so on. He had also done consultating work on management, soft ware and e-commerce for national and international companies. He was also partially responsible for the foundation of several famous domestic websites.

When he was in Shanghai, he made an acquaintance with Ji Qi in a business activity. Later, the two became very good friends. They used to drink together and exchange ideas about the Internet business. In the end, they came up with the plan to build a website together.

The plan for making a travel website specifically

"What kind of website should we make?"

Liang Jianzhang had once considered making an e-bookstore when choosing the direction. They had noticed that an American website called Amazon. com was selling their books very well online. By the end of 1998, the stock price of Amazon had broken through 300 US USD. And in February, 1999, the market value of Amazon was as high as 25 billion US USD.

Apart from Amazon. com, Liang Jianzhang had also considered making a website for online job application. In America, such a website Monster. com had made a huge success, so had the two Chinese counterparts 51job. com and Chinahr. com.

But Ji Qi was thinking differently. He had an idea that was triggered by the booming house decoration market in mainland China. In 1996, the interior decoration industry in China had an output value of 45 billion RMB. By 1998, the money spent on house decoration domestically had reached 100 billion RMB. In Shanghai, the decoration industry had a sales volume of 20 billion RMB, taking up one fifth of that in the whole country. Therefore, Ji Qi wanted to enter the online decoration business. He had even chosen a name for his website-Online IKEA.

Later, upon second thoughts, Liang Jianzhang and Ji Qi found that there was a fatal weakness of both Amazon. com and Online IKEA-logistics. Owing to the vast land and lagging logistics facilities in China, no one could solve this problem completely at low costs. As to job application websites, there were a few of them already. So there wasn't too much competitive advantage for Liang Jianzhang and Ji Qi at that time.

Their ideas were denied one after another. Exactly what was their best solution? On a weekend, Liang and Ji drove to a nearby scenic spot, and Liang said, "Let's make a tourism website!"

"Good! This is worth giving a shot. " Ji Qi agreed for he was also a fan of travelling. He continued asking, "Do you like travelling?"

"Yeah. I like it Very much!" After his idea was agreed to by Ji Qi, Liang shared with Ji his stories about travelling.

"When I was little, I fell in love with travelling. But it was just a phase where my enthusiasm was about looking for new stuff and taking adventures. When I was in middle school, I went on my first trip to Wuyi Mountain. I played with my mates and fell into the water uncarefully. I swam like a dog in the water. But it was a great experience. And now I think about it, the happy memory still lingers on. "

Liang went on, "My second experience of travelling was to Zhang Jiajie, followed by natural scenic resorts in and out of China such as Mount Huangshan and the Grand Canyon in America. I especially admire the great pieces of work in the nature. I have been to some of these places for many times, still, I would have a totally different experience each time. Once I went on holiday in an outskirt in the United States, and I met a girl, who has now become my wife. "

"Ah! Your relationship with travelling is predestined! You have got a wife out of travelling. Maybe this time, we will ascend into world's leading magnates if we build up a tourism website. "

"Hehe! I especially like budget travelling. When I was in the United States, I used to go on trips as long as I was free, particularly on weekends. Once, I took my girlfriend to a forest. It was quite late and we got into the forest under guidance of a map. We never thought the route could be so long that before we realized it, it got dark. Fortunately we found a path to the expressway. We followed the path and got out of the forest before it got completely dark. Since that incident, I have thought that a tourism website should be set up to help myself and other people. " That was how Liang Jianzhang showcased the reason to make a tourism website.

"You were too romantic! Why did you choose to go into a primeval forest when you had so many other choices? You deserved it!" Ji Qi began to laugh.

The more they talked, they more they found they could talk about with each other. But, two people could not make a team. There was lacking a third guy-a guy who could get money.

Ji Qi soon realized this problem and said to Liang Jianzhang, "We should recruit someone who knows about finance into our team. "

"Yes. I think we should find such a person as our partner. " Suddenly, Liang got all excited and said, "I have one. He is even a schoolmate of yours!"

"Who is he?"

"Shen Nanpeng. He is doing a great job in venture capital business." said Liang Jianzhang.

"Shen Nanpeng? He is indeed a schoolmate of mine. I had a dinner with him back in the United States. Ok! Let's find him now!"

Would Shen Nanpeng join them? Please continue reading!

Section III   The master of capital Shen Nanpeng

The prodigy from Zhejiang

Shen Nanpeng was undoubtedly a good investor of venture capital.

Shen Nanpeng was born in Haining, Zhejiang in 1967. When he was 7, his grandfather passed away. His mother was a factory director of a state-owned enterprise. She was too busy to take care of Shen Nanpeng. So she had to send Shen to Shanghai to live with his aunt who had no children of her own.

Shen was a hard working child. Compared to children of his age, he didn't have much time for playing around or seeking pleasure. He was interested in mathematics and solving mathematical problems like a robot. He spent his time either at school or in the Olympic Mathematics Class in the Youth Center.

He had spent every weekend in learning mathematics and had gained respectable a-chievements-he had won the First Prize of National Mathematics Competition; on the First National Middle School Computer Competition in 1982, the 15-year-old Shen Nanpeng won the prize together with the 14-year-old Liang Jianzhang; in the high school entrance examination, he got scores of 594 out of total 600, which made his teachers start to worry about him-Shen had such high scores that it was possible for him become a student with "high scores and poor ability" and unable to adapt to the real society when he grew up.

It would take many years to prove whether he could adapt to the society or not. What was known was that upon graduation from middle school, he got recommended for admission to the major of Application Mathematics in Shanghai Jiaotong University. And later in 1989, he was enrolled by the Mathematics School of Columbia University in the United States through examination.

Columbia University was founded in 1754 in the center of New York and has a history of more than 250 years. It is one of the eight Ivy League universities and has more than 18,000 students, ranking among the top ten in the U. S. academically. There are exceptional majors in Columbia University such as Medicine, Law and Philosophy. It also has top-ranking natural science majors-Mathematics, Chemistry, Biology and Computer, to name just a few.

We could imagine that Shen Nanpeng went into the Mathematics School of Columbia University with a great ambition, hoping to realize his dream of becoming a leading mathematician in the world, for the school was the cradle for world's best mathematicians.

Regretfully, half a year later, Shen discovered that he was not capable any more compared to the plenty of other superior students. Shen Nanpeng began to lose himself, "How could this happen? I used to win all kinds of prizes all the time. Am I not talented in math?"

One day, Shen finally thought it through and got the answer-he had mistakenly been practicing math for the name of talent. From the first grade in middle school to the third grade in senior high school, Shen would spend his Sundays going to the Shanghai Youth Center to attend the 3-hour long mathematics classes. Through such training, one could become somewhat talented even without any real talent. The problem of Shen was that he could accomplish the required academic credits with his mathematical logic easily, but it was far from being a superior mathematician overtaking other talents.

Upon realizing that he could never make it to a mathematics prodigy, Shen Nanpeng began to reflect upon himself, "I probably couldn't be a mathematician, but there are plenty of other fields where I can put mathematics into use. I can go to the College of Commerce, or I can do jobs related to mathematics such as securities or bonds."

At that time, the story of a Chinese student studying abroad motivated all students who came from foreign countries. He wasn't keen on making progress and didn't apply for a doctor's degree. He didn't even pass any of his exams. But, things turned out that he had entered one of the best companies in Wall Street.

Without further consideration, Shen Nanpeng quitted from Columbia University in 1990 and then applied for the MBA program in Yale University.

The job in an investment bank upon graduation

In 1992, Shen Nanpeng was graduated from the College of Commerce of Yale. He was so happy to accept the diploma certificate from the Dean, which he thought was the gate for him to enter a brand new world. After the ceremony was finished, Shen didn't immediately go back to his dormitory. Instead, he had a stroll on campus, unwilling to leave.

When he walked out of campus with the diploma certificate in his hand, he watched the street with people coming and going and got completely lost. He didn't know where to go. It was a time when the Americans were suffering from a grim job market. Though Shen was graduated from a top university, he seemed incomparable to so many MBA graduates-there were 200 MBA graduates from Yale, 700 from Harvard, and 400 from Stanford. All graduates from famous universities could amount to 1300, let alone those from less well-known universities. What was worse for Shen was that Chinese students like him never had any re aexperience in commerce. He had never read *The Wall Street Journal* before he went to College of Commerce of Yale. Shen Nanpeng went for interviews with investment bankers in Wall Street time and time again he went with great passion, only to find himself turned down coldly again and again.

It was not an easy time for him, about which, he talked to a journalist several years later, "What you could only see are the words typed on the screen. What you could not see are the tears that I've cried and dropped on the keyboard. "

In the end, he got an interview from Citibank. The interviewer was a doctor from Mathematics Department of Stanford University. He had Shen tested in two intellectual exercises.

The first one went like this, "An America was doing trades in a food market. First, he bought chicken at eight USD and then sold it for nine USD; then he bought the same chicken at ten USD and sold it for eleven USD. So, has he lost or gained? If lost, how much had he lost? If gained, how much has he gained?"

The second exercise was this, "There is a gambling agency (casino) in which you could bet on the winner of each game of this season's NBA. If you have bet on the right team, your money would be doubled. But if you have bet on the wrong team, you would lose all of your money. According to the gambling agency, you need to have 1000 remained in the finals. Then how much should you put in in the first game of this season?"

The interviewer wanted Shen Nanpeng to admit the difficulty and back off. In his eyes, Shen was just a drop-out from Columbia University and could never finish theses two exercises.

What the interviewer didn't know was that Shen Nanpeng had been doing mathematical exercises for six years in his middle schools Years. He might admit that he was not a mathematical prodigy, but he would never back down from these intellectual exercises.

That morning, three people were interviewed-an American, a Japanese and a Chinese (Shen Nanpeng).

They got the same answer to the second exercise. But they were different on the first one-the American thought he businessman had gained 2 USD; the Japanese thought he had lost 2 USD; the Chinese (Shen Nanpeng) thought he had lost 4 USD.

The American presented his reason like this,

The same chicken was bought for the first time and then the second time.

In the first trade, it was bought at 8 USD and sold at 9 USD. 9-8 = 1. So the businessman had gained 1 dollar.

In the second trade, it was bought at 10 USD and sold at 11 USD. 11-10 = 1. So the businessman had gained 1 dollar.

Adding what he had gained in the two trades-1 + 1 = 2, he had gained 2 USD.

The Japanese presented his reasoning like this,

The same chicken was bought twice at the same time.

In the first trade, it was bought at 8 USD and sold for 9 USD. 9-8 = 1. So the businessman had gained 1 dollar.

In the second trade, it was bought at 8 USD and sold at 11 USD. 11-8 = 3. So the businessman had gained 3 USD.

Adding the two trades together-1 +3 =4, he was supposed to gain 4 USD. But he had actually just gained 2 USD-{(9-8) + (11-10) =2}.

So, he had lost 2 USD-2-4 = -2

The Chinese (Shen Nanpeng) presented his reason like this,

The same chicken was bought twice at the same time.

If the two trades were done as on trade, the businessman could gain 6 USD-the chicken was bought at 8 USD and sold at 11 USD. (11-8) ×2 =6

But he had actually just gained 2 USD —{(9-8) + (11-10) =2}.

So, he had lost 4 USD-2-6 = -4

Shen Nanpeng's thinking greatly attracted the interviewer. Thus, he got a job in Citibank working in the Investement Banking Department related to bonds and shares in emerging markets.

Agreement on the golden value of website

Life in Wall Street was not so wonderful as Shen Nanpeng had imagined. It had opened a door for him to a place where there were many people like him who had dreams but only a few could succeed. Every step was very difficult for him working in a large company like Citibank. Shen Nanpeng found a stage for his talent, but he still needed to wait for his chance.

Finally, his chance arrived. Ever since Brilliance China was listed on New York Stock Exchange in October 1992, foreign investors had been having high expectations on Chinese companies. In 1994, without any reason and over almost just one night, Shen Nanpeng and many other Chinese people working in Wall Street changed from being marginalized to being extremely flattered. Shen had become particularly popular among investment banks for he had a perfect CV-he was graduated MBA from Yale; he had two-year working experiences in Wall Street; and he was from Shanghai, China. The same Shen Nanpeng was turned down by these investment banks again and again before, but now the tide had been turned.

Among the investment banks that were chasing after him, Shen had chosen America's third largest securities company —Lehman Brothers Holdings. It was an investment bank founded in 1850 and entered China in 1993. It had set up agencies in Beijing and Shanghai and was just in need of investment experts like Shen Nanpeng.

Ever since then, Shen Nanpeng had been moving forward rapidly on his career path. After two years' work in Lehman Brothers, he wanted to find other place for more rapid development. In 1996, he jumped to DMG & Partners Securities-an investment bank under Deutsche Bank, and became a director.

When he was in DMG & Partners Securities, Shen had run his business differently from other investment banks. In 1997, DMG & Partners Securities, under his leadership, helped China issued debts worth 500 million marks in the European market. The best story was the project he had done to save the "small company" Wai Gaoqiao. It was a financing case that caught all attention from the entire industry for him.

It happened like this. There was a Peruvian company called Wai Gaoqiao Bonded Area Development Ltd. located in Wai Gaoqiao, Pu Dong, Shanghai. This company was growing rapidly, and was needy of capital to expand its business. But the most valuable one among its fixed assets was the Gaoqiao Mansion, which had already been put in pledge. It would be difficult to use this mansion again for financing purpose. The other assets were not valuable enough financially to finance its further development.

Through careful and thorough analysis and observation, Shen Nanpeng said to the person who was in charge, "You could get loan without pledging your mansion as a guarantee according to your credit. " The person in charge thought what he said made sense and followed his advice. As expected, with Shen's help, Wai Gaoqiao raised 100 million USD using the mansion, which otherwise could only get 50 million USD if it was put in pledge. Thus, Shen Nanpeng assisted this company to get double financing without pledging the mansion.

This was just one of the many good performances of Shen Nanpeng's work in the investment banking sector. It happened in the late 1990s, a time when China's economy was developing very fast. There were many small and big scale companies with uncertain future waiting to be saved by investment bankers like Shen Nanpeng.

However, at this time, Shen Nanpeng was surprisingly approached by Liang Jianzhang and Ji Qi. The two invited him to join them in founding an Internet company. Shen thought that the Internet was blossoming across the world and many people had talked about Internet to him. Considering he was familiar with Ji and Liang, he said yes without any hesitation.

Shen Nanpeng agreed to join the entrepreneur team. It flashes back to the scene mentioned at the beginning of this article—Liang Jianzhang reasoned and persuaded everybody into believing that it was most promising to establish a tourism website.

Soon, they began to invest in the new company which was about to be born-Liang Jianzhang and Ji Qi each brought 200,000 RMB, holding 30% of total shares respectively; Shen Nanpeng took up 40% of the shares with 600,000 RMB.

Through continuous discussion, the plan of founding a tourism website appeared more and more achievable. However, before too long, someone just found out that there was a piece missing from the puzzle. They lacked a person who was familiar with tourism-Liang Jianzhang was dealing with technology; Shen Nanpeng was doing investment; Ji Qi was in charge of icorporate management.

Therefore, Shen said, "Now we are making a tourism website, why don't we find someone who knows tourism pretty good?"

Just when they were wondering whom to look for, Ji Qi tapped on his own thigh heavily and shouted, "I have a perfect choice! He is the boss of Chunqiu Travel Agency, Wang Zhenghua. "

"Wang Zhenghua? He is doing well in his travel agency business. He might not take seriously a company such as ours. Besides, he is much older than us. "

"We haven't even talked to him yet. How could you be so assertive? Ji Qi, you are the one who can make this deal done. " Liang Jianzhang followed.

"OK! I'll go!" Ji Qi answered powerfully.

Could Ji Qi get this deal done? Please keep on reading!

Section IV The authority of travelling—Wang Zhenghua
The leader of travelling business—Chunqiu

Wang Zhenghua whom Ji Qi had mentioned was indeed a leading figure of tourism business in Shanghai.

Wang Zhenghua was born in Shanghai in 1944. In 1981, he was the Party Committee Deputy Secretary of the Neighborhood Committee of Zunyi Street, Changning district, Shanghai. He was assigned with a mission to help educated young people who returned from the countryside to find jobs. At that time, the 37-year-old Wang felt his blood was all flowing because he knew it was time for him to establish an enterprise.

Thanks to the good policy, with the money gathered all by him alone, Wang Zhenghua had established six companies without break, including a garage, a passenger transportation company, a cargo transportation company, a travel agency, and so on. Three years later, Wang's garage was witnessing thriving business; he had 40 passenger buses running between Shanghai and Yangzhou everyday carrying passengers to and from the two cities; he could have 70 deals done every day in his cargo transportation company. The unexpected success had brought him pride he had never experienced before. He sighed with emotion, "What a time! Those who dare could get fulfilled while those who are timid could only be left to starve. " Thereupon, Wang Zhenghua decided to quit his job and plunge into the commercial sea in his 40s.

On hearing his decision to quit his stable job, his family objected first and then the organization he was working for tried again and again to persuade him into staying. Nevertheless, Wang had made his choice and no one could stop him. With no other choice, his leader told him that he could only bring one of the six companies that he founded with him if he had to go away.

Comparatively, the travel agency required least amount of capital, and that's why Wang Zhenghua brought it with him eventually.

At the beginning, the business wasn't good, and the agency had only got revenues of 10,000 RMB. China Travel Service and China International Travel Service had already taken up almost all of the group travel business at that time, leaving no opportunity for the inexperienced new bird Wang Zhenghua.

It made it more difficult for Wang when he had lost more than one hundred RMB in the first business. It was advertised as a one-day tour of 40 people from Shanghai to Suzhou. They sold only 20 tickets after waiting for customers over a long time, and the fees collected weren't even enough to conpensate for transportation costs.

His dream was far away from being realized. Wang Zhenghua suddenly got the picture that it was not enough to only have a dedicated mind, but also sufficient professional knowledge. Thus, he began searching for professional books on tourism. Owing to the environment which lacked information at that time, he couldn't find one suitable book after searching around in bookshops and libraries in Shanghai. Later, he overheard that there was a book about tourism written by a tutor back from Europe, which was then printed into teaching materials. This book was named *World Tourist Industry and Its Philosophy*. He used all his relationships and contacts to look for this book. The book read, "With the development of China's economy, there would emerge more and more people wanting to travel at their own expenses. What was neglected by the state-owned tourism giants is going to be the main stream profit source in the future. Why not make the move now?" Upon reading this, Wang suddenly felt enlightened and determined to focus his business on independent tourists.

As predicted, more and more people had become interested in personalized travelling, leading the independent tourism to begin to take up a larger market share. Chunqiu had found the right path. As a result, its business was growing unbelievably well-in the next year, Chunqiu's business volume had increased to 640,000 RMB and by the third year, over 1.2 million RMB. Before the other state-owned travel agency giants could realize what they had missed, Wang Zhenghua had already been running ahead with Chunqiu and had expanded its business everywhere in Shanghai.

The relationship not meant to be

1994 was the year when Wang Zhenghua was just 50 years old, and it was also the year when Chunqiu ranked the first place in the domestic tourism industry. The question for Wang was how to keep the advantage from fading away.

Wang Zenghua was experienced and made the decision to take two measures at the same time.

On one hand, a computer network system must be set up. At that time, most of the agencies in this business were still doing their work manually. On the contrary, Wang invested 20 million RMB in computer network systems. It was a big move, but didn't show any obvious effects. However, it did show its advantages when Wang Zhenghua was competing with his rivals to take up the markets. Once, Chunqiu opened several new agencies in the urban districts of Shanghai. Other travel agencies led by CYTS (China Youth Travel Service) began to encircle and suppress the newly opened ones of Chunqiu's. CYTS took the strategy to open agency offices nearby Chunqiu's, which was imitating McDonalds' competeing strategy against KFC. But, in the end, CYTS closed half of its agencies while almost all of Chunqiu's agencies survived.

On the other hand, Wang Zhenghua began to apply the agency model that was widely applied in abroad-Chunqiu attracted small and middle-sized agencies under a favorable commission system. Out of every tourism project, Wang would take only 10% of the profits and the rest went to partners.

In addition, Wang Zhenghua improved his managerial system into a vertical one. In those years, most domestic agencies were using a horizontal way of management, in which tour guide was holding various sources in the business. The horizontal management turned out to be an inefficient one-in 1992, dozens of employees from the Eastern China business region of Chunqiu, led by their manager, hopped to another agency, resulting in huge losses of business of Chunqiu's Eastern China Region. That's why Wang Zhenghua decided to apply the vertical management system, in which functional departments of tour guiding, purchasing, route planning and supervision were separated from each other.

After a series of reform measures, by the beginning of 1999, Chunqiu had already formed "over 50 stores in Shanghai, and more than 30 branch offices and thousands of agencies across the country. " Chunqiu had also been collecting independent tourists from all over the country constantly.

Fortunes found their way to Wang Zhenghua. In the meantime, Ji QI showed up.

Ji first expressed his admiration towards Wang and his willingness to learn from him. Then, he began to talk about the promising future of the Internet industry.

Through Ji Qi's great efforts, Wang Zhenghua understood his real intention.

Wang said, "Are you inviting me to join you to build a tourism website?"

"Yes! I am really looking forward to having you join us. " Ji Qi answered, and waited for Wang's answer.

"I am sorry, but I'm not interested in the Internet. " Wang rejected Ji Qi at once, lightly. Wang Zhenghua could never have imagined that the young man in front of him would one day have Ctrip become a listed company. Ji Qi could also never expect Wang Zhenghua, the man with no interest in the Internet, would open an airline in the future.

Apart from the Wang Zhenghua mentioned above, Ji Qi and Liang Jianzhang had contacted several management staff of other tourism companies. None showed any interest in this newly founded company, let alone give up their jobs for it.

Coincidently, Ji Qi heard that Fan Min, the General Manager of Shanghai Continental Hotel, was also a graduate from Shanghai Jiaotong University. She was once in the tourism business and had been living in Switzerland for futher study. Ji Qi thought, "Isn't she the one we need?"

Ji Qi detected the hope. Could he persuade her into joining them? Please read on.

Section V The expert of management Fan Min

The bitter-sweet years

At that time, Fan Min was not as mighty as Wang Zhenghua. Nevertheless, he was leading a sustainable life and was doing well.

Fan Min was born in 1965. In 1983, he was admitted by the Industry Management Engineering Department of Shanghai Jiaotong University. Four years later, he furthered his education for the Master's degree of Management without taking the Entrance Examination. Among over 1000 undergraduates that year, he was one of the two excused from the examination because of their good performances in grades. Therefore, he had spent seven years on campus of Shanghai Jiaotong University.

The memory was still fresh to Fan Min that the time when he was a student was one in deficiency of material sources. People were intensely hungry for knowledge and culture.

Fan Min remembered clearly the time when he queued to buy a *Les Miserables*. It was indeed a miserable memory for him too because he had to get there at seven o'clock before the bookshop opened, but when he got there, people were already lining up.

Fan Min remembered clearly the time when a roommate of his got a recorder from a relative in Hongkong. The little machine was working 24 hours a day after it had arrived at their dormitory. It was a luxurious "electric appliance" to all of them and had made all the other roommates jealous.

Fan Min remembered clearly in the 1980s, every time when an expert gave a lecture, the hall would be crowded. And among the crowd, there must stood Fan Min.

This phase might have played an influential part in Fan Min's life. In *On the Aesthetics* by Zhu Guangqian, there was a saying which became Fan Min's motto, "One should be an honest person, say honest words, and do honest things." The impression others had on Fan was that he was dependable, mature and steady. Years later, his classmates would still recall the Chairman of the Student Union who had conducted business like a true leader.

Somehow, this steady leader would "go out of line". When he was a senior in the university, he, together with several other students, founded a company called Jiaoda Angli Student Technology Development Company. He was the deputy manager of this company, which was mainly doing project consultation and scheming for companies and other cities.

It was a pity that this company founded by Fan Min had collapsed. But the name of the company Angli had dramatically remained and found itself become another company's name. Fan Min's first entrepreneurial experience ended in vain, but it was a good practice for him.

The career in a state-owned enterprise

In 1990, Fan Min got his master's degree. He wondered what job to look for. There were many choices for him-to work in the government, in a financial institute, and so on. In the end, Fan Min chose to work in the tourism industry which seemingly could not provide him with a high social status then.

Why did Fan Min chose tourism industry? In the 1990s, tourism was very hot. Once, it happened that when the Hilton Hotel was hiring attendants, many under graduate students enrolled eagerly. Another reason for Fan's choice was that he believed "The less people there are in a business, the easier for one to stand out, just like a monkey could become the king in a mountain where there is no tiger. "

Fan Min worked in Shanghai Xinya Group.

There, Fan Min seemed to have obvious advantages. During those years, post graduate students were more precious than pandas in China because there was a shortage of them. Xinya had only got two post graduates that year. From the very beginning, Fan had been the highlight among the new employees.

Fan Min's first job was being responsible for the planning and coordination in the corresponding department in Shanghai Xinya International Travel Service, which belonged to the old stated-owned enterprise. His regular work was to send and receive faxes, to arrange tourist groups, and to communicate with suppliers. After a while, in December 1990, Fan Min was transferred upwards to be an assistant to the Enterprise Office.

One and a half year had passed before one day Fan Min went to have a talk with his leader and expressed his will to work in Hailun Guest House. Hailun Guest House was a newly established unit which belonged to Xinya Group.

The Office Director Zhao Huan said to Fan Min, "Xiao Fan, are you out of your mind? Your job in the office is perfect. Why do you have to make yourself work in a place with worse condition?"

"Director Zhao, I haven't been familiar with work in the office, which the boss isn't happy about. I want to go there even if the working condition is much worse. " Fan answered.

"But even if you go there, you could only start from the bottom. There's no chance for you to become a head immediately. " Zhao Huan wanted Fan Min, the top student from Shaghai Jiaotong University, to think twice before making his decision.

Fan Min persisted in choosing to work in Hailun Guest House.

On 18th February, 1993, Hailun Guest House officially opened on Nanjing East Road, Shanghai. On Fan Min's chest, the employee tag read, "Management Trainee".

Being in a low position didn't matter to Fan Min because he believed, "Only by burying itself under the earth, could a seed gain its value. It could never be germinated flying in the air. " Compared to the office work, this was a better stage for him.

The sweets await right after the bitterness. Four years later, Fan Min got recognized by his directors and was sent for further education to Switzerland in the Hotel Management School in Lausanne. In a state-owned enterprise, such opportunity meant a forth-coming promotion.

This education in Switzerland was organized by Shanghai Tourist Administration. It was a one-year-long project with over twenty people from Shanghai. During this one year, Fan Min had a better understanding of the service industry.

Since the first class, Fan Min had felt something different. It was a class on etiquette lectured by a French professor. He emphasized that the tourism service industry was a hospitable industry in which its workers must have a good command of hospitality and pay attention to details as carefully as possible. He gave examples such as how and which side to take to walk stairs, which showed the exquisite details in tourism service.

There was another thing that had a great impact on Fan Min. Once, they were asked to write and send recommendation letters for the school back to China. Done with writing the letters, Fan Min and the other students causally handed them to their head teacher. To their surprise, they got criticized instead of being thanked. The head teacher said, "You are all managers from hotels. What you have just done showed your unprofessional quality, which you shouldn't have. These letters should be put away in order in the basket, faced up and corners aligned. By doing so, you can save the letterman much trouble. They could put the postmark on each letter quickly. "

This had made Fan Min truly realized that detail was the decisive factor in the service industry. A servant could make a difference by paying attention to every inconspicuous detail and make his customer satisfied. There was a saying, "Being different is key to being successful. "

The new home Ctrip

Back from Switzerland, Fan Min was promoted to the Deputy General Manager of the Hotel Management Company of Shanghai Xinya Group. Ever since then, he had been smooth on his career, and was later promoted as General Manager of Shanghai Travel Service and Continental Hotel. By 1999, he had been working in the tourist industry for ten years.

In the 1990s, it was quite satisfying to be a general manager in a state-owned enterprise. He was equipped with an apartment, a car and even an assigned driver for him. This ought to have stopped him from going off into wild flights of fancy.

Things are not always as you though. One day, a couple of people broke into his life and changed his life path.

These people were Ji Qi, Liang Jianzhang and Shen Nanpeng.

Upon deciding that they need a partner in tourism business, they spared no efforts looking fora suitable person and had finally found Fan Min.

One day in 1999, the 34-year-old Fan Min was invited by a friend to Lulu Restaurant in Shanghai. When he got there, there were already three people waiting for him-a current senior manager of Deutsche Bank Shen Nanpeng, the Consultation Supervisor of Oracle's China Business Region Liang Jianzhang, and the man who had founded many high-tech enterprises Ji Qi.

During their first talk, Fan Min's facial expression didn't change much.

When they got back, Liang Jianzhang and Shen Nanpeng had discussed that maybe they should look for other candidates. To many people, it seemed impossible to get Fan Min, who was the general manager of a state-owned enterprise with an apartment and a driver appointed by the enterprise.

In Ji Qi's mind, he thought that he had the incomparable advantage of being Fan's schoolmate. And he thought that nobody else could get Fan Min except himself.

In the following days, Ji Qi had regularly visited the Continental Hotel in 200 Xizang Central Road in Shanghai. He went there to discuss dreams and futures with Fan Min. Ji Qi showed his persistence just like when he was in sales business before.

It was quite strange that every time, Fan Min would keep Ji Qi waiting for him outside the office, even if Fan was available. It didn't bother Ji because he thought it was very common for a leader of a state-owned enterprise to do so. However, thing got better after Ji's several visits. The time that Fan kept him waiting reduced from 10 minutes to 5 minutes.

The last time Ji Qi went there, he asked directly, "My schoolmate, have you made up your mind?"

Fan Min responded, "Ok! I am willing to take the gamble. Actually, life is like a gambling game. One should not gamble on his life. But if necessary, one should take the risk and win."

Probably because that he was moved by Ji Qi's persistence, or that he was tempted by the big picture Ji Qi had drawn, Fan Min had finally agreed to join the team. Seeing that Ji Qi had no purpose on giving up, Fan was awakened and once again became passionate.

Thus, the team members were gathered and the Ctrip team was founded. What was their next move? Please continue to read Chapter Two *Enterprising and Financing*.

Summary

The four members of the Ctrip team had already made their appearances in order. But could the four of them form a Roman Army and sweep away all the obstacles? We have a human resource management system to give this team an initial assessment and evaluation.

I. The elements in an entrepreneur's development

According to the Theory of Success, there are three elements related to the development of an entrepreneur.

1. Environment. It is needless to mention that in the 1990s, Shanghai had provided entrepreneurs with a favorable environment. This element is especially important. Pan Shiyi once said that he could have been a poor villager in Tianshui, Gansu Province if not owing to the environment.

2. Education. This includes the high education in school (educational background) and the reconstructive education in the society (experience). All of the four people are qualified for this element. There was a difference, however. Liang Jianhang and Shen Nanpeng received their education in abroad, but in contrast, Ji Qi and Fan Min did it in the domestic.

3. Heredity. A quality model must be introduced first to explain this element. In an onion-shaped quality model (p1-1), the quality of an individual is divided into 3 levels and 8 factors-in the first level, there are Motives and Traits; in the second one, Self-Image, Social-Role, Value and Attitude; in the third one, Knowledge and Skills. The factors in the first level are innate, which are hard to change, whereas the factors in the third level are acquired, which could be obtained by training.

p. 1-1 \onion-shaped quality model
\ easy to be trained and evaluated
\ can be trained and evaluated
\ hard to be trained and evaluted

Combining the theory and the growing-up experience of the four team members, it's easy to see that they had strong motives for success and clear self-images. They had accurate and proper career planning for themselves.

Many people are reluctant or unable to make changes in their lives, however, there are people who could do it perfectly-

Ji Qi left Shanghai Computer Service for Zhonghua Yinghua, and then established his own company Ctrip;

Liang Jianzhang had himself transfered from the Technology Department to the Customer Service Department without a second thought;

Shen Nanpeng hopped from Citibank to Lehmam Brothers, and then to DMG & Partners Securities;

Fan Min volunteered to work as a management trainee in Hailun Guest House and left his work in the head office.

All these truth prove that they are of good quality.

Individually, they are all qualified for entrepreneurs.

II. A common model of an efficient organization

A Chinese organizational behavior expert Dr. Chen Quan believes there are two ways of efficient organizations.

1. All-round organization. In such an organization, every member is an ideal talent. What is an ideal talent? Here is the formula-

   Xing-Compatibility.

   Ge-strong physical build and easy-going character

   Qi-ambition, brilliance and luck

   Neng-capability of thinking, doing, speaking and writing

To understand compatibility is rather important, which means one team member should judge other's choices without any personal bias. When assembling a computer, a motherboard of any brand must be compatible with graphics cards, memory cards and hard disks of any other brands. Just like this motherboard, when forming a team, the members should not be over picky and partial. Once there was a man who wanted to start a business and he looked for partners, but in the end, he couldn't find any. Why? Because he was pickier choosing team members than when choosing a wife. He thought that people from Guangdong were too astute, Shanghai too penny-wise, Hubei too sneaky, Hunan too dominating... In the end, he gave up on all of these choices.

Secondly, the team members must be physically healthily built because sometime they have to take bus 11 (to walk). They should also have a good temper. If a team member scholds a lot, others would not be able to stand him.

Thirdly, the team members should have great ambition, and the will to make a difference. They should be brilliant. They need luck, and probably so good luck that they couldn't be stopped by the Diwang Mansion-the highest building in Shenzhen.

Last, the four skills are required. The team members should dare to think and speak out, to dash against anything, to tell stories and to master with their literal works.

2. Complementary Organization (p1-2). In such an organization, each member is irreplaceable. Here is a Blood Type Theory of talent-

   Type O-good at being a boss. The O-type people are characterized as being predictive. They like to make plans in ahead and are good at making use of the sources they have.

   Type A-good at finance. The A-type people are characterized as being cautious and sensitive to numbers. They are excellent at analyzing and want to do everything perfectly.

   Type B-good at market. The B-type people are characterized as being outgoing and passionate. They are energetic and impulsive. They like jobs of challenge.

Type AB-good at management. The AB-type people are characterized as being cool and humble. They also stay neutral and have special viewpoint. They do their work rationally and can hardly be affected by their emotion.

From the above theories, we can see that the four of them couldn't make an all-round organization. There is hardly any all-round organization. But if they had clear self-positioning, they could work the team into a complementary organization. Here is the result-type O (Liang Jianzhang), type A (Shen Nanpeng), type B (Ji Qi), type AB (Fan Min).

p. 1-2   real-life employee type

Type A-good at finance

Type AB-good at management

Type O-good at being a boss

Type B-good at market

red cell antigen A

red cell antigen B

III. 5P elements of a team

An organized group doesn't necessarily mean a team because not all organizations are all teams. The 5P elements (p. 1-3) of a team have decided that its difference from an organization.

The 5P elements are Purpose, People, Place, Power and Plan.

Among the 5 elements, the most important are Purpose and Place. Only by placing each one in the right position, could the team be kept from conflict between members. Only by setting a clear purpose, could the team survive any disturbance.

p. 1-3   the 5P elements of a team

To explain thoroughly, let me introduce the Team Xiyou (a Chinese literature *Pilgrimage to the West*) and the Team Shuihu (a Chinese literature *Heroes of the Marshes*).

In Team Xiyou, every team member has his shortcoming

Tangseng always mistakes the evil for the good. He himself couldn't fight against the evil, but could only torture the badly-behaved Sun Wukong with the Inhibition.

Sun Wukong is of capability but also a trouble-maker. He would always run back to Shuilian Hole as soon as he has been wronged. The Zhu Bajia in charge of HR has to the ideological work on him. For this reason, Zhu Bajia almost had his ears cut off and cooked by the monkeys on Huaguo Mountain.

Zhu Bajie was libidinous, lazy, greedy, and incapable. Before leaving Gao Laozhuang, he says to his father-in-law, "Don't let my wife get remarried. Tell her to wait for me. If I couldn't get the sutra and come back, the marriage will continue."

Sha Heshang and Bai Longma have practically no skills. They are just obeying. However, each one of the team has a very accurate self-placement. Tang Seng is the boss. Sun Wukong is the general market inspector. Zhu Bajie is the general human resource inspector. Sha Heshang is the general finance inspector. Bai longma is the general logistic inspector. At the same time, the team leader has a firm goal to go on a pilgrimage for Buddhist scriptures, which has never changed. So, the team has achieved final success through the 81 hazards.

In Team Shuihu, there is a wealth of talents. There are the "36 Big Dippers" and the "72 malignant stars". There are intellectual talents like Wu Yong and Gong Sunsheng and physical talents like Ling Chong and Wu Song.

However, these team members don't have accurate self-placements. One doesn't defer to another. There is a scene in which they get into a big fight all because of the seat order. What is worse is that Song Jiang does not have a clear goal in his head. He is always talking about acting for God and exercising morality. He also promises his team members to share the fortune, which turns out to be a lie. Later, he was offered amnesty by the Song government, and he has betrayed all of his brothers for wealth and rank. In the end, the team was destroyed. Many of the Liangshan heroes died with no shame, and Song Jiang was no exception.

There are 5 stages (p. 1-4) in a team's development-the foundation period, the unrest period, the stabilized period, the high production period and the adjustment period.

p. 1-4   Stages in a team's development
the foundation period
the unrest period
the stabilized period
the high productivity period
the adjustment period

During the foundation period, the team members are excited and nervous. They have high expectations. They would feel anxious, confused and insecure. They begin to give themselves positioning and to carefully try out their positioning on others

During the unrest period, the team members find the reality different from their expectations, thus they would begin to feel frustrated and emotionally beaten. Tension arises between the members. They begin to complain about their leaders.

During the stabilized period, the team members begin to trust and accept other members after blending in the team. They begin to transfer their focus onto other matters, and their skills get improved. The standard and routine will be built.

During the high production period, the team members become confident. They have a good command of various techniques to solve problems together. They share their view and gained knowledge with each other. They have the sense of mission and honor.

During the adjustment period, the team members become independent. One would feel that he is the one who contributes the most to the team. He begins to think that what he does deserve more what he gains and he want to start his own business.

Among the five stages, it is most difficult to get through the unrest period. Then how did the Ctrip team get through the valley of death on their entrepreneurship road safely? Please look for the answer in the next chapter.

Application

Ⅰ. Is he an ideal partner?

In his first experience of entrepreneur, Hun Hun had some disagreement with his business partner and then left the team.

One day, Hun Hun met a friend on the Internet, who was 40 years old and was just back from abroad. Hun Hun was feeling depressed and wanted someone to talk to, so he started chatting with him. The more they chatted, they more common interests they found they had. Then, Hun Hun talked to this "Hai Gui" (a person back from abroad with educational or work experience) about his idea.

Hun hun said, "I want to make knockoff laptops. What do you think about this idea?"

Hai Gui said, "Good! We can form a partnership. I have the business platform."

Hun Hun asked, "Do you?"

Hai Gui answered, "Hehe! I am the Chief Consultant for Beijing University Students Entrepreneur Alliance, which I could use as a platform to promote the knockoff laptops. In the meantime, we could do OEM and make our own brand. If we make use of this platform and promote our product in universities in Beijing successful, we can copy this model to other big cities around the country."

Hun Hun kept asking, "Do you have control over this platform?"

Hai Gui responded, "Of course. We can also promote related marketing on own laptops and gain profits from advertisement."

According to the above chatting records, would you work with Hai Gui if you were Hun Hun? Please specify your reason!

Ⅱ. Who would you choose?

In the end of 1997, a time when the stock market was flourishing, the author was approached by an inspector from a securities company in Shenzhen. They requested me to design a paper test for a job interview. They specifically requested-

1. They are interviewing for the position of a Customer Manager, which required the reading ability equalling to a high-school graduate.
2. This should be a test of the interviewee's awareness on investment. And it should allow interviewees to give different answers based on their different awareness.

That evening, the author sent an email to the inspector including the test and key to the test. It read like this,

Test

One brought 100 RMB to a Shiduo shop. He bought a commodity at 25 RMB, which had a prime cost of 20 RMB. The shop owner didn't have enough change, so he took the 100 RMB to the shop next door to make some change.

Half an hour later, the shop owner from next door came and said the note was a counterfeit one. The shop owner had to give him another 100 RMB note.

How much had the shop owner lost? Please give a specific answer.

Choices for the answer

A. 195 RMB

B. 95 RMB

C. 100 RMB

The next day, the inspector had over 70 test papers return during the first round of the interview. But the answers varied from one another, and were beyond the choices given- there were answers like 225, 205, 200, 195, 100, 95··· Some interviewees even wrote answers that read, "The answer is however much you think he had lost."

The author didn't specify the reasons for the three choices. The inspector was totally confused by all the answers he had got.

If you were the inspector, what would you think of the efficiency and credibility of this test? If you approved of this test, which answer would you choose? Please tell me your reason.

Chapter II
Enterprising and Financing

We can't deny that the Ctrip team is terrific. It started with the initial capital of only one million RMB. But surprisingly, they had swayed venture capital investors into investing three times in a row, gaining investment of over 10 million RMB. In their first round of financing, they got half a million from IDG; in the second one, they got 4.5 million RMB from 5 companies including Softbank; in the third one, they got 12 million RMB from companies like Carlyle Group.

Quotations
Reflections on the business market 1-5

To succeed, one must first go mad, and rush forward with a simple mind. In the end, success will come easily.

—reflection on the entrepreneurial story of Ctrip team

Be a person, then be a businessman; make friends, then make deals. Personal quality always comes before product quality.

—reflection on Ji Qi's work experience in the state-owned enterprise

Don't be regretful if you have been running around for it, if you have been talking until your mouth is out of shape, if you have run into the ghosts, or if you have wasted your saliva talking too much. You need to believe that one day you will be successful.

—reflection on Ctrip team's financing in Hongkong

An employee should work in the mind-state of a boss. A boss should manage in the mind-state of an employee.

—reflection on the entrepreneurial story of Ctrip team

If you could get it done, so could I. If I could get it done, you might not. If I could not get it done, nobody ever could.

—reflection on Ji Qi's fighting spirit

A fable
The hare and the tortoise

One day, a hare and a tortoise were discussing which one of them could run faster. Neither of them was willing to admit that itself was slower. Hence, they decided to have a race.

The first time, they raced on the highway. The hare lost the race. Why? Because it went to take a nap during the race, however, the tortoise kept on running and had finally won the race.

This tells us that diligence is more important than intelligence. One must become a diligent worker to be successful.

The hare didn't recognize its lost, and went for the tortoise. The hare said to the tortoise that it would never give up unless it had won the race. Thus, they had another six rounds of races.

The second race was held on a playground. The hare had already lost the race after it had begun. Why? It was because that the hare was running towards the opposite direction.

This tells us that direction is more important than effort. The efforts will end up in vain if you are going for the wrong direction. One must be aiming for the right direction in order to succeed.

The third time, they raced on the grass. The hare went missing during the race, and the tortoise won. Why? It was because that the hare fell into the slough.

This tells us that in order to be successful, one ought to be good at discovering and avoiding traps. No pies would fall from the sky, however, there are always traps on the ground.

The fourth time, they raced on a hill. The hare ran and ran, but still lost the race. Why? It was because that the tortoise rolled itself down the hill, which was obviously a faster way than the hare's.

This tells us that one should make the best of his advantages in order to become successful. It would be easier for one to succeed if he could bring his strong point into full play and amending his own weak point in the meanwhile.

The fifth time, they raced on the express highway. The hare kept running, but he had still lost. Why? It was because that the tortoise took a taxi.

This tells us that one should be able to command how to integratie sources.

The sixth time, they went back to the playground for the race. This time, the hare ran very fast and almost got to the finishing line. Suddenly, it saw a banner hung by the tortoise that read, "The first one to finish is the son of a tortoise". The hare became extremely angry and immediately stopped running.

This tells us that success requires emotion management. Once one loses his temper, everything will be ruined.

The seventh time, it was still on the playground. The hare ran and ran, seeing the finishing line ahead of itself. Out of nowhere, it felt its tail bitten. The hare swayed its tail, and the tortoise got thrown to the front. As it turned out, the tortoise put his mouth on the hare's tail. And when the hare got near to the finishing line, it gave the hare a hard bite that made the hare so painful that it wanted to die.

This tells us that one should make use of power and strength of his rivals. Success is gained by making friends, and bigger success if gained through making use of the rivals.

The story of the hare and the tortoise shows us that there are 7 conditions required for success.

1. Diligence
2. Direction
3. Avoiding traps
4. Bringing strong point into play
5. Integrating sources
6. Emotion management
7. Making use of rivals

Text

Section I   Positioning of the website
Fan Min's and Shen Nanpeng's viewpoints

With the direction set and team members gathered, the four of them began to operate this website in May 1999.

It may sound incredible that they had a very poor working condition at the beginning. They rent half of the 17th floor in Qixiang Building south to the Xu Jiahui Church. They shared this floor with Xiecheng in an office of only 200 square meters. Fan Min and Liang Jianzhang didn't even have a used table to work on.

They had a high expectation on this small company with over 30 staff members. Even their job titles seemed hilarious. Shen Nanpeng was the CFO because he had invested the most. Liang Jianzhang was the CEO. Ji Qi was the President. And Fan Min was the Executive Vice President. "Small as the sparrow is, it possesses all its internal organs-small but complete."

In the next step, they needed to decide on the positioning and planning of the company's future. They expressed their viewpoints in Ji Qi's office.

Fan Min was the first one to go, he said, "I have a hunch that the tourism industry is going to be bigger than we could image. In 1998 alone, this industry was worthy of 239.1 billion, which made it the second largest industry in China. Chinese people have spent more on tourism than on automobiles. In such big a market, the workers in the tourism industry could survive on the 'internal organs of the chicken' and the 'chicken soup', and they didn't even need the 'chicken legs'. They could get full."

"But the situation is that today's tourism industry doesn't match the demand in this market. Besides, the tourism service companies don't qualify the service needed. Our only and wise choice is to go for the combination of tourism information and e-commerce."

Shen Nanpeng made a speech next, "Actually, the e-commerce business was already born in the summer of 1997. At that time, a guy named Wang Juntao established an experimental website called 'Software Bay' to sell software online. Later, they separated this e-commerce department from the company, which later became the Everest E-commerce Internet Service Company (8848. com). When 8848. com was first founded, there was a program called 72-Hour Internet Survivor. 8848. com had its image advertisement showing during the gold hours on CCTV-2 for several days in a row. 8848. com got famous and began to control the e-commerce market in China. In 1999, 8848. com sold MP3 player for Chuangxin on its website. Half a year later, 8848. com became the sales champion among all agencies of Chuangxin's MP3 player product. The sales volume surpassed greatly that of the traditional agencies offline, which proves the prominent future of e-commerce."

"Speaking of the application of e-commerce in the tourism industry, we are not the first one to make the move. There are already many such companies in the United States, some of which are listed companies. The question for us is to choose between B2C and B2B according to the environment in China. Should we focus on travel agencies aiming at independent tourists, or should we incline towards those enterprises with growing business trips? Should we gain more profits from ticketreservations which is less flexible, or from hotel reservations which is a broader platform? We need to try to find out the answer."

"It has been ten years since the Internet was born in China. I remember when Zhang Chaoyang went back to China from abroad, he was too financially broken to fly and had to take a ship. However, with an idea of setting up a portal website, he got investment. This shows us that the Internet is an abundant land for wealth and fortune. But the time has passed when heroes like Zhang Chaoyang and Wang Zhidong ran business on their own. To survive in such a competitive environment, there must be a powerful management team. I think we are one of such teams and this is our advantage. If we were to become a listed company, we could stand any investor's challenge, and we don't even have to rap ourselves in a beautiful package."

The decision made by Liang Jianzhang

Liang Jianzhang continued the conversation with a long speech, "Now that all of us have agreed on the e-commerce model, I must introduce the 3 models of successful e-commerce in America."

"The first model is priceline. com. It is a price-bidding website, on which users could post their demands, a price, and a deadline. The first one to respond wins the bidding. For instance, some tourist fan wants to go to Seattle and he posts his requirements on this website-50 USD a day and accommodation in a three-star hotel. Then, priceline. com would check if there is any hotel in favor of this deal. If a hotel is in favor of it, the deal gets done without the confirmation from the user. "

"The second model is lonelyplanet. com. It is the world's largest independent tourism publisher which provides tour guiding and city guiding all over the world. On this website, there is free information on self-supported travelling and the users could look for information of all the places across the globe. "

"The third model is represented by travelcity. com and expedia. com. The former one is a comprehensive website that works with thousands of travel agencies in the world. The users could make ticket reservations and hotel reservations, and could rent cars through the relative system on the website. The later one is the world's largest online tourism website whose service covers every aspect, including air tickets, hotel reservations, car-rental service, and so on. "

"In China's tourism environment, the price-bidding model like priceline. com couldn't work. Anyone who wants to copy this model is doomed to end in failure. The second and third models are worth consideration. "

"Between the second and the third models, which one should we choose? As far as I am concerned, the third one is the best choice for us. Here is my reason. People have been shocked by the amount of information the Internet can provide us with once they get in contact with it. People are intoxicated by thevarious possibilities on the Internet, so we should offer them as much information as possible so that our users can find anything they are looking for. Now we are in a stage where we are exploiting the possibility of each model. Without a clear answer, we must make our contents and applications of our website as wide as possible to graspe the opportunities in the market. "

"To conclude, I think we should aim for a portal tourism website. And I have a temporary name for it-Youhu (Later, this temporary name was changed to Ctrip). "

It was Ji Qi's turn to express his idea. Abruptly, Liang Jianzhang switched the topic and said to Ji Qi, "I will be in charge of the technology. Why don't you go first and run this company?"

What? The four of them formed a partnership to build a company, and now Ji Qi had to run this company first by himself. The rest were going to share Ji Qi's fruit. Would Ji Qi say yes to this arrangement? Please keep reading.

Section Ⅱ The first round of financing
Ji Qi's pioneering

"OK! I can be a pioneer. After all, I have been swimming in the 'ocean of business', and I have got nothing to lose. " Ji Qi said, "I have a feeling that we are having a relay. The first baton is in my hand-I am in charge of exploiting markets; the second one is in Liang's hand-he is in charge of website technology; the third one is in Fan's hand-he is in charge of product management; the fourth one is in Shen's hand-he is in charge of listing and financing. "

Ji Qi agreed to this arrangement open-heartedly.

Now, this entrepreneurial story had become different from other ones. During the early operation of this company, the four all of them didn't invest equal time and efforts in it. During the early period, Ji Qi was basically fighting all by himself. In the meantime, the other three members would only work with Ji Qi on their leisure time as if they were doing part-time working in this company.

Why didn't they quit their jobs and throw themselves into the entrepreneur of Ctrip regardless of the sacrifice?

In fact, this was not their fault. They were very clear that the success of a new company call for lots of factors. If there were a minor error on any link, the company could be destroyed. People usually say, "One careless move leads to the loss of the whole game. " They made an excellent team and each team member had extraordinary experience and business model. Despite this, faced with the wave of Internet, no one could make the promise of success without a clear vision.

Hence, they could only wade across the stream by feeling the way.

Now that they were exploiting the way, they had to take the financial cost into consideration, meaning that had to choose the one with the lowest cost as a pioneer during the early stage. Undoubtedly, Ji Qi was the right choice.

Ji Qi had advantages and possessed what the other three didn't have-he knew the rules in the business of China, which was still an immature market. He knew how to survive, that is, he had to make the best of the limited sources at hand, and cook with whatever there was in the grocery basket. Compared to the turtle (a person back from abroad) in an international enterprise and the shark in a state-owned enterprise, Ji Qi, the tortoise (a complete local Chinese), was more capable of finding the right path through the distractions for their company.

Ji Qi was the one with the lowest cost, but the new born company was in need of money. Just like Ji once said, "It wastes a large amount of gasoline when the car starts. " Within three months, they had almost run out of the one million RMB they invested. (On their business license, the registered capital was two million.) The company could die if they couldn't get help from an investment bank.

Liang Jianzhang and Ji Qi had predicted this to happen, and that's why they asked Shen Nanpeng to join them when they were forming the team.

But things were not as easy as they had expected. Shen Nanpeng could not bring his skills into full play. First, Shen did not have many chances with the venture capital investors. Secondly, the projects he used to work on were all big ones. Comparatively, their small project could not get attention from any of the investment banks. In short, the "Giant Ship" Shen Nanpeng got stranded at the "Harbor" of a small company.

Making the first acquaintance of a venture capital investor Zhang Suyang

The team members of Ctrip were wondering what to do next. At this point, a name came up upon Ji Qi's head-Zhang Suyang, a partner in IDG.

Here is a brief introduction of the company IDG. Nowadays, speaking of the Internet in China, IDG needs to be mentioned. What IDG is to China's Internet industry is what Washington is to the U. S. and what Napoleon is to France. However, looking back at it, we unexpectedly find out that IDG had accumulated its fame little by little.

IDG Group was founded in 1964 and headquartered in Boston. Its parent company is famous for being good at data processing. There are sub companies and branch companies in 90 countries in the world with more than 10 thousand senior research experts and data collectors and processors. Ever year, over 90 thousand market research reports and technology development predict reports gets published by IDG, which has a strong public opinion influence on world's information industry.

In 1981, McGovern, the Board Chairman of IDG Group, founded the Pacific Entrepreneur Investment Fund, aiming for the Asian market, especially the Japanese market. In 1993, the IDGVC (the short term for IDG Technology Venture Investment Company) was founded in Shanghai, China. Xiong Xiaoge was its first General Manager.

How did Xiong met with McGovern?

It was like this. In 1986, Xiong went to Boston University in the United States for his Doctor's Degree. In 1988, he joined Reed, the world's largest publisher, and was editing for the Chinese Edition of *Economics Guiding*. In August 1991, Xiong Xiaoge was assigned to Hongkong. But in his opinion, the publication could only be performed well in China. His proposal got denied by the company, and he felt depressed. At this moment, he thought of Mr. McGovern, who he had met at a dinner party at Fletcher School in the fall of 1988. That time, he was an interpreter for Rong Yiren. Therefore, he wrote a letter to McGovern immediately.

McGovern got his letter and gave him a call that night to invite him to join IDG, and send him a letter of appointment. Thus, Xiong Xiaoge officially began his work in IDG in November 1991.

At first, Xiong was also in charge of making e-magzines. Later, he had helped the Pacific Bite Sports Ware Company get foreign orders and this company had made a fortune. This company was the first Chinese company McGovern had investment in. Seeing this, McGovern thought that the venture investment in China should be expanded. Thereupon, Shanghai Pacific Technology Entrepreneur Investment Company was established.

In 1999, the Internet industry was blossoming. He formed partnerships with other companies to run this Shanghai Pacific Technology Entrepreneur Investment Company as an interior department of IDG. So IDG had many partners in China, such as Zhang Suyang and Zhou Quan.

When Pacific Technology Entrepreneur Investment Company was founded, IDG did not have much fame and experience in the field of venture investment. The company was not in possession of large sums of capital, so IDG had to choose small investment in order to minimize the risk. They would invest in any project of the Internet just like scattering pepper powder because the Internet industry was a heated one at that time.

Besides, IDG couldn't afford those projects in latter stages because they were in need of a large sum of investment. So they had to choose those projects stil in their early stages. They could not foresee the future of these early-staged projects and could only base their investment vaguely on the profession. Now that they had chosen the profession, they had to live or die together with them. They would never miss any opportunity to invest in a new-born profession. The company's concept in its early stage was "to invest in and to have shares in every company".

During the two years between 1997 and 1999, IDG had invested continuously in over 40 China's Internet companies such as Sohu, Dangdang, Yiqu, 3721 and Baidu Online. After these companies began to earn money, IDG began to become famous. But this story can be saved for later. Now is the story of Ji Qi's search for venture investment.

Ji Qi had known Zhang Suyang because of his idea of purchasing the Shanghai Office of Zhonghua Yinghua. Ji Qi had got the advanced payment from the integrating wiring and was in demand of other's investment to finish the purchase. Ji Qi requested for investment from two IDG investors and they explained to them about the Shanghai Office. Zhang Suyang replied, "If this company were as good as you have described, we IDG would consider putting some money in." On hearing this, Ji Qi went straight to Beijing to negotiate on the purchase. He could not get the deal done in the end. But, he had made an acquaintance with Zhang Suyang ever since.

Later, IDG had invested in a company in Nanjing-the Sino-America Joint-Venture Nanjing Top Information Network Ltd. Company. Before too long, something happened in this company. The General Manager ran away with the coffer and the company was in danger of being shut down. This company was majored in system integration, about which Ji Qi was familiar. Then Zhang Suyang went for Ji Qi and offered him the position of an executive director, hoping that he could use his power to stabilize the company.

It took a while for Ji Qi to save the company. When it was stabilized, Ji Qi left it.

After this, Ji Qi and Zhang Suyang didn't keep in much touch for there was no business between them. But now, Ji Qi thought he needed to talk to Zhang Suyang because Ctrip was running out of money.

In the late September of 1999, Zhang Suyang was invited to Ji Qi's office.

Zhang Suyang became interested when Ji Qi told him it was about the Internet industry.

Zhang smiled and said, "You are in this Internet business as well?"

Ji Qi smiled back and said, "Yes! The whole world are opening Internet companies. Why can't us?"

"You choose to make a tourism website?"

"Yes. We think it's a promising business."

"Could you be more specific?" Zhang Suyang carried on.

Ji Qi replied confidently, "We have been discussing every possible field for over half a year. We have taken many choices into consideration-an online bookshop, an online employment website, an online house decoration website, and so on. But we have found that these choices have their limitations. So we finally decided on making a tourism website."

"Did you think up of this idea first?"

"No. It was our CEO Liang Jianzhang. Once, he got lost with his girlfriend on a trip. It took forever for them to find the way. That's why he wanted to make a tourism website. He wants to do good to himself and other people."

"Hehe! That's interesting. How many members are there in your team?" Liang asked with a smile.

"There are four of us. The other three are Liang Jianzhang, Shen Nanpeng, and Fan Min. Liang Jianzhang is the Technology Inspector of Oracle's China Business Region. He was a prodigy since being a child and an expert of Internet technology. Shen Nanpeng is the director of DMG & Partners Securities of the Deutsche Bank. He was the man who lead the project to save the 'small soldier' Wai Gaoqiao. Fan Min is the General Manager of Shanghai Continental Hotel and he has been working in the tourism industry." Ji Qi explained.

Among the three partners Ji had introduced, Zhang had already known two of them. Once Ji Qi invited Zhang Suyang for dinner and Liang Jianzhang was there too; in a dinner with several other people working in the investment field in Jiangan Guest House, there sat Shen Nanpeng.

When Ji Qi was finished with the introduction, Zhang said, "Let me think about it." Then, he stood up and was about to leave.

Hearing this, Ji Qi thought to himself that maybe IDG wouldn't be interested in this deal. At that time, the most popular websites were the portal websites. Portal websites like Sina.com, Sohu. com, 163. com and Chinanet. com had already been listed in NASDAQ. Their performance had excited all people in the Internet industry and those in the investment industry. Many people believed that to invest in portal websites was the right and best choice. Few was convinced that tourism websites had a promising future.

Then, Ji Qi grabbed Zhang Suyang hurriedly, "Suyang, you have a wide connection with people in your field. Could you introduce some venture investors to me?" Zhang answered, "No problem!" After Zhang said this, he left without giving Ji Qi any further information to follow.

Ji Qi thought, "Now. We are screwed." He kept pushing Shen Nanpeng, "Nanpeng, go look for investors! If we couldn't get financing soon, we'll end up being dead awkwardly."

Shen Nanpeng didn't get any financing, however, Ctrip didn't die. Why? Please read along.

The second meeting with Zhang Suyang

Three weeks later, Ji Qi got an unexpected call from Zhang Suyang saying that two of his IDG colleague wanted to meet the founders of Ctrip. Ji Qi got so happy that he almost fell off the chair, and asked hurriedly, "Suyang, how is it looking? Could we get it?" Zhang did not give him a clear answer, but just said, "I'm not sure yet. Let's have a meeting first. You'd better bring your partners."

Thus, Ji Qi brought Liang Jianzhang with him to a restaurant serving home dishes on Tongren Road where he had arranged to meet Zhang Suyang. They met in a cabin on the second floor.

One of the two colleagues Zhang Suyang brought with him was Zhou Quan, the General Director of the Technology Investment Fund of IDG. The other one was a technology specialist from IDG's Boston headquarter.

To Ji and Liang's surprise, these two investors did not ask them about the business model and profit model of Ctrip. They did not throw at them the three normal questions that venture investors usually asked-"What is your business and what are you doing?" "Who are in your team, and how do you know them?" "What's the current capital situation of your company?" Instead, they asked some questioned that got Ji and Liang all confused.

Zhou Quan asked, "I am just wondering what your purpose was when you founded Ctrip."

Ji Qi answered, "We think that the Internet is a great platform for people to further elaborate their personal abilities. We could make our products more customer-friendly through the Internet."

Zhou kept on asking, "If Ctrip were to be a bigger company ten years from now, what are your plans as members of the entrepreneur team?"

Ji Qi and Liang Jianzhang found the second question difficult to answer because they had never thought about things in such a long term.

Ji Qi took a glimpse at Liang Jianzhang, and responded, "We haven't thought about it yet. Everybody is doing business in the Internet business, so we think that we should do it too. I think we can have expansion in the Internet industry." Then, Ji Qi told IDG investors about his first experience with Internet in Oracle when he was in America. He expressed that he had been looking for a point through which to cut into the Internet industry ever since he went back to China.

This meeting between the Ctrip team and the IDG investors ended with these confusing questions. After Ji Qi and Liang Jianzhang had left, Zhang Suyang asked the other two, "Brothers, how's this team? Don't I have a keen insight?"

The specialist from Boston said, "They do not have a clear long-term goal and are not sure about the combination of tourism and Internet. However, this is indeed a complementary team in terms of the members' skills."

Zhou Quan furthered his view, "The Internet industry is very hot now. Besides, Internet companies are our major investment targets. Let's put some investment in it first! If this team could not make it, I don't think any other team could."

"The four of them are like an organization with four different backgrounds-the big and small gears coordinate with each other perfectly. We investors firstly pay great attention to the potential quality and secondly to the potential quality and thirdly to the potential quality of people who we would spend our money on. This team comes with an attractive background and would be able to have control over the company." Zhang Suyang said, "OK, let's put some in first. If things go well, we can add extra investment to this project."

One week later, the result came from IDG. It gave an evaluation of two million USD on Ctrip, and promised an investment of half a million USD, which took up 20% of Ctrip's shares.

What's worth mentioning was that Ctrip wrote a 10-page Business Plan to IDG. Zhang Suyang had made the decision without even finish reading this business plan.

In October 1999, they got the investment of half a million USD from IDG and the four co-founders started this website on a grand scale with over 30 employee.

On 28th October, Liang Jianzhang changed the website's name from Youhu to Ctrip. From then on, Ctrip. com was officially online and advertised on *Shanghai Microcomputer* magazine.

"Ctrip. com is a portal tourism website specialized in online tourism service and tourism product promotion for tourists, tourist groups, and relative industries. We cover all natural spots and artificial sceneries across the country, and offer the attractive tourist tracks. We provide you with comprehensive information on travel agencies, hotels, restaurants, entertainment, shopping and transportation, and online reservation, including for tickets, rooms, groups and restaurants. We have an all-round service of tourist news, hot-spot recommendation, BBS and clubs. www. ctrip. com is a dynamic multi-media encyclopedia of tourism in China."

Later, in an interview with *Internet Weekly*, Ji Qi exemplified the market positioning and development route of Ctrip.

"The market positioning of Ctrip is the combination of tourism information and tourism e-commerce. Ctrip provides its users with the self-help tourism based on the Internet. We emphasize on four aspects, the site, the agency, the BBS and the club. "

"The 'site' means that this is a website established for the Chinese tourists as well as foreign tourists. We want to make it in China and of China. Ctrip. com will be managed as an all-roundly dimensional website. We will have extensive cooperation with other synthesized or specialized tourism websites, tourism agencies, hotels, inns and other industries related to tourism. "

"The 'agency' means that Ctrip, in the meantime, is a large-scale e-commerce website, namely, a virtual travel agency. We can cover all tourism products including the six aspects of food, accommodation, transportation, travelling, shopping and entertainment. On our website, our users can choose directly from over a thousand hotels, 800 tourist tracks and 30 travel agencies. They can also book air tickets online. "

"The 'BBS' means that we have an online community in which the tourists could share their information of tourism and bitter or sweet memories of their trips. They can state their opinions on each tourist spot and hotel. They can even gather friends to travel together in this community. All of these things could make travelling a true love of their own and provide them with opportunities to meet people who share the same interest with them. "

"The 'club' is going to be a salon for people interested in travelling and a shelter for hardcore lovers of tourism. It is a place where people could go and take part in all kinds of activities. This is going to lead the fashion in tourism. "

The failure of the road show

Why was Ji Qi the one got interviewed by the journalist? IDG's half-a-million investment not only changed the share percentage of Ctrip team, but also changed the structure of the Ctrip Company. Liang Jianzhang had been the CEO for only a few days before he was replaced by Ji Qi. It turned out that Ji Qi was the one Zhang Suyang trusted. Liang Jianzhang was switched to the position of a COO.

After Ji Qi got on the stage, under the guidance of setting up a website combining tourism information and e-commerce, he had improved the website into almost an encyclopedia. On the other hand, he tried every possible business just like when he started his companies in earlier years. He sold everything that could be sold on this website, including entrance tickets, air tickets, reservations for hotel rooms and group tickets of travel agencies.

From 1999 to 2000, the Internet industry had peaked across the world. Nobody could give an accurate number of the Internet companies opened during this time. It was no exaggeration to say that the number of Internet companies was larger than that of the tadpoles in the river. Take the tourism websites as examples, they were countless-Ctrip. com, Yilong. com, CYTC Online. com, City Tourism. com and Green Path. com···

Though there were countless of tourism websites, they were basically in the same business model-tourism information and tourist e-commerce.

All tourism websites were using the same model, they wondered if there was a way to judge the success of their websites. Was there such one way? There was one! At that time, the only measurement was the CTR (Clicks Ratio).

So, to make their CTR look more considerable, the Internet companies began their expensive money-burning competition-to advertise open-handedly.

Ctrip was no exception. They had burnt a lot of money on the CTR. Soon, they were out of money again.

In the Internet wave in 1999, the half-a-million investment IDG had put in was just "drizzle". The Ctrip team had to start working their brains and tried to find a second investment.

This time, the four founders of Ctrip was greatly enlightened by Yiqu's road show to Hongkong, and they thought, "Why don't we have a road show?" Thus, they wrote a business plan that roughly introduced Ctrip's business model, future prospects, and the current situation. Shen Nanpeng made a list of all the venture investment companies in Hongkong, which the four of the Ctrip team meant to use to seek for investment one by one there.

Regretfully, this road show in Hongkong turned out a failure. "Moscow doesn't believe in tears. "

Ji Qi still remembered vaguely about the conversation he had with an investor in Hongkong.

"What kind of company is yours?"

"Ours is a company that is specialized in tourism website. "

"Do you know that many tourist companies are promoting zero-cost group tours?"

"Zero cost? What does that mean?"

"What does that mean? Let me tell you, travel agencies could hardly survive in this business now, let alone tourism websites like yours. Young man, go for another business before it's too late!"

In short, venture capital investors in Hongkong thought the tourism market was a big but scattered one, which was a mess. Besides, they thought tourism websites were outdated comparing to portal websites and e-commerce ones.

If there was anything gained from that trip to Hongkong, it was the enhanced familiarity of Ctrip to all. At least, Ctrip was known to those venture investment companies as an Internet company making tourism websites.

But it was a time when they needed money the most! It was like playing a computer game. However high the level of your avatar is, it will fail the battle without sufficient blood and energy.

Please read the next section to find out if the Ctrip team could get a second round of investment.

Section III   The second round of financing

Success of the second round of financing

With the road show failed in Hongkong, Ji Qi smoked alone in his office in a depression and wondered what to do next.

Ji Qi had been scratching his head for a solution for the financing when Zhang Suyang suddenly showed up.

Zhang Suyang was just back from Beijing, where he had been for the investment in another tourism website.

Why would he invest in two companies of the same feature? During the end of 1999 and the beginning of 2000, nobody could predict the prominence of an Internet company. In each business model, the investors had to choose several promising companies in order to grasp the opportunity while evading the risk.

"What? You have invested in another tourism website?" Ji Qi was not happy about it.

"Yes. Over the past two years, IDG have invested in nearly 40 companies, among which there are several that have the same nature. But we don't put in too much investment during the first round." Zhang said.

"Do you still have faith in our Ctrip?" Ji Qi stared into Zhang's eyes and asked.

"Of course I have faith in you! It's needless to ask. There are already nearly 10 tourism websites in this country. However, your job for Ctrip now is to improve your core competitiveness so that no other companies could compete against you. It's like what Liu Chuanzhi has said, 'Spread a layer of soil, and tamp it down; spread another layer of soil, and tamp it down again.'" Zhang Suyang replied.

"Come on! Ctrip is out of money, and its life is hanging by the thread. The urgency is the financing, and any other issues are nonsense for Ctrip right now. If you are really confident in Ctrip, please hurry and introduce some new investors to me." Ji Qi had lost his patience.

After a while of silence, Zhang Suyang opened his mouth, "Alright! I'll give you another famous investor. You are all on your own to get the investment done."

"Who is that? What investment company does he work for?" Ji Qi was so excited that he even had sparkles in his eyes.

"Softbank. Shi Mingchun, the representative of Softbank's China Region. He is already quite famous in this field of investment."

"Softbank?" Ji Qi had no deep impression on Softbank. But he trusted Zhang and believed it was a good company.

Actually, at that time, few people were familiar with Softbank, which was formerly in the field of industrial corporating. It was not too long ago before Softbank entered the field of venture investment.

The chief leader of this company was a legacy-Sun Zhengyi. Here, we need to have a brief understanding of his growing-up experience and investment concept so as to comprehend the special bond between Softbank and Ctrip.

In August 1957, Sun Zhengyi was born in a middle class family in Saga, Japan. In September 1975, he went to America for study, and majored in Economics in the Berkeley School of California State University.

He had spent a year in America before he suddenly realized that there was a time-saving way to make a lot of money there. It was the business of applying for and selling patens. Having thought in this way and that, he used an instant way of combination-he discovered electronic dictionaries through the combination of sound equipment, a dictionary and a screen. Thereupon, he gathered specialists on this research. He succeeded in this research and got his company listed in the stock market. Sun Zhengyi had dug his first bucket of gold out of this research.

In March 1980, Sun Zhengyi graduated from university. He decided to go back to China to start his own business, and gave up the high salary in America. Upon a one-year scientifical research through 25 standards on 40 projects, he decided to focus his business on software distribution. In September 1981, the 24-year-old Sun Zhengyi founded Softbank with the registered capital of 10 million Japanese yen.

On the opening day of Softbank, he stood on a fruit case and announced to two new employees, "Our goal is to become a company with trillions of Japanese yen and thousands of staff members. " These two employees thought this speech was off-key and their boss was mad, so they quitted on the spot.

But, after 1992, Sun Zhengyi got the dealership in Japan of the Cisco Sytems. By the end of that year, Soft had controlled 70% of the software sales channel in Japan. His career was in the ascendant.

In July 1994, Softbank got listed and got the financing of 140 million dollar. Sun had become a billionaire at the age of only 37.

In the same year, Sun was determined to transform his business into venture investment. In November 1995, Sun invested two millions in Yahoo,com, which had only several staff members. This move seemed incredible even to Yang Zhiyuan. He thought Sun was out of his mind. What surprised Yang more was that later Sun had put more money in Yahoo. When Yahoo got listed, Sun Zhengyi cashed in 5% of his share into 450 million dollar, still being the biggest share-holder of Yahoo. This time, Yang admired Sun so much and described him as "the man who could see the 15 to 20 years coming ahead".

Finished with first successful battle in America, Sun wanted to make his move back to the Chinese market with his team. At the same time, his schoolmate, Lu Hongliang, from Berkeley school came for him. Lu Hongliang, Wu Ying and three other people had founded UT Starcom. They had met with the bottle neck of money shortage and were in need of venture fund. Wu Ying made a 30-minute speech about the current and future development strategy and objective. Sun Zhengyi was deeply impressed by Wu's career ambition. He immediately invested 30 million USD in UT Starcom, taking up 30 percent of its share. Later, UT Starcom developed well and gave Sun Zhengyi multiplied payback. Thus, Sun made the decision to open an investment company.

Softbank set up its first venture investment fund in China, and it was named Softbank China Venture Investment Limited. It got registered in Hongkong in July 1999 with the capital of 50 million dollar. Shi Mingchun was the representative in China of Softbank China Venture Investment.

In terms of style of investment, Softbank China was very different from IDG. The former one liked to cooperate with IDG-normally, IDG would put in the first investment as seed money, and Softbank China would join in during later time. Shi Mingchun had a concept about investment that went like "Venture investment is like a wolf hunting-the more hunters, the braver they get." With his support, Softbank China had invested in Internet companies such as Sina, 163, 8848, and Dangdang in succession. Shi Mingchun himself also had a special affection for Internet companies.

IDG had such cooperation with Softbank China, Zhang Suyang called Shi Mingchun right after he had left Ji Qi's office and told him that Ctrip was a company worth putting venture investment in.

Before long, Shi Mingchun showed up in Ctrip's office.

Just like the investors from IDG, he had a casual conversation with no limitation with the founder of Ctrip. He asked where the four co-founders came from, what the liked to do and what their interests were.

Shi Mingchun discovered that the four of them had very different characteristics-Ji Qi and Shen Nanpeng were good at words while Liang Jian had a few words which showed his keen insight; Fan Min's talk unfolded his affinity with people.

After the "investigation", Shi Mingchun got down to business.

"Could you use several sentences to briefly describe the business model and the development outlook of your company?" Shi asked with a smile.

"There are three reasons for choosing this product. First, there were successful examples of such kind in America. Secondly, there is no such service in China yet. Thirdly, people will be in need of such service with the development of the China's market and economy." Liang Jianzhang responded.

Shi Mingchun was quite satisfied with Liang's response, so he made a quick decision to put investment in Ctrip. In the end of 1999, Shi Mingchun decided to invest in Ctrip himself, and he had also pulled four other investment companies-Shanghai Industrial Corporation, US Orchid Fund, Hongkong Morningside Group and IDG. The five companies had a total investment of 4.5 million USD, taking up 29% of Ctrip's share.

Later, when Shi Mingchun talked about Softbank China's investment in Ctrip, he said, "We had chosen Ctrip because, on one hand, this industry is suitable to be conducted on the Internet-this model is simple and clear, and easy for people to understand; everybody will think that they need this service. On the other hand, this company is lead by a pretty good team. This was a choice based on comprehensive consideration. Ctrip was not the first one in this business, but definitely is the fastest one, which has a lot to do with its market positioning and team. Ctrip's value will gradually appear because it has the technology and brand. "

The start of the "money-burning" competition

In the late of March, 2000, Ctrip got its second financing investment. Seeing that they had got another 4.5 million USD, the three of Liang Jianzhan, Shen Nanpeng and Fan Min wrote their resignation to their current companies over night, and packed their stuff to work in Ctrip, deciding not to turn back.

Now that venture investors had put so much money in Ctrip, what did they want Ctrip to do?

Zhang Suyang said, "Ji Qi, we have money now! What do you say? Let me tell you, the current situation is that any Chinese Internet company could go public now. You need to work on the click ratio and user number, without thinking too much about the profits. Don't think about the long term development. Our goal is to get Ctrip listed. Once Ctrip goes public, we will become billionaires over night. "

"What if we can not get Ctrip listed?" Ji Qi joked.

"If we can not get Ctrip listed, merger and acquisition is another choice!" Zhang Suyang carried on, "Don't think too much. Go and advertise. "

Actually, at that time, Zhang Suyang was not the only person among others in the Internet business to think like this-advertising, improving click ratio, getting listed and cashing in.

What was odd was that nobody was working on how to make money through the websites. CEOs of Internet companies had no concern over this problem. They believed that as time went by, they would find a way to make money, but the urgent step for them to take was to advertise.

Such concept had made Internet companies so eager to promote their websites that they were burning RMBs and USDUSDs like burning faux paper money (a kind of money resembling real bills made to be burnt to memorize the passed-aways) on Tomb-Sweeping Day-they were spending USD and RMBs like papers. Ji Qi had described such passion like this, "I had the feeling that there were loud noises in a fair, and in order to get heard, I had to yell louder than anybody else."

It was necessary to burn some money, but they needed to know how to burn the money.

The Ctrip team thought that the time had passed when any advertisement could bring profits-"The advertisements are in the sky and the channels are on the ground. The bosses are happily bending their backs to pick up money." The strategy on advertising was that "with no advertisement, a company is waiting for death; with disordered advertisements, a company is doomed for death; with great advertisements, a company is going to make money till its death."

How to make great advertisements? The answer is to make a big difference with a small amount of money. So, Ctrip had a strict control over the cost on their advertisements-they controlled the cost for marketing and promotion within 30% of the company's finance.

To have a better control over the cost, they decided not to make random attempts. They gave up on roadside billboards, body advertisement on buses, and even advertisements in the subways.

Ctrip aimed at business travelers and high-end tourists who flew around frequently, focusing on the air travelers. Therefore, they built advertisement lamp boxes in several major airports, each one of which cost over one million RMB a year.

Finished with the advertisement lamp boxes in the airports, they began on other promotions.

In April 2000, Ctrip cooperated with CAAC (Civil Aviation Administration of China) to hold the first air stewardess beauty pageant in the domestic aviation industry-Shanghai International Air Stewardess Centurial Elegence Competition. Ctrip aired the live competition exclusively online.

Ctrip had put many human and financial resources into this event. The theme of that competition was to showcase the "one-hundred year history of the world's aviation industry and the elegance of air stewardess across the century". Ctrip. com provided the netizens with a complete community in which they witness the appearance of the air stewardesses and obtain their personal profiles. In the meanwhile, Ctrip. com had set up an award for the audience's favorite contestant, voted directly by the Internet users online. All of those who had taken part in the activity would get a present from Ctrip. com, probably a Lenovo MP3 player.

Ctrip had spent a fortune on this public event, however, the repercussions were so plain that Ji Qi felt frustrated.

The Ctrip team were at lost when their investors made an appearance again.

"Zhang Suyang, Shi Mingchun, you are both here!" Ji Qi said.

"Chief Ji, how much have you spent on the promotion?" Shi asked.

"Two or three million RMB each year-that's about over ten million RMB together these months. But the repercussions were not so great!"

"Only ten million RMB? You are burning the money too slow! Go faster. In this market, it's sometimes like boiling water-in order to get the water boiled, you must maximize the flame; if it's only a tiny flame, the firewood will run out before the water gets boiled." Shi said.

"Chief Ji, Shi Mingchun was right. We never requested that the Ctrip team must succeed. If you have really tried your best, but still fail, it wouldn't matter. I mean, you shouldn't be so conservative. Seize the opportunity, and spend money courageously. After all, it's not your money. What are you being afraid of?" Zhang Suyang followed.

But, the Ctrip team, who were personally in this market, knew very clear that it would be a move meant to lose, and it was pointless.

Would the Ctrip team follow their investors' advice? Please read the following!

The continuance not to earn profits

The advice from the investors seemed convincing on the surface-"You are spending my money on your advertisement. Why do you hesitate?" But Ji Qi did not think so. He thought, "If one out of ten companies invested by venture investment companies could make profits, the investors would have enough reason to bet on them. But it's different for the entrepreneurs. Once they lose, they will not have a second chance. Just like the saying goes, 'If you lose over years of fighting, you will go back to the time before the liberation.'" There would not even be another chance for them in another life if they failed.

Compared to those Internet entrepreneurs who had no experience of running a business, Ji Qi knew deep in his heart that it was not going to work out if his company could only live on investments rather than making profits. When people were losing direction in the passion of Internet, Ji had stayed conscious and knew that "it is a crime for a company not to make any profits".

With this realistic idea, Ctrip was looking for the most profitable business among hotel reservations, entrance tickets, group tourism and air ticket reservations.

On 9th January, 2000, the Ctrip team attended the Tourist Industry and Internet Economy Forum held by *China Business Journal*, in which Ji Qi had somehow apprehended something.

Ctrip. com, CYTS Online, 51yala. com, byecity. com, Chinagc. com, BTG Travel & Tours Group and Hasee Group had joined this forum. The topic was "Do tourism websites have impact on traditional industries?"

On the meeting, the General Manager of Hasee Group Zhu Yongde said, "Personally, I think that nowadays, people's living standard doesn't match what is required by the Internet economy. The Internet doesn't have a great impact on traditional industries. I have once worked with some websites, which wasn't as ideal as I expected. However, the Internet has done great help to us, through which we can get to know tour tracks and tourism products. Thus, our communication and service awareness has been enhanced. "

The Deputy Manager of Yjita. com Long Yuanzhao followed and said, "In my opinion, there are some impacts created by the Internet to traditional travel agencies. First, there are room and ticket reservations. These two had brought us quite a lot of profits. But now we are losing both with the development of information technology. As to the question whether Internet will take up all the business of traditional travel agencies', I think that the Internet could only play a catalytic part. We would have to depend on traditional travel agencies for actual tourism. Or else, where could the tourists get transportation, tour guides, or even WC if they need to use the toilet?"

The General Manager of Byecity. com Wu Gang also expressed his viewpoint, "The Internet has its advantage in terms of new tourism products. We could provide tourists with personalized tourism products according to our online inquiry and provide them with whatever they prefer. Take our tour group to Australia several days ago as an example, we have formed this group through only e-mails instead of any other forms of advertisements. This is something a traditional travel agency would not be able to do-they could not even afford the cost for the promotion. What's more worth mentioning is that new products bear high gross profit margin. "

With the finishing of the "Kong Fu contest at Mount Hua", could Ji Qi was inspired by the ideas exchanged among those people in his business. Could the Ctrip team find a most profitable business? Please read the third chapter *Transformation and Purchase*.

Summary

There are three questions related to this chapter-

I. How can a team get through an unrest period?

There is an old saying goes like this, "People get together because they don't know about each other. They break up because they have known about each other. " When a team develops into the unrest period (p. 2-1), the team members will find each other not so perfect as they have expected them to be and they will have conflict because of their different opinions.

This is a problem that causes a headache not only to the Ctrip team, but also to almost any other teams.

At this moment, what measures could a team leader take to keep his team from falling apart and make the members continue to cooperate with one and another?

p. 2-1   a team behavioral curve

team characteristic

job efficiency

a group

a false team

a potential team

a true team

an efficient team

There are many solutions on textbooks-to comfort team members, to encourage team members into participating in strategy, to establish work rules, and so on. But, Ctrip did not take any of the measures which sounded reasonable. The reason why Ctrip did not collapse during the unrest period was their unselfish dedication.

Wasn't this the reason? When they formed this partnership, Shen Nanpeng put in 600 thousand RMB, taking up just 40% of the share, while Ji Qi and Liang Jianzhang had each put in 200 thousand RMB, taking up respectively 20% of the share. Wasn't this the reason? When the company was first founded, it was only Ji Qi who was running it. The other three partners joined in when it had moved onto the right track.

I have a fellow who wanted to build a real estate company with a best friend of his. Upon reading his business plan, this friend of his said, "We don't have to partner up. If you need money now, I can lend you some in ahead." My fellow got confused, and posted his business plan on a QQ group for discussion, hoping to find what the problem was.

One e-friend replied, "This is a precise business plan with absolutely no problem in format. It's just that you have emphasized too much on the distribution of benefits."

My fellow explained, "He is my best friend, and that's why I did so! What if there is going to be a dispute if we don't get this straight in ahead?"

My fellow could not understand his best friend's feeling after reading his business plan-"If we are haggling over every penny now, wouldn't things get worse in the future?"

Until now, my fellow have never understood the meaning of the story of shooting a wild goose-when shooting a goose, is it better to shoot it down first and then discuss about how to distribute it, or otherwise?

Ideas make lifestyle; attitude makes altitude; horizons make a state of mind; patterns make ending. At that time, Ji Qi and Shen Nanpeng probably both thought, "Let's build up the business first, and leave the problem of money distribution to be worried about later."

II. Discovery of the opportunities in the market

1. Market opportunities can be categorized into three types (p. 2-2) based on the clarity of supply and demand-the identified market opportunities, the discovered market op-

portunities and the invented opportunities.

p. 2-2　categories of entrepreneurial opportunity
　　　　supply demand
　　　　discovered clear on one aspect
　　　　the identified clear on both aspects
　　　　the invented clear on neither aspects

(1) The identified market opportunities-such kind of opportunity is clear on supply and demand, and it would only take the effort of the entrepreneurs to identify them. .

(2) The discovered market opportunities-such kind of opportunity is only clear on either supply or demand, and entrepreneurs have to dig the other aspect.

(3) The invented market opportunities-such kind of opportunity is clear on neither supply nor demand, and entrepreneurs have to invent them by using economic methods.

To better exemplify the three kinds of market opportunities, here is a small story named "Selling shoes to the South Pacific".

It is said that during the 1950s, three shoes factories had sent three salesmen to the small islands on the South Pacific in order to expand their business there.

The three salesmen got there and were surprised-nobody wore shoes in that damnable place.

The first salesman felt depressed and wondered whom to sell his shoes to. He sent a telegraph to his boss at once saying, "Nobody here wears shoes. I am taking the first plane back tomorrow."

The second salesman did the exactly opposite thing. He was so happy on seeing the situation there. "Haha! I am going to be rich. See, nobody wears shoes here. It is a virgin market." H sent a telegraph to his boss at once, "Boss, nobody here wears shoes. I've decided to stay."

What was the third salesman's thought? His idea was more amazing! Not only had he found out this virgin market, he had found another market-the coconuts on this Pacific island were useless to the local people. He thought to himself, "Why don't I sell some coconuts to the outside, and use the money to stock some shoes and sell them here?"

Thus, the three salesmen began their three types of lives-

The first one got fired and left the business of sales; the second one became a marketing manager; the third one became a boss.

How could the three salesmen see three markets through the same opportunity?

Because the first salesman used the method of confirming, failing to identify the market; the second one used the method of discovering, ending in finding a market; the third one used a comprehensive method, being able to find and create a market based on the one found.

So, in this world, there lacks no opportunity, but the awareness of transferring opportunities into markets.

Looking back at the time when Ji Qi was in Oracle with his school mate, he looked for *Mona Lisa* using the Yahoo search engine developed by Yang Zhiyuan, which surprised him. He could never have imagined that he was able to find anything through the Internet. Immediately, he realized that the Internet could change people's lifestyle and the current business model of itself.

When he returned to China, he was looking for a point to cut into the Internet market. He wanted to integrate traditional industries and discover a new market through the platform of the Internet.

However, discovering an opportunity doesn't mean the success of entrepreneurship because this opportunity needs to be developed.

2. In chronological order, there are three steps-discovering, seizing and transforming the market opportunities.

Among the three steps, the first two are the most important.

Chen Tianqiao had once said, "An opportunity is like a fast revolving door-you must enter without any hesitation when you see an interval." He meant that one must grab the opportunity as soon as he saw it.

Jiang Nanchun had another saying, "I wasn't the only person who thought it was a pioneering work to have advertisements on the LED screens just next to the elevator gates. But I was the only one who acted on this idea." Jiang meant that one must seize the opportunities which had been discovered but had not been acted on yet.

To exemplify the importance of seizing any opportunity before anybody sees it, here is a story of "Catching the bull's tail".

There was a young man who was unconditionally and madly in love with the beautiful daughter of a farmer. One day, he decided to propose to the girl in the farmer's house.

The farmer said to this young man, "There are many excellent boys who want to marry my daughter. If you want me to agree on your proposal, you have to do one thing. I want to see if you have the bravery and wisdom."

The young man asked hurriedly, "Uncle, what is it that you want me to do?"

"Come over here," the famer took the young man near a cattle pen and said, "Later, I will let out three fierce bulls. Catch any one's tail, and you'll succeed."

The young man hesitated for a while, but finally agreed. He was afraid of the fierce bulls, while still hoping for miracles to happen.

The first one came out. It was a fearful young bull. It roared and was very fast. The young man was still in hesitation when it rushed towards him. The young man thought, "I'll wait for the next one. If I'm lucky enough, the next one will probably be less fearful."

The second bull came out. It was a very tall and strong bull. The moment it broke out of the fence, it showed its incomparable physical strength and range. The young man got shocked and lost all courage. He thought, "I can't be that unlucky. I'll wait for the next one. I'll catch the next one's tail no matter what."

The third one came out. It was a skinny old bull which couldn't even run. "Haha! Finally." The young man was so happy that he ran straight towards the bull and tried to catch the tail on its bottom. Suddenly, he found that the bull had no tail, feeling so astounded.

In fact, there are many opportunities like the above ones in the business market.

When you can't see the opportunity clearly, you'll have to wait and see; when it becomes clear, you'll find that the market is already full of competition; when you have eventually made up your mind to enter this market, the opportunity will have already been unattractive.

Between the years 1999 and 2000, portal websites were very popular. However, the Ctrip team focused only on tourism websites with great passion. Did they really have keen insight on the market?

Actually, they were crossing the water by searching for and feeling the stones-they were uncertain about what's beneath the surface. What Liang Jianzhang only knew was that such websites in America were successful. But they were not certain whether they could survive if they transplant this model to China.

What the Ctrip team had done right was that they seized the opportunity.

III. How to negotiate on financing with venture investors?

The three elements of entrepreneurship are people, money and projects. With the team assembled and project picked, the next step is financing. There are four normal ways of financing-from shareholders, banks, venture investment and going public. The initial capital must be from the shareholders, and the following-up capital can be loan from the banks, investment from venture capital investors. When the company gets into the right track, it could go public.

Among the four financing choices, the shareholders are unable to bring in large sums of money; mortgages from banks requires pledge; going public would be a long to go. Thus, venture investment seems the best choice for small and medium sized enterprises.

Many people think that to gain favor from venture investors, there must be an attractive business plan. How to write a good business plan? The answers are clarity, brevity, logic and figures. Only by matching the four requirements, could a business plan be convincing to a venture investor. Once an entrepreneur concluded, "To get the investment from a venture investor is as difficult as pursuing a divorced woman. "

However, is this true to venture investors? Do they think the same? On a general survey of the companies who have got investment from venture investors, to our surprise, venture investors value the entrepreneurial teams more than the projects. In the TV show *Winning in China*, Guo Fansheng once said to the teams, "What you lack is not money, but the trust from people who have money. "

So, they think that the risks lie in the people, not in the projects. They would attach great importance to the communication with the entrepreneurial teams to understand their thoughts and ideas.

What questions would venture investors ask the entrepreneurial teams?

1. The normal model. Investors would give them three questions-

(1) What are you doing?

To answer this question, you must follow the rule of KISS (Keep it Simple & Stupid), meaning the simpler, the better. Venture investors think that the easier the business model is, the more possible for it to succeed.

(2) Who are in this team? How do you know each other?

To answer this question, the entrepreneurs need to inform the investors the number of core members in this team and how you got to know each other. It's better if these questions are answered in person rather than by the CEO.

(3) What's the current capital situation?

The true intention for this question can be concluded into three points-

First, it is to know the general situation of the company's operation; to know how much cash the company has; to know how long the cash could sustain for. If you tell the investors that the cash could only last for 10 days, there would be no need to talk to the venture investors.

Secondly, it is to know the how well you master the capital of your company. If you could not answer this question, the venture investors would feel incredible-you are the CEO, how could you not know about it?

Thirdly, it is to know about your control over the turnover of the capital. You are in need of cash, which means it is unrealistic to say that you don't want any money. You can answer that the current business could maintain the cash in an optimum state, and that it could last until the next year if the business does not get expanded.

2. The extraordinary model. Investors would give irregular questions, not following basic rules-

IDG asked Ctrip the following questions.

(1) What was your purpose to found Ctrip?

(2) If ten years from now, Ctrip gets bigger. What would you team members plan to do?

The first question was to understand why they chose to start an enterprise. They second one was to understand the thoughts of the core members and how big they wanted to expand their business to.

Softbank China asked Ctrip the follow questions.

(1) Where are you from?

(2) What do you like to do?

(3) What's your hobby?

These are simple and useful questions. During an interview, it is better to ask open questions in order to get overall information. The unnecessary detailes will be saved.

In all, venture investors inspect the entrepreneurial teams so strictly because they could not have a direct hand in the company's business, neither could they control it. The only choice is to choose the right people.

During the two years between 1999 and 2000, large scales of capital went into this industry. Some Internet companies were born over night, and some died over night.

However, in this case, the Ctrip team did not let the venture investors down. They had done a great job in this "Internet Bubble". Next, let's read the Chapter III *Transformation and Purchase*.

Application

I. Should I enter the market of cactus drinks?

In the afternoon of 19th January, 2009, a former colleague of mine flew from Hainan to Shenzhen to discuss something with me.

At eight o'clock, we met in the North Huaqiang Shangdao Café.

"Zhang Chao, it's been six years. You must be doing pretty good, aren't you?" I said directly.

"Heihei! My former leader, honestly, I'm doing so so. I have at present opened a beverage factory in Hainan, which is specialized in producing cactus drinks."

"Cactus juice? This is new to me!" I was quite surprised.

"Yes, I wanted to take the road nobody else dared to take. You know that in the market of mineral water, there are Robust and Nongfu Spring; in the market of tea beverage, there are Uni-president and Master Kong; in the market of soda, there are Coca Cola and Pepsi; in the market of herbal tea, there are Wanglaoji and Guangdong Herbal Tea; in the market of energy drinks, there are Red Bull and Jianlibao… There is currently no famous brand in the market of cactus drinks."

"That' a good idea! But, I wonder what the market positioning of the product is. That's to say, what's your appeal to the customers?"

"We have a great product with a special taste and delicate fragrance. It's good for your skin and stomach. It helps to diminish inflammation, to reduce blood sugar and to reduce blood fat. If well promoted, this product will have a prominent future in the market. "

"Yes. I've meant to mention the promotion-why would customers want to drink this? You should know that this is a new product. There are already similar products in the current market. But no company could really build up this market. " I said seriously.

"So, I came to you! Would you please join our team? We'll give you the job position of Market Inspector if you are willing to join our team. "

"Would you be willing to burn money on the advertisement?"

"Our boss is a billionaire and is confident in this product. He is a local resident in Hainan, and had contracted thousands of mu's land to grow cactus. "

......

According to the above conversation, do you think there is a prominent market for his cactus drinks? If there is one, then how to construct the selling-point of this product?

Ⅱ. How much shares should an one-hundred-million RMB investment take up?

I have a friend from Chaozhou who had fought for his business in Shenzhen for twenty years, owning eight inns. The current situation is that he invests around 5 million RMB in each inn every year. And 7 inns are profiting, earning 200 to 300 thousand RMB per month. The seventh one was opened one year ago and is still in a deficit, losing 4 to 5 thousand RMB each month.

This friend began to have some ideas when he saw the chain hotels are developing rapidly in these years. He hired a management consultation company to give his inns a unified name. He had also spent 150 thousand RMB on a VI brochure.

Soon, a venture investor had an eye on his company, offering 100 million RMB to hold 70% of the share.

The question is-is the percentage of shares reasonable? If not, then what do you think the percentage should be?

Chapter III
Transformation and Purchase

The company which was only half-a-year old and had no experience in hotel reservations found the most profitable model in this new business, which turned out to be the perfect transformation. In a situation of deficit, the company purchased the most profitable BizExpress and Modern Yuntong with a small amount of cash and shares. "Currently, for Ctrip, the best choice is to purchase the best reservation agency on the market."

Quotations

Reflections on the business market 1-5

You have to be good in the first place; then you need someone to praise you; the one who praises you have to be good too; you have to practice what you preach.

—reflection on the Ctrip team members' mutural recognition

Don't dread a rival like a wolf. You need to be more afraid of a teammate like a pig.

—one has to be cautious when choosing a teammate

What you lack is not money, but the trust from people who have money.

—reflection on the Ctrip team's second financing

Great efforts might not end in success; zero effort will definitely end in failure. You can choose to give up, but never should you give up on choices.

—reflection on Ji QI's remarks on purchasing

Whether being a lion or a sheep, you have to keep running; whether being poor or wealthy, you have to keep on hard-working.

—reflection on Wang Shengli's entrepreneurial story

A fable

The bees and flies fleeing for their lives

This was an inspiring experiment designed by Professor Karl Weick from University of Michigan.

One day, Professor Weick was in a large room with dim light. He opened the only window in the room and the window was small. He put six bees and six flies separately into twelve narrow-necked bottles. Then he laid the bottles down, facing the bottle neck towards the window. He wanted to see if they could manage to fly out of the narrow-necked bottles.

Normally, it should be a bee that came out first. But the result had people drop their glasses.

The bees hit the bottom of the bottle hard, trying to find the way out. They continued on this until they got too tired to fly or starved to death; but the flies did something different-they flew around for a while, but within two minutes, they had flew out from the bottle neck on the other side of the bottle.

Professor Weick could not believe what he had witnessed. He decided to do several more experiments, each of which is more serious than the former experiments he had conducted.

After these experiments, Weick finally came to the conclusion that bees were sensitive to light. They would think that the way out is where there is light according to their experience. The glass is a supernatural mystery to them, but they had never come into contact with the atmospheric layer in nature which they could not get through. They considered it unacceptable and incomprehensible that they could not get through the obstacles. So, they repeated the moves which seemed logical to them without stopping. It was such persistence that lead to the death of the bees.

The flies seemed not to care about logic. They ignored the light and flew around. They scored a lucky hit by trying over and over again in the bottle. They finally found the exit they had hoped for, gaining freedom and new lives where the seemingly experienced bees withered away.

This story tells us-

1. Experience form previous jobs might be a stepping stone, or a stumbling stone to the present job.

2. Faced with the ever-changing and unpredictable situation, you should persist on and weave your way through for the success. Don't be afraid of making mistakes. Be brave in taking risks and dare to take risks.

3. Continuous attempts are more important than experience and intelligence.

Text
Section Ⅰ The trend in websites
The first one to try tomato—Info Highway

Speaking of China's Internet industry, there is a name that need to be mentioned—Zhang Shuxin. This woman was born in Fushun, Liaoning and graduated from University of Science and Technology of China. She was the first one to try tomato in China's Internet industry. In 1995, a time when people had no clue of what Internet and e-commerce was, she established her own company Info Highway. The advertisement board of Info Highway was set at the intersection on Zhongguancun Road in Beijing. The advertisement board read,

"How far away are Chinese from the information highway? 1500 meters to the North."

As the first company to provide ISP (Internet Service Provider) and ICP (Internet Content Provider) in the domestic market, Info Highway was walking with great difficulty.

According to Zhang Shuxin, when she went to apply for the Internet in Post and Telecommunication Bureau, the employees there felt at lost what to do, not knowing how to categorize her application and how to charge.

When the company was first started, it only registered with the capital of 7 million RMB. Zhongxing Facan shared Info Highway's by increasing its registered capital to 80 million RMB. The later one took up 73.5% of its share, so Zhongxing Facan's Chief Director Liang Yeping became the Board Director of Info Highway and Zhang Shuxin was transferred to being CEO.

When asked about the business of her newly founded company, Zhang would say, "Info Highway is a platform on the Internet, on which our terminal users could enjoy the service and contents."

Looking back, such business model seemed not profitable in 1995. At that time, Info Highway had eight branch companies across the country with 50 thousand users. In the business circumstance in its Beijing branch, it could profit with 20 thousand users. Accordingly, Info Highway was in need of another 110 thousand users. What was worse was that in June 1997, the Post and Telecommunication Bureau had invested 7 billion RMB in the 169 National Multimedia Telecommunication Network. As a result, the life of Info Highway was in jeopardy.

Based on the current situation, the choices made for Info Highway by the decision makers had to be so cautious because it would affect the future development of this company. Zhang Shuxin thought the future for Info Highway was to become a public website "for people"; Liang Zhiping, on the other hand, the business of Info High should be transformed into financing information service specialized for corporation users.

Different minds think apart. After rounds of negotiation, Liang Zhiping and Zhang Shuxin couldn not reach an agreement. Holding larger shares, Liang Zhiping had the power of speech. In result, Zhang Shuxin had to leave the company she built by herself.

Therefore, Zhang Shuxin ended in a complete lost. Why did she lose?

Reflecting on it, Zhang thought, "It was most unfortunate that I've entered the Internet business. I entered the right business at a wrong time, ending in an error. I've made three mistakes-first, I did not have any checking on background resources of this industry; secondly, I agreed to an unreasonable capital structure; thirdly, my business model was not designed with multiple value chains."

But, an enterpriser who had once cooperated with Zhang had an different opinoin about this. His assessment on Info Highway was, "There are three limits in Info Highway's development. First, the powerful promotion gave people illusion. Secondly, as a manager, the macroscopic strategist Zhang Shuxin failed to perform management strategies that should be aimed at the market. Thirdly, Info Highway was just an experiment in the development of China's Internet industry, and it was meant to end in this way. "

Though everybody had different opinions about this, one thing was certain to all-as the CEO of a company, you will have to step down if the company could not earn money. This is what Info Highway had enlightened the followers in the Internet industry.

The two models of making profits

The failure of Info Highway did not mean that of the Internet industry's. Zhang Shuxin was outed because there were problems in her business model. Now let's take a look at a successful business model and learn how they made money.

The first company is Yahoo. Yahoo was built by two doctors from Stanford Unviersity-Yang Zhiyuan and David Filo.

It was founded on the 5th, in May 1995.

In August 1995, Yahoo sold its first advertisement, making a small amount of money.

Unexpectedly, Yahoo got listed in NASDAQ in April 1996. The stock price rose 154% on the day it got listed, increasing its market capitalization to 800 million USD.

As time went by, the Internet wave got higher across the world. And the stock price went upwards incredibly. Somebody did a math-if you had bought one-thousand dollar shares on 31st January 1997, they would turn into 56 thousand dollar the exact same date three years later. Its yearly return on capital was as high as 380%.

The above are about the development of Yahoo. The following are the exploitation about its business model.

When Yahoo was first established, its major functions were website categorization and search engine. Later, it expanded into every possible aspect, including news, chatting rooms, real-time stocks & shares quotations, economic and financial information, broadcasting, e-mails, billboards, online payment system and many other services.

How could Yahoo make profits? The answered can be concluded into one sentence-"By making the better, the larger amount of advertisements, and faster alliances. " Apart from over four thousand advertisers, Yahoo also had worked with over ten thousand businessmen in its online shopping system, and with more than one thousand strategic partners.

This is the portal website model invented by Yang Zhiyuan. Timothy Koogle once described Yahoo like this, "Yahoo is the only place one can go if he wants to have anything do to with anything or anybody. "

However, Yahoo was not the only successful Internet business model in those years. In the U. S, there was another one-the AOL model.

On 10th January 2000, the world's largest ISP AOL (American Online) and the world' s largest media group Time Warner announced that the two enterprises would merge into an enormous Internet and media group-AOL-Time Warner Corporation.

This was the biggest purchase in the business history, amounting to as much as 184 billion USD. After the merger, the company would become the world's seventh largest company with a yearly business volume of 30 billion USD and a market value of 286 billion USD. With the announcement, the stock price of Time Warner rose from 75 USDto 95 USD, and reached 102 USD the next day.

After the merger, the stock price of Time Warner did go up. But, people were confused, "Time Warner is an old brand with a 70-year history. It controls TV networks such as CNN, Cartoon TV, and Warner Bros Picture. It also has power over famous newspapers and magazines like *People*, *Fortune* and *Entertainment Weekly*. It ranks top among traditional media, having assets worth 83 billion USD. How could it be that such a company is willing to be purchased by AOL, which had only a history of over ten years?"

The spokesman for Time Warner explained after the merger, We have known the impact on traditional media from the Internet for a long time. We have tried to march into the Internet industry, but we failed. With only a ten-year history, AOL has made profits four times that of the Time Warner's in the second financial season in 1999 alone. Besides, there are only over 10,000 employees in AOL, but we have more than 60,000 in Time Warner. The disparity is very clear. "

Meanwhile, AOL had expressed that they had purchased Time Warner for the use rights of its TV networks, gigantic user profile systems, TV shows and newspapers. AOL did not get satisfied with only being the largest ISP, it wanted to expand itself in the future world of Internet. That's to say, it wanted to realize the all-round life on the Internet-it would be a combination of not only words and graphics, but also sound, light, and vision.

One example of a business model-Sina. com

In the market, there lacks innovation rather than methods of duplication.

Soon, the business model of portal website was copied to China from across the Atlantic Ocean.

In 1997, Wang Zhidong established Sina. com; Zhang Chaoyang established Souhu. com; Ding Lei established 163. com.

Among the three new companies, the story of Sina (the former Stone Lifang) is worth illustration. This company had seen the bubble of Internet inflating and bursting.

In October 1997, three venture capital companies including Walden International had invested 65 billion USDUSD in Stone Lifang. Thus, the first portal website in China was born, the founder of which was Wang Zhidong-"the Wang (King) of China's Internet Indudstry. "

Wang Zhidong explained that he had got this name only because of his family name

"Wang". Nevertheless, Wang Zhidong was indeed the first person to have introduced venture capital investment in China's IT industry.

Stone Lifang had a dramatic development ever since it was founded.

In September 1998, the General Manager of Huayuan's China Business Region called Wang Zhidong and said that his boss wanted to merge with Stone Lifang. Huayuan wanted to purchase the latter company, having capital four times that of Stone Lifang. Unexpectedly, when they met for the merger, the percentage was revised; Stone Lifang-purchased Huayuan with the capital proportion of 2:1. Later, when Wang talked about this merger, he said secretly, "I threw a bomb at them."

After the merger, the new company was founded in December that year and was named Sina.

It was clear that Sina wanted to go public with their efforts to get venture capital investment and merger.

What was regretful was that in July 1999, Chinanet got listed in NASDAQ ahead of Sina, when the latter one was still in preparation for getting listed.

The board members got very upset because the title of "China's first portal website" was stolen by Chinanet.com. So, they decided to initiate IPO and road show immediately.

On 30th Martch, 2000, Wang Zhidong set off with his Sina road show group from Hongkong. What was odd was that during the time they were having the road show, their stock prices on NASDAQ dropped dramatically. By the time they finished the road show, they had dropped over 500 points.

They couldn not wait any more-they need to go public as soon as possible. On 13th April 2000, Sina was officially listed on NASDAQ with an opening price of 17 USD. After the opening, it raised to 22 USD, increasing 22%.

Chinanet, also as a stock within the China concept, was subscribed 10 times when it first went public. Its opening price was 20 USD. After the opening, the price went up to 60 USD, increasing 200% on that day. In contrast, Sina was disappointing. Several other Chinese companies gave up on going IPO seeing Sina's experience.

The Internet bubble burst. No one could figure out which one was the cause between the burst of the Internet bubble and the drop of NASDAQ.

One thing clear was that when NASDAQ began its "diving" slump in April 2000, the CEOs of these websites were having miserable times.

One year ago, Internet companies were having a money-burning competition-all the best advertisement boards had names of Internet companies printed on. Now, many websites were having problem surviving.

Meanwhile, foreign investors were moving around in Zhongguancun with money in their hands. In Zhongguancun, even a beggar who held a bowl with .com on it could get venture capital investment of millions of USDs. Now, venture investors from America got smarter. They needed not only a good story, but also predictable profits behind the story.

At that time, many Internet companies died over night, among which, there were some of the 40 companies that IDG had invested in. However, could Ctrip, the one IDG had an eye on , survive from this depression?

Section Ⅱ Decision on transformation

Which product is promising?

Now that the Internet bubble had burst, would the Internet industry be faced with a recession?

The Softbank China Representative Shi Mingchun had a view that "Not the whole Internet industry is a mistake, neither is it a bubble. It is normal that in the development of this industry, there might be certain companies that need to be adjusted for high stock price, and it is also normal that a company dies abruptly. There are opening and closing in every business every day. If Amazon dies one day, the model of B2C should not be the one to blame. It's a sigh that we need to look for new business models. "

Ji Qi, the founder of Ctrip, thought that he had to thank the Internet bubbles. In one of his speeches, he said, "The success of Ctrip is related to both our team and historical opportunity. " Ctrip was born in the Internet, and the Internet bubble made Ctrip. The bubble made Ctrip seemed over-estimated, helping it gain the investment worthy of over 100 million RMB. What the Ctrip team had done best was that they seized the time to integrate the traditional industry.

However, this was a long process that can not be concluded in just one sentence.

From the day it was founded on, Ctrip had been aiming for tourists, tour groups and online services related to tourism, providing users with online reservations for tickets, rooms, tour groups, restaurant and so on.

Seemingly, selling tour group projects was Ctrip's highlight. In the Ctrip team, they had Fan Min, who was the General Manager of Shanghai Travel Service and had been in this business for ten years. He ought to know about this business better and be more familiar with it than everyone else.

Logically, this was a perfect plan. But, in reality, itthis plan was not so easy to execute. First, the profits were small-no more than 10% ; secondly, this was a competitive market. Every travel agency had formed their mature business channels. It was difficult for Ctrip to get tour groups and, besides the independent tourists were very fewof a small amount; thirdly, they had to go through travel agencies for tours. Travel agencies had higher authorities compared to tourism websites. In all, it was impossible for Ctrip to survive on this business of tour groupgroup tourism. This was not expected by the Ctrip team.

They thought, "If we can not make money out of tour groups, why don't we consider selling entrance tickets?"

The New Year's Eve of 2000 was the joining point of two centuries. Many businesses wanted to grasp this once-in-a-hundred-year opportunity, and Ctrip was among them. In December 1999, Ctrip had got the distribution right to sell the tickets online to ring the bell on New Year's Eve in Longhua Temple in Shanghai.

This event of Bell Ringing in Longhua Temple to Celebrate New Year's Eve was one of the special tourism activities in Shanghai. It was held every year from the year of 1989 on.

Accordingly, it was a grand and meaningful ceremony. In that evening, the gate of Maitreya Buddha Palace of Longhua Temple would gradually open, followed by the welcome speech from the Abbot. Then, 108 bell-ringing guests would gather in the bell tower. The Abbot would put the ribbons with their names and time of bell ringing on the lucky guests. Later, the monks would begin to sing the *Song of Three Treasures* to the guests, who walked upstairs, rang the bell, and prayed for happiness of the forthcoming year.

The ceremony usually started at 23 o'clock. With the 108 guests finished ringing the bell, it would be exactly the start of the first day of a new year. Only those who had been there in person would be able to experience the holiness and satisfaction.

This was supposed to be a good business and Ctrip was supposed to sell the tickets very well and to make a fortune out of it. However, it came as a surprise that there was not a single ticket sold on Ctrip.com. With no other choices, the Ctrip employees had to sell their tickets at the entrance of Longhua Temple in the icy wind, being taken as "scalpers".

Selling entrance ticket did not work out. They wondered whether it would work out if they sell air tickets on their website.

After some specific exploration, the Ctrip team found out that this would not work out, either. This was an industry with a history of twenty years. Let's take a look at the services already in this industry-ticket delivery, air ticket agency and free transportation to the airport. To Ctrip, what was worse was that there was a period in which they had to wait for the money to be transferred once the tickets were sold on their website.

They had tried tour groups, entranced tickets, and air tickets. The only choice left for them is hotel reservation. Could it bring a new hope to Ctrip?

The most profitable service-hotel reservation

This time, Ctrip had made the right choice.

Hotel reservation is a new business less than three years old. It is different from selling tour groups and air tickets, which had been developed too much.

Now, in this business, there was obvious unbalanced factors between demand and supply.

In the planned economy, tourists had to have a recommendation letter to check in a guest house. There was no intermediary agency back then. But, ever since the opening up policy in China, tourists could check in with only an ID and did not need any recommendation letters. Recommendation letters were out-dated. However, with the old fashioned guest houses still existing, there emerged not only more traditional guest houses, but also various hotels and inns of uneven qualities.

Tourists were confused with the choices for acommondation. They had no means to check the availability of a guest house, nor could they bring a tour guidance brochure with themselves to look up for the telephone numbers of the hotels in their destinations.

They could either ask the travel agencies for help on room reservation, or just settle for any inn near the train station. Neither was the ideal choice. Then, tourists needed an agency for room reservations with simple procedures and reasonable prices.

Ever since the opening up in 1978 in China, for the hotel industry, it had been a spring. There born a bunch of joint-venture hotels such as Guangzhou White Goose Hotel, China Grand Hotel and Beijing Jianguo Hotel.

After 1984, the Holiday Group and Accor Group had entered China. Ever since then, international hotel groups had been "enclosing the land" in the mainland of China.

Especially during the ten years between 1985 and 1995, the number of hotels in China had grown with a rapid speed, causing the temporary excess in supply of the hotels.

According to the data, there were six thousand star hotels, half of which were in deficit of 7.2 billion RMB. The profit in this whole industry was -5.46%. More than 30% of the hotel rooms were not being used.

Under such circumstance, they were in urgent need of intermediary agencies for distribution.

Ctrip was not the first one to find this empty market. Someone was already doing an impressive job before Ctrip was founded.

Ji Qi led his team into this market because he couldn't make money in other businesses, and that he was inspired by Long Zhaoyuan's speech. It was when he attended the Tourism Industry and Internet Economy Forum. The Deputy Manager of Yjita. com Long Zhaoyuan said, "In my opinion, there are some impacts done by the Internet to traditional travel agencies. First, there are room and ticket reservations being affected. These two had brought us quite a lot of profits. But now we are losing both with the development of information flow."

In November 1999, Ctrip had developed and began to use an online reservation system on hotel reservation. It had made hotel reservation Ctrip's primary business in the next two years.

However, Ji Qi made a wrong move. Unfortunately, hotel reservation was a sunrise industry in which Ctrip strove to enter but failed.

The shortcut of purchasing

Why couldn't Ctrip get in this industry? The answer is quite simple.

For a half-year-old Internet company with no experience in hotel reservation, the result would be predictable if it wanted to expand itself into hotel reservation service.

Here is what usually happened.

In some luxury hotel, a young man managed to get into the hotel manager's office.

"Hello, manager! This is my business card. I am an employee of Ctrip. com. " The young handed his business card to the manager passionately.

"What do you do?" The hotel manager threw his card into the corner of his table, casting a sidelong glance at this young man.

"We are hoping to work with you on hotel reservations. " The young man smiled.

"What? Online hotel reservations? Don't you know that we have our own website?"

"Yes, I do. But ours is a professional website faced with users across the country. " The young man answered awkwardly.

"Ok. Got it. But I am busy now. I'll contact you when I get free. " The hotel manager did not let the young man finish, and send him away.

In fact, it was normal to be sent away. Imagine that an infamous small company which was new in the hotel reservation service wants to work with you, would you consider? It was lucky for him not to be kicked out.

Promoters of Ctrip tried to knock the doors of hotels open and got refused again and again. However, they did gain something out of this. At least, the name of Ctrip was remembered by these hotels. In the meanwhile, some hotels had tried working with Ctrip after their continuous visits. Of course, Ctrip had treated their partners decently in return-it would bring one tourist to the hotel oneday and ten tourists one month later.

In this way, Ctrip had established cooperation with over one thousand hotels in the country within three months.

However, this did not help Ctrip earn profits. With the development of Ctrip's hotel reservation service, Ji Qi came to realize that it was not as simple as he had thought. With a platform, Ctrip could gain commissions out of room reservations. But the problem was that the number of tourists making room reservations online was small even if Ctrip could get the hotels to agree on this business.

Ji Qi wondered what to do next. He decided to hold a general meeting of the shareholders.

Ji Qi said, "Fellows, things are not looking good now. Hotel reservation service is not working out. What should we do?"

Fan Min said, "Let's go back to tour groups and air tickets. "

Liang Jianzhang said, "How about headhunting?"

"There's no turning back now. But, can headhunting be a solution?" Ji Qi asked.

"What do you think?" Liang Jianzhang asked back.

"In my opinion, it has to be a whole purchase. The operation and development of this industry are related to the structure and client relation of a company. Headhunting alone can't be the answer to the problem." Ji Qi carried on, "Currently, there are four best companies leading the business in hotel reservation-Modern Yuntong, be88. com, baideqin. com and jsj. com. I want to talk to them."

Then, could Ji Qi get the deal done?

The companies which were the not bad

Could they enlarge their hotel reservation business on their own without purchasing other companies?

The answer was yes. However, Ji Qi knew very clear that "efficiency is life; time is money". Currently, for Ctrip, the best choice was to purchase the best hotel reservation agency on the market. It was not easy for these companies to have such a big scale.

The first company to choose from was Modern Yuntong, which was the first company to discover this market and to rush into this market without any hesitation.

In 1996, an employee in the External Trade Department of Blue Sky Industrial Enterprise made a discovery on his business trip-the price varied greatly among different clients. There were the Major Client Price and Independent Client Price. This employee told this situation to his Section Chief Wang Shengli, and suggested that they should enter the market of hotel reservation.

On hearing this, Wang Shengli thought it made sense. He himself had notice this on his business trips as well. Wang Shengli made a call to the Board Chief of Blue Sky Industrial Enterprise at once.

The Board Chief responded, "This is a good suggestion. Is it possible to do another research on the recognition of this market?"

To verify whether their judgment was practical, Wang Shengli followed the Board Chief's suggestion and lunched a market research.

In the beginning of 1997, there held the Spring Canton Fair. The Blue Sky Group would attend this fair every year. Wang Shengli thought that participants of the fair coming from all across the country could be the target group of hotel reservation. Therefore, Wang Shengli and his partners handed out over six thousand inquiries asking questions such as "Will you pay 600 RMB for a room introduced by us which was priced 800 RMB?" and "What do you think of paying afterwards instead of the traditional way of paying in ahead for a room?" As it turned out, they got 4000 inquiries in return, ending in good reverberations.

There seemed indeed to be a market. What was left to be done was the preparation.

On 18th December 1997, along with the Blue Sky Industrial Enterprise, Wang Shengli and several others invested two million RMB to found the Modern Yuntong Buisness Service Limited Company. The Blue Sky Industrial Enterprise was the majority shareholder. Wang Shengli and the other joined in. Wang Shengli was pointed as the general manager of Modern Yuntong.

But when they first opened the reservation service, they had only 36 hotels to work with. At that time, many hotels did not approve of such means. The kept asking, "Could you bring more customers to us with such low prices?"

If they go through Modern Yuntong, they had to charge a room for 600 RMB which was priced at 1000 RMB. No wonder they would have doubts.

Wang Shengli was confident though the hotels had doubt about him. He thought that Modern Yuntong might be an Internet company, but it could form a national hotel reservation network. And as long as it could link the hotels together, it could bring more customers to the hotels. This was something that one single hotel could not accomplish all by itself.

To dispel their doubts, Modern Yuntong had to persuade them, and deposit millions of cash to their contracted hotels.

As they had predicted, this was a large market, and maybe even larger than they had thought. Hotels worked with Modern Yuntong with doubts, but later they would cheer on the amount of customers Modern Yuntong had brought to them. Modern Yuntong had an outstanding achievement. In the first few months, the business volume grew 200% every month. Before long, it had become the largest hotel reservation distributor in the nation, offering hotel reservation service for over 700 star hotels in more than 100 cities across the country. At its peak, 20 thousand people made reservations for hotel rooms nationwide through this company in a month.

Modern Yuntong was not only a pioneer in hotel reservation inside the nation, but also one in the business modle of hotel reservation-it had established the 800 Toll-free Hotline and its Call Center.

At the time when Modern Yuntong was first founded, travel agencies were doing their work manually and would use a computer for accountant at most. However, as soon as it was founded, Modern Yuntong had introduced a reservation system-a Call Center. Meanwhile, they bought the telephone number 800-810-6666 which cost them 60 thousand RMB.

At that time, they had two options-the traditional way and the advanced way of computer system. In the former one, they only needed to set up a switchboard to switch the calls. In the latter one, they would have to spend 50 or 60 thousand RMB on a Motorola microcomputer.

Should they buy this microcomputer? Some people in the company thought that manual accounting would be enough for the company with only dozens of cases at most. They thought there was no need for a company with only two million RMB to spend such a fortune on a Motorola microcomputer. Nevertheless, Wang Shengli had a keen insight on this market and was certain that this it was going to expand.

Wang Shengli's insight was confirmed. At first, Moder Yuntong advertised on *China Aviation*, "China Hotel Reservation. com is officially online!" On the first day, the hotline was almost paralyzed from calls made by people for consultation. In the first few months, they calls received grew at the speed of 200% and the number had only got stable at 10% per month half a year later.

Wang Shengli had triumphed. He was the first one to find this empty market, and he was going to be rich very fast.

However, in the market of hotel reservation, Wang was the first one, but not the only one. There is another person worth mentioning. He is Wu Hai, who had found this market through another channel.

Wu Hia graduated from Central University of Finance and Economics. He was a major in Economics Information Management. He was trained in abroad for some time and had worked in a state-owned enterprise after he came back. Later he joined Hainan Phoenix Corporation as its General Manager of Northern China.

Hainan Phoenix was a joint-venture company by Soros Investment Group and Hainan Airline Company. Its main business was air ticket reservation system. It was a platform through which the ticket agents could issue the tickets for air travelers.

Hainan Phoenix invented this system and intended to sell them to air line companies in the first place. But when they were promoting this system, they had met with unsolvable problems.

Here was what happened. At that time, all the data for air tickets (flight number, seat, discount and so on) were in the information center of CAAC. The CAAC had a ticket reservation system developed by themselves; they could never hand the data to their competitor Hainan Phoenix.

Helplessly, Wu Hai had to turn to the air line companies. But these air line companies had concerns that it could damage their relationship with CAAC if they were to work with Hainan Phoenix. They gave their responses to Wu Hai perfunctorily.

Wu Hai was so frustrated because he could not work on CAAC, nor air line companies.

Nevertheless, Wu Hai had soon switched his thought, "It is meaningless to put the terminals of Hainan Phoenix in the existing ticket agencies, for they have already got ticket reservation systems from CAAC. What would happen if I make a change on the distribution channel and put the terminals in hotels? There are currently no ticket reservation systems in hotels. They would be willing to work with me if I could bring them extra profits. "

Thus, Wu Hai began his market research in hotels one by one.

After the observation of half a month, Wu Hai had discovered the jaw-dropping demand in the market. In many hotels, there were guests checking in without making reservations, which meant that there was greater potential in hotel reservation than in ticket reservation.

"A watched flower never blooms, but an untended willow grows." He had gain an unexpected result from this research. When he got back to his company, he immediately made a suggestion that they start on hotel reservation.

His leader agreed without too much consideration upon realizing the difficulty in ticket reservation. Unfortunately, just when the project was about to begin, there began a major staff transferring within Hainan Phoenix, leading into an internal dissension. Wu Hai hated scheming against each other, and wanted to prevent himself from the conflict. Thereupon, Wu Hai handed his resignation letter and left.

After he left Hainan Phoenix, he had pulled together some investors and founded BizExpress Information Technology Company. BizExpress was born a few months later than Modern Yuntong and had gone through some obstacles, but it had soon become one of the largest room reservation centers in the nation.

Wang Shengli and Wu Hai had discovered this market through researches by themselves. Differently, Li Zizheng and Liu Zhigang came into this market through their business partners.

Let's look at Li Zizheng's story first.

In 1997, Li was chosen as the Board Director of Henan Jinboda Business Hotel. On his term, he had met with a difficult problem-room service industry was different from the catering industry. In the catering industry, if he could not get his products sold one day, he would be able to sell them the next day. And the price of his products would not vary too much. But, if he could not get the rooms sold one day, it would be a permanent lost. Besides, hotels were restrained regionally, and they had to spend a fortune on the promotion advertisements if they wanted to be known by people everywhere.

Li Zizheng had been obsessed with this problem for a long time until he received a membership request letter from an Internet Hotel one afternoon.

This request letter was sent from a British company. This letter read, "If you could offer sales commission to our Internet hotel and discounts to guests, then you could have all of the guests using our online hotel."

"Great! This is a good idea!" Li Zizheng remembered that he had got into contact with similar models on his business trips-Universal Card, Profit Card, and so on. He believed he could make a difference if he was to enter this market now.

He approved of this business model and was certain about this market opportunity. Thus, in May 1998, Li Zizheng went north to Beijing and founded the Golden Century Internet Hotel Reservation Limited Company. It was targeting at business travelers with the membership system. It launched the Golden Century Hotel Reservation VIP Card with a national unified price of 398 RMB.

At first, the response they got from the market was intense, and the reservation business was going on colorfully. But then, Li met with some problems. Some of the hotels did not obey the contract and offered discount secretly to attract customers, resulting in that the VIP price was higher than that of regular customers'.

Facing the complaints and the leaving of the clients, Li had to take forceful measures. He said goodbye to those hotels that had repeatedly broke their contracts. In the meantime, the Golden Century Hotel made a solemn promise that any client would be compensated twice for the lost if things mentioned above happened.

Because of his effective measures, Golden Century Hotel had gained a firm foothold in the market of hotel reservation in Beijing.

Then, let's look at Liu Zhigang's story.

In 1997, Liu had taken part in founding the Beijing Modern Yuntong Business Travel Service Limited Company. He was the Deputy Manager of this company.

Two years later, Liu Zhigang left Modern Yuntong. Again, he founded a room reservation discount service company named Beijing Baideqin Travel Consultant Limited Company, and launched its e-commercial website Lohoo. com.

Why would he found a new company?

Because Liu had made a discovery-in 1998, in the room reservation channels of hotels with average room prices between 300 and 500 RMB, 12. 8% were reservation websites, and 77% were traditional ones like direct hotel reservation, travel agencies, hotel representative a-gencies and so on.

From this point, he could see that there was a large scale of demand in online room reservation. It would not be a problem to open a few more such companies. Upon this, Liu Zhigang decided to do it on his own.

The four companies mentioned above were all targets of Ji Qi's purchasing. Which companies did Ji Qi want to buy? And would the purchase succeed? Please read the next section.

Section III Start of the purchasing
The real difficulty in negotiation

It was a midnight in January 2000, and there was swirling snow outside the window. At this moment, Ji Qi was sleepless. It was not because the espresso he drank a couple hours ago, but the news he had seen in the daytime-AOL had bought Time Warner.

This piece of news was a sign and hint to Ctrip. Ji Qi was in Beijing for business, and he was quite excited about this piece of news.

Ji Qi's went to Beijing for the opening of Ctrip's Beijing branch and the following media conference. More importantly, he was in Beijing to choose a company to make the purchase.

Which company should Ctrip purchase? Ji Qi made contacts with these companies in

Ctrip's office in Beijing Changan Mansion in the morning and met with them in the afternoon-Modern Yuntong, BizExpress, Golden Century, Guoxin Business League and Baideqin.

These names were not resounding in the IT field, but they were well known in the business of hotel room reservation. No less than five thousand room nights (the professional term used in hotels indicating one night in a hotel room) were reserved through these companies every month. Ctrip was nothing compared to them.

The first one among them Ji Qi had met was Wang Shengli, the General Manager of Modern Yuntong.

Before his meeting with Ji Qi, Wang Shengli had only heard of Ctrip and had no particular impression about it. Wang Shengli had once browsed Ctrip. com and searched the Room Reservation Center, which he thought was no particular.

Knowing that Ji Qi wanted to meet him, Wang Shengli thought, "These young men have collected some money and want to make use of it. They must want to ask me for advice because they are not familiar with hotel room reservation. Let's have a talk and see if there is any chance that we can have some cooperation. "

When they met with each other, Ji Qi talked to Wang Shengli about his experience in America and about the shock he got when he first got into contact with the Internet. Then he introduced to Wang Shengli the hotel reservation Ctrip had been running.

As Wang had expected, this was an unknown and small company which was new in the industry. But what Ji Qi said later had made Wang drop his jaw.

"Is your company available for selling?" Ji Qi stared at Wang and asked.

"I've never thought about it. " Wang felt confused.

"You might as well think about it. How much are you going to sell it if possible?" Ji Qi kept asking, "It's either that we invest jointly and form a strategic alliance, or that we become rivals. "

"Well, then. I've got to go. I'll inform you if we want to sell our company. " Wang Shengli left the Changan Mansion with questions in his mind, "Is there something wrong in this young man's head?"

Actually, when he met with Ji Qi, Wang Shengli knew nothing about the four founders of Ctrip. At first during their talk, Wang thought this young man was daring even though his company was young and infamous. But later, when asked whether he wanted to sell his company, Wang felt it abrupt, and thought that the young man was too arrogant. Wang wondered if Ji Qi knew the status Modern Yuntong had in the hotel reservation market when Ji mentioned the purchasing. He also wondered if Ctrip could afford to purchase his company.

The second person Ji Qi had met was Wu Hai from BizExpress.

Wu hai thought Ji Qi was agreeable maybe because of their experience in sales.

Wu hai told to Ji Qi honestly about his situation and his view on hotel reservation.

Wu said, "Once a company has enough business volume and wants to expand itself, the absolute choice is financing, for it can not depend on the capital at hand."

Wu Hai continued, "I have talked to my brother company Soros, and I'm planning on selling the majority shares to it and keep the rest for myself. The Project Manager agreed on my terms-purchasing my shares one year later with a price no less than the present one, covering the insurance for BizExpress's employees, and so on."

Ji Qi was surprised, "You want to sell your company to the Wall Street investment bank?"

"Yes. But the Project Manager and their lawyers have been busy recently, or else I'd already have sold my company." Wu Hai said.

"Why don't we cooperate?" Ji Qi must have seen the hope.

"I'll have to wait for their response first, and we'll see!"

Wu Hai didn't give Ji Qi a clear answer whether he wanted to sell his company to Ctrip. Ji Qi had to personally walk him outside to the elevator and watched him go.

Ji Qi had later met with the persons in charge of Baideqin, Guoxin Business League and Golden Century.

Baideqin's Board Director Chen Yalin said that their talk with Yilong's boss Tangyue was almost done. Yilong had offered 12 million RMB. Baideqin could only work with Ctrip if they could offer a higher price, or he would have to say no to Ctrip.

The owner of Golden Century Li Zizheng said, "It's better for us to sit down and talk rather than fight in blood on the market. Chief Ji, what you have just said made sense. But in my faith, the true warrior dies on the battle field, not on the negotiation table. We can have a talk on other cooperation projects, but not on purchasing."

The person in charge from Guoxin Business League rejected Ji Qi decisively. They were not going to sell the company they had founded themselves to others.

Among the five companies, Modern Yuntong and BizExpress had impressed Ji Qi the most. He thought that Wu Hai had a comprehensive and systematic view while Wang Shengli's thought was clear and unique. As to the other three companies, Ji Qi gave them ordinary evaluation, especially the last two-they would not sell their companies, neither would Ji Qi buy theirs. However, Ji Qi was not sure if he was able to purchase the first two companies.

Wu Hai's being moved

Ji Qi decided to focus on Wu Hai because he had decided to sell BizExpress. Besides, there was another important reason-Shi Mingchun, the partner of Softbank China had promised Ctrip an immediate investment on condition that Ctrip could purchase BizExpress.

Ji Qi had made several calls to Wu Hai to talk to him about the cooperation continuously. But Wu Hai refused him tactfully on the phone.

Ji Qi didn't become less persistent though he had been refused so many times by Wu Hai. Ji Qi would not stop "until reaching the Huanghe River". Once he had found a target, he would try to communicate with him because he believed that "faith moves mountains".

As expected, in the last call, Wu said to Ji, "Chief Ji, I have to admire your sincerity and persistence. Fine, I'll go to your company and we'll see."

Knowing that Wu Hai was coming to find out the operation in Ctrip, Ji Qi borrowed a Nissan from his friend to pick him up. In the car, Ji Qi introduced the development situation of Ctrip's hotel reservation business to Wu Hai-they could get 900 room nights every month, and with the market opened, the number would double in the future.

When Wu Hai arrived at Ctrip, it was worse than he had expected. Ctrip sold the rooms at the price given by the hotels. They could not get attractive discounts because of the number of reservations they made. They had not established a call center, depending only on the Internet for reservations. As the 900 room nights, to Wu Hai, who had already expanded his business to 30 thousand room nights, it was not even worth mentioning.

Wu Hai said, "Chief Ji, you will have a fat chance if you keep doing this. This is not how you play the game of hotel reservation."

Qi Ji was shocked, "Chief Wu, you mean……?"

"I can come to Ctrip, but you'd have to make a change." Wu Hai smiled at Ji Qi.

"No problem. Whatever you say, I'll do it!" What Ctrip needed was Wu's experience in hotel reservation. Ji Qi agreed to Wu's requirements-shares in addition to cash (the number of which was never publicised).

In March 2000, Wu Hai joined Ctrip with his senior staff in BizExpress. Ctrip offered him the position of Senior Deputy Director, leading the sales, marketing and online promotion.

After joining Ctrip, Wu Hai copied his methods in BizExpress to Ctrip. He established a call center, sales team, and a negotiation team to hotels. Before too long, Ctrip had taken the market. Its monthly reservation volume rose from hundreds to hundreds of thousands.

Wang Shengli's hesitation

Ctrip got its second finance investment after purchasing BizExpress. Ji Qi wanted to strike the iron while it was hot, so he went to talk to Wang Shengli in Modern Yuntong on the purchase.

But, it was a difficult negotiation. In those months, Ji Qi and Shen Nanpeng would fly from Shanghai to Beijing. And as soon as they got off the airplane, they would go to the appointed restaurant or club to meet Wang Shengli. If they got fed up with North-eastern cuisine, they would change to Hunan cuisine, and then to Guangdong cuisine. Over different meals, they had the never-changing topic going on. Ji Qi talked to Wang Shengli again and again about his dreams and future while Wang Shengli studied Ctrip over and over again.

They tried to reach a consensus by adapting to each other.

Why was Ji Qi so persistent? It came from the experience when he was in sales-"Negotiations are like dates. As time goes by, they develop into ambiguous relationships." There was another reason-if Ji Qi could get this deal done, Shen Nanpeng could get a third round finance investment from the venture investment bank Carlyle.

Time went by quickly. Before they knew it, nine months had passed. To their disappointment, they couldn't come to terms with Wang Shengli.

A friend advised Ji Qi, "Chief Ji, just forget about it! Even if you could come to terms with him, you probably could not afford the purchase."

What the friend had said made sense. At that time, Ctrip did not have much money. They had run out of the money from the first round financing, and used some of the money from the second one. The company was in a deficit.

However, Ji Qi thought, "Internet companies are highly evaluated. They can not make money, but have value in the capital market. Traditional companies such as Modern Yuntong could make profits, but are worthless in the capital market. For Ctrip, a valuable company in the capital market, to purchase Modern Yuntong, a worthless company in the same market, it would not cost too much."

So, Ji Qi never mentioned that Ctrip was valuable to Wang Shengli. He only emphasized that if he could join Ctrip, they could work together, indicating that in Ctrip, Wang Shengli could accomplish what he could not do in Modern Yuntong.

What did Wang Shengli think of Ji Qi's heart to heart proposal?

In fact, Wang Shengli was aware of the power of the Internet. He had once opened a website E-hotel. Lacking money and talents, he never promoted his website online, using it as just a poster.

Then, Wang Shengli met a problem-the new national policy forbade army forces from running industrial business. Wang had to sell Modern Yuntong as soon as possible.

Who could he sell it to? There were some more competitive rivals of Ctrip's-Huaxia Travel. com and Shanghai Huachen. Huaxia Travel. com was backed up by Li Jiacheng's Hutchison-Whampoa and Changjiang Industrial Enterprise; the Board Director of Shanghai Huachen was rich and ostentatious, who once said to Wang Shengli, "You are lacking no money, nor talents, but an innovative leader and a company that has already formed a scale." There were other companies offering cash that equals to, or was even higher than Ctrip could offer.

Wang Shengli was having a headache over this problem.

In the early half of 2000, Ctrip purchased BizExpress and Yilong purchased Baideqin. As the number one company in hotel reservation, Modern Yutong had naturally become the main target for purchasing among many tourism websites.

Among the companies negotiating with Wang Shengli, the person in charge of Huaxia Travel. com was the one with the clearest objective. He knew very clear that Huaxia Travel. com could become the strongest if he could purchase Modern Yuntong, or else, it would be fraught with grim possibilities.

The second most clearly objected person was Yangrong from Shanghai Huachen. He was a master of employment of capital, owning several listed companies. Once he opened his mouth, he would present himself as confident and arrogant. He threw the question in Wang Shengli's face, "For how much will you sell Modern Yuntong?" He emphasized for a couple of times that money was not a problem to him.

Wang Shengli had served in the army for twenty years, and was sharpened in the business market. He had quite rich experience of people. He balanced among the companies wanting to purchase his company, and decided to throw the olive branch to Ctrip.

Why did Wang Shengli carry a torch for Ctrip? On one hand, he was moved by Ji Qi's sincerity, and on the other, he was attracted by Ji Qi's Ctrip entrepreneurial team. Modern Yuntong needed money for its development. But at that time, money was not a problem to Modern Yuntong because there were many companies that wanted to purchase it. What was more important was the human resource structure. After contacting with the founder of Ctrip, Wang Shengli thought they were of knowledge, of culture, of insight, and of courage, which was different from the other companies that wanted to buy Modern Yuntong. Ji Qi, the Southern Chinese graduated from Shanghai Jiaotong University, in particular, was vigorous, capable and loyal. And Liang Jianzhang was a meticulous person with a few words, and a specialist on technology. Wang Shengli thought to himself, "If Modern Yuntong and Ctrip could work together and enhance our business, we could make profits of hundreds of millions every year even if we fail to go public."

Wang Shengli agreed to sell his company to Ctrip. The next step is to negotiate on the purchase plan. Liang Jianzhang gave Modern Yuntong an evaluation of 60 million USD, and they would pay in share and cash.

Wang Shengli agreed on the purchase plan. Thus, on October 16 th 2000, Ctrip made the whole purchase of ModerYuntong with several millions of RMB in cash and parts of Ctrip's shares.

The real number one Ctrip

When Ctrip successfully purchased Modern Yuntong, the whole industry felt an earthquake. Many CEOs of tourism websites were stunned. They could not understand why Modern Yuntong was purchased by Ctrip.

This event left room of elaboration and imagination for the finance and economics journalists.

Information Industry Journal reported, "With Ctrip and Mordern Yuntong joining together, they are running far ahead of their competitors. The other tourism websites could only help-lessly watch the Ctrip team count their money. "

China Business Journal commented, "The recent purchase of Yuntong by Ctrip has solid Ctrip's number one status among tour e-commercial websites. This purchase has brought more resources and clients to Ctrip. Moder Yuntong is an old brand in this industry with abundant resources in this industry-it had 400 thousand members. Adding it up to the 600 thousand members Ctrip owned, it now has more than one million members. In a time of relationship marketing, clients make a winner. "

Other media had also given comments on this purchase, long or short. They basically shared the same opinion.

In fact, before purchasing Yuntong, Ctrip was already the largest hotel room distributor in domestic market. Its purpose to purchase Modern Yuntong was not the 400 thousand members. What was important was that Wang Shengli had exploited the northern market and brought to Ctrip the third round of financing.

In June 2000, Ctrip was negotiating its third round of financing with Carlyle Group, the world's largest private share investment company. This time, it was much more difficult than the last two times. The project managers knew the traditional market very well and cared about Ctrip's finance data and plans to make profits. During the interview, they asked macroscopic question such as-

"What would Ctrip do if China's economy went bad?"

"Wha would Ctrip do if China's hotel industry grew too fast?"

"What would Ctrip do if China were to join the WTO?"

After they were done with the questions and got satisfactory answers, they still did not felt secure. Carlyle put forward another condition-the investment agreement would only be effective on condition that Ctrip purchased Modern Yuntong successfully.

Now that Ctrip had successfully purchased Mordern Yuntong, Carlyle was more than hap-py to keep their promise.

In November 2000, Ctrip received the third round of financing investment mainly from Carlyle. Carlyle invested eight million USD in Ctrip, taking up 30% of its shares. IDG, Soft-bank Japan, Shanghai Industrial Enterprise and Orchid Fund had put in additional invest-ments, adding the total up to 12 million USD.

The Internet industry was in a cold winter, and many companies were struggling to sur-vive, to whom the 12-million-USD was an enormous figure. At that time, the NASDAQ col-lapsed. Plenty of investors ceased investing and pulled themselves out of the Asian market. Some investors were even broken. Carlyle's decision seemed quit bold.

Carlyle's representative of China explained afterwards, "The Ctrip team is the best among those I've seen. I could probably never found a second team like this anymore. "

Investors believed in Ctrip. However, at that time, Ctrip had a monthly trade volume of 10 million RMB, the expenditure of 2 million RMB, the income of one million RMB and the net loss of one million RMB.

What? If Ctrip was still in a deifict, would it "die"?

Don't worry. Because Ctrip would not "die". There emerged a sharp person who could lead its achievement into a speed faster than Shenzhou-7 (the Spacecraft launched by China on 25th September 2008). Who is this person? Please find the answer in the fourth chapter *Growth by Leaps and Bounds*.

Summary

The following are the knowledge points related to this chapter.

Ⅰ. The formation of the team spirit

A team is formed by numbers of team members. The individuals are put together into a whole. The objective of forming a team is to obtain a whole greater than putting the individuals together. However, in reality, not every team could have members making concerted efforts and realize their original goal and hope. Some team could have members scheming against each other, leading to the internal exhaustion of the resources. Why do these happen? The answer can be illustrated in two points.

1. The relationship between team members

According to years of research and observation, the author has found out that in entrepreneurial teams, there are five categories in their relationship.

(1) $1+1>2$ Team members share mutual appreciation, mutual trust, mutual understanding and mutual cooperation. (cooperative relationship in the mature period)

(2) $1+1=2$ Team members share mutual respect, mutual exploration, and mutual adaption. The relationship is not deep. (cooperative relationship in the early period)

(3) $2>1+1>0$ Team members share mutual suspicions, mutual restriction and guard against each other. (competitive relationship in the early period)

(4) $1+1=0$ Team members expose and have a grudge against each other. (competitive relationship in the mature period)

(5) $1+1<0$ Team members exclude and fight with each other. (dog-eat-dog relationship)

Trust (Trust Model p. 3-1) is very important. Under normal circumstances, team members of an entrepreneurial team form their relationship from point 2 on, and then to point 3. At this moment, if this team grows healthily, it will get to point 1. If the internal conflicts keep going on, the team will get to point 4 and point 5.

Either the good or bad results have something to do the following point.

p. 3-1　three bases of the trust in a team

　　　　potential trust level

　　　　trust based on status based on the value, the trust is gained through the high status

　　　　trust based on knowledge based on the capability, the trust is gained through the professional performance

　　　　trust based on psychology based on the intimidation, the trust is gained through the worries for punishment

2. The self-recognition of team members

The team's cooperation spirit is decided by its members' self-recognition. Here are the four aspects.

(1) One team member trust and places his hopes in other team members.

(2) One team member's contribution can not be replaced by another one's.

(3) One team member tries to win understanding and support from others.

(4) One team member examines his shortcoming and errors.

How were the relationships between Ctrip's team members? And how did they evaluate their contributions to the team?

Let's talk about their relationships first.

Ji Qi thought that the personal connections between team members were very important. If they did not have personal connections with each other, the team would split up in the face of difficulties. He traveled with Liang Jianzhang and enjoyed some "snakes and drinks" with him. He was Sheng Nanpeng and Fan Min's university schoolmate. Such personal connections could ease off the crisis brought by conflicts and contradictions. What's more, self-knowledge of each member was also quite important. Everybody had to know their limits in ability and be aware of what to do and what not to do.

Then, how did they evaluate their contributions to the team?

Some might think that Ji Qi had made the greatest contribution during the process of entrepreneurial financing and transformation and purchase, and that Ctrip could not make it without Ji Qi. But, did Ji Qi think so?

Faced with the public, he said to a journalist, "The four of us are like four pieces of a puzzle. No one of the four of us can be missed. We have made a pact that we don't refer each one of ourselves as a member of somebody else's team."

Similarly, Fan Min had said no less than once to the media, "We are constructing a building. Ji Qi is passionate and has connections. He is the one who could get the permition documents and land for the construction. Shen Nanpeng is good at financing. He is the one who could get money. Liang Jianzhang knows about IT and can explore business models. He is the one who is in charge of piling and working out the whole structure. I was in the tourist industry. I am the one who stirs the cement and sand to make concrete and fill in the structure. That's how we build this building. "

To summerzie, the Ctrip team could overcome the obstacles one by one and get closer and closer to success all because that the team members' wise self-recognition and perfect cooperation.

II. The importance of market research

There are two types of market researches-direct research and indirect research. Three methods are used in direct research-interviews, observations and experiments; there are four forms of interviews-face to face interview, mail interview, phone interview and retained questions.

Why do I write such long a piece on this problem of market research? Because it has great importance to entrepreneurs. As an entrepreneur, one may hear somebody say that a certain project is good, or that he knows somebody who has succeeded in a project. If this entrepreneur enters this market impulsively without doing preliminary market research by himself, he would be meant to lose rather than win, unless he is really intelligent and lucky.

Here is a classic case in ancient China. It is a story about Jiang Ziya's four experiences in business before becoming a government official.

It is said that he had been cultivated by his master, the Yuanshi god, for 40 years in the Wangxu Palace on Mount Kunlun. At the age of 72, he left there with no relatives to go to. He had to depend on his sworn brother Song Yiren in Chaoge City. He felt sorry that he had to depend on Song Yiren and his family, so he decided to undertake some business to make money.

He wondered what to sell. Suddenly, he remembered that he could make bamboo filters when he was young. Thus, he chopped some bamboos and made a load of bamboo filters to sell in Chaoge City. Unfortunately, he was not able to sell a single one bamboo filter that day.

Failed to sell his bamboo filters, Jiang Ziya decided to sell flour. He thought that this time would be different because people would want to buy flour. He ground a load of flour to sell in the Chaoge City. But he could not sell one kilogram after he had walked around the four city gates. Finally, somebody came and wanted to buy the flour of one wen (the smallest ancient Chinese currency unit). Jiang Ziya felt angry but funny, so he unloaded the flour to scoop some up. Unexpectedly, just at this moment, there came a startled horse which knocked his bamboo basket over. The flour spread all over the ground. A sudden gust of wind blew it away.

Failed twice, Jiang Ziya was determined to open a restaurant near a training field at the northern gate of Chaoge City. He was confident that he could have successful business here.

So, he ordered his shop assistants to prepare pork and lamp for their guests early in the morning. They waited for half a day, and there was no guest at all. The meat began to smell and the alcohol went sour. As it turned out, there was no training that day in the field. It was very hot that day, so nobody came to his restaurant.

Failed three times, Jiang Ziya did not want to give up. He bought a herd of cattles and horses to sell in Chaoge City. This time, he thought that the living animal could not go rotten. What he could not have predicted was that when he got to the city gate, the gate keeper confiscated all of his animals. The Chaoge City had not received any rain for half a year and it was very dry. The king ordered a ban on livestock trading to pray for rain. Anyone who broke the ban would be considered breaking the law.

Thus, Jiang Ziya failed for a fourth time. He was a smart man, but he never understood that he had failed because he had not done serious market research.

His first failure was caused by his products. Jiang Ziya could make bamboo filters with good quality, but they are out-dated. He had no idea that his products were dozens of year behind the style in bamboo filters because he had not done market research.

The second, he failed because he had not done market research on the distribution channel. In fact, flour is sold in stores. Direct distribution was not going to work on selling flour.

He had not done market research on the demands of his products, so he failed for the third time. If it was the first time for him to enter the fast consuming product market, market researches were more important.

The fourth time, Jiang Ziya failed because he forgot to do market research of the political environment. He broke the law by selling livestock blindly. He almost lost everything and ended up in prison.

What would the results be if he had done enough market research? Let's take a look at another case familiar to all-the legend of Shi Yuzhu, the Board Chairman of Giant Group. In his second entrepreneurial experience, he launched a health care product called Melatonin which had been popular for many years.

In 1997, the Giant Mansion was constructed within expected time. Meanwhile, the "Three Battles" of the Giant Group ended in failure. Shi Yuzhu was in a debt of 250 million RMB, and vanished.

Shi Yuzhu concealed his identity. He had always been thinking about one question, "What have I done wrong to end up in such a failure?" Finally, one day, Shi Yuzhu figured it out-he had not done enough research on the target customers of his product.

In January 1998, Shi Yuzhu borrowed half a million RMB from a friend and started on Melatonin. This time, he decided to start in Jiangyin which is a city of county level in Jiangsu Province. It was close to Shanghai and Nanjing, with a strong purchasing power. If he could succeed in this model city, he could copy it to other cities around China.

Shi Yuzhu prepared himself with a detailed market research before initiating the Jiangyin market. He carried door-to-door surveys in every village with a pair of sun glasses on his face. At daytime, the young people in the village were out and in the big cities doing labor work, leaving the old men and women all by themselves with no one to talk to. They were very happy seeing and talking to Shi Yuzhu , who would chat with them sitting on a small bench in the yard.

"Aunt, have you ever had any health care food? Would you buy a product that can improve your sleeping quality and can take care of your stomach?"

Normally, these uncles and aunts would answer, "If this product you referred to is really that good as you've described, I would want to have a try. But it's too expensive that I couldn't afford it. I could only depend on my son to buy this for me. "

Shi Yuzhu kept on asking, "If you feel that this product is really effective after you have taken it, what you would do if you want to have more?"

"I'd put the empty box in a place where my son could see easily, so he'd know that I want another one. "

Shi Yuzhu heard this, and realized that he should put the health care products in the gift market and it could make a difference. Thus, there born the advertisement of Melatonin, "We take nothing but Melatonin as a gift for this Spring Festival. "

Many people thought this advertisement was tasteless and it was selected as one of the "Ten Most Awful Advertisements" by CCTV for eight straight years. However, the judges who gave this advertisement such criticism could never have imagined that it would have brought humongous sales volume to Melatonin, turning Shi Yuzhu into a billionaire within a couple of years.

Selling is practice with the feature of "based on research" rather than "based on imagination". It should be based on the result rather than on logic to testify the effect of selling.

Likewise, in this chapter, the market of hotel reservation was also discovered through market researches. They had some differences-Wang Shengli discovered this market through the six thousand inquiries and his staff's advices; Wu Hai's discovery was made through the researches on the platform of air ticket reservation; Ji Qi made the discovery indirectly by participating in the Tourism Industry and Internet Economics Forum.

To draw the conclusion, for entrepreneurs, through whatever means, market research is an indispensible link before initiating the business.

Ⅲ. The benefit of market positioning

In modern marketing theory, there are four steps in target marketing-specifying the market, choosing the market, positioning the market and competing in the market. That's to say, before entering a market, you should divide it into smaller markets, from which you can choose the one you are most confident to compete with others in.

How to specify the market? There are normally five ways (p. 3-2) to divide a market. Take the tourism industry as an example, the five ways are separately-

1. Market unification. E. g. Reservation of economic hotels only with no attachment to other tourism products.

2. Product specialization. E. g. Specialized in hotel reservation, including non-star and five-star ones.

3. Market specialization. E. g. Specialized in high-end tour products, including five-star hotels and first-class travel.

4. Choice specialization. E. g Specialized in both five-star hotel reservation and economy-class ticket reservation.

5. Comprehensive market. Play the "All-round" competition.

Why is there such a complicated theory? Why can't a company just cover all the products in tourist industry?

p. 3-2　Five regular models of target marketing

　　　　Market unification Product specialization Market specialization

　　　　Choice specialization Comprehensive market

To demonstrate the reason, let's read the story *The Head Sheep* first.

Once, a photographer went to travel in the Inner Mongolia Grassland. One day, he saw a crowd of adorable sheep. So, he used the camera in his hands and took a picture. After the picture was developed, he found something very interesting.

In the picture, there were numerous sheep which looked alike. But there was one sheep looked very different—it lifted its head and stared into the lens while other sheep buried their heads into the grass, which was very cute. Every person who had seen this picture was attracted by the sheep. They were impressed by this sheep and have no impression on the others.

The photographer named his photo *The Head Sheep* and took part in a photography competition with it. As a result, the photo had won the first prize with the comment that read, "The different are the outstanding and the attractive."

From the above story, it is not difficult for us to see that in the case of Ctrip, it had no difference from other tourism websites in its early development-it covered everything. In result, Ctrip became a master of none, failing in every business. Later, they changed their market positioning to focusing on the hotel reservation. They wanted to succeed in this market, and then head towards other markets. Thus, the right positioning got Ctrip through the "cold winter" steadily in the Internet industry.

Ⅳ. The rapid growth brought about by purchasing

There are fifteen ways in four categories to reorganize an enterprise, and purchasing is one way of those in the first category (expansion). There are three ways to make a purchase based on the form of capital in the purchase-in cash, in share and in mixed payment (cash plus share).

In the three categories, a company has to possess enough cash if it wants to make the purchase in cash; if a company wants to make the purchase in shares, the current shareholders would have to minimize their percentages. Which exactly is the best way?

The answer lies in Ctrip!

Ctrip purchased BizExpress and Modern Yuntong with shares in addition to cash. Ctrip did so because there was not enough cash in Ctrip at that time. Besides, their benefits were tied together once the other side had parts of Ctrip's shares. So, Ji Qi had to persuade the other side from another angel. He told Wu Hai and Wang Shengli that the shortages of their companies were not marketing and products, but technology and service capability. Ctrip was a prominent company which was good at both technology and service, and its shares were valuable.

After Wu Hai and Wang Shengli had been persuaded, they sat down to talk about the share price of Ctrip. Ji Qi said that Ctrip's shares were worthy of 40 million USD. This was an unreasonable price because Ctrip was not profiting and had only millions of cash. However, Wu Hai and Wang Shengli were eventually persuaded. The purchased were to be made in the combination of options, shares and cash. Thus, with only several million USD and parts of its shares, Ctrip had purchased the two companies.

From Ctrip's purchasing case, it is not difficult for us to see the things needed to be taken into consideration to choose the purchase methods.

1. Does the acquirer have enough cash?

2. Does the acquirer want to control the company?

3. Is the acquirer's share price high?

4. What is the scale of the purchase?

5. What is the cost for financing?

In the meanwhile, from Ctrip's purchase case, we can also understand the importance of purchasing for an enterprise. Purchasing could not only enhance the competitiveness of an enterprise, but also could raise the value of the acquirer. Take the company of Ctrip as an example, without purchasing Mordern Yuntong, its over-300-million value could not have been discovered.

In my opinion, what Ctrip had done the best was that they negotiated with the other companies on purchasing and on financing at the same time during the process. They purchased for financing and financed for purchasing. This is what we could learn.

This reminds me of another story *How to marry Bill Gate's daughter and be a Deputy Di-*

rector of World Bank at the same time?

There was a businessman named Jack. One day, he told his son, "I have sought out a girl for you to marry. Now, you go and marry her!" His son replied, "Dad, I am the one who get to choose who to marry. You don't get to worry about this for me. " Jack smiled, "Hehe! The girl I mentioned was Bill Gate's daughter!" His son was surprised, "Ah? If that's the case, I'd agree unconditionally. "

In a party, Jack said to Bill Gates, "I have a husband to introduce to your daughter!" Bill Gates replied, "Jack, stop joking! My daughter is still young, and she is not going to get married soon!" Jack said, "But this young man I've mentioned is the Deputy Director of World Bank!" Bill Gates was surprised, "Ah? If that's the case, my daughter would take him into consideration. "

Then, Jack went for the Chief Director of World Bank. He said directly to him, "Chief, I have a young man to introduce to you to be the Deputy Director. " The Chief Director said, "I already have dozens of Deputy Directors, and that's enough! I'm even planning on downsizing them!" Jack said, "But this young man I mentioned is the son-in-law of Bill Gate!" The Chief Director shouted, "Ah? If so, I'll have a talk with the young man first!"

In the end, Jack's son got married with Bill Gate's daughter and became the Deputy Director of World Bank.

The above story naturally reminds us of Ctrip's case. At that time, Ji Qi used the same means to "deceive" venture investors and hotel reservation companies. He promised venture investment companies that they could purchase Modern Yuntong right away; at the same time, he urged Modern Yuntong to cooperate with Ctrip because he could get venture investment soon. In result, Ctrip had a successful financing and purchase.

V. Serious consideration on share holdings

Holding means that a shareholder could control the internal operation of a company by holding the certain amount of shares.

There are two types of holdings-absolute holding and relative holding. The absolute holding means that a shareholder holds the shares more than 50%. For example, if he holds 51% of the shares, he would have the right to make major decisions for this company. The relative holding means that a shareholder holds the shares less than 50%. For example, if he holds 40% of the shares, but he is the one holds the majority shares more than any other shareholders, he would also have the right to speak on condition that the others are not united.

So, to play it safe, the original founders of the company had better hold more than 51% of its shares unless they want to sell their company.

In Ctrip's case, it had three rounds of financing. In the first round, IDG invested half a million USD in Ctrip, taking up of 20% of its shares; in the second round, five companies including Softbank invested 4. 5 million USD, taking up no more than 30% of its shares (probably 29%). After the two rounds, the Ctrip team was still in control of the holdings. But after the third round, they were no longer an absolute holding shareholder because Carlyle had invested 8 million USD, taking up 30% of its shares.

In fact, the Ctrip team were very clear that capital meant right of speech-now that they no long hold the majority of the shares, they could get laid off in any minute. But they had no other choice because the company was still not profiting. They'd rather give up on the control and make money than die for the control.

Speaking of purchasing, I'd like to give you another story of Danone's almost purchase of Wahaha.

In 1996, Hongkong Peregrine brought Danone as a strategic partner to negotiate with Wahaha on cooperation. The two sides on the negotiation table had agreed that Jinjia Investment Company, a joint-venture by Peregrine and Danone, and Wahaha form a joint-venture company. Jinjia Investment Company would invest in cash, taking up 51% of the shares and Wahaha would invest with its current factories, equipments and trademark, taking up 49% of the shares. A few years later, Peregrin sold its shares to Danone because of the Asian Financial Storm, ending in that Danone became the solo controlling shareholder of Jinjia.

At that time, Wahaha was in urgent need of capital for its development. Being inexperienced in joint-venture, they signed the agreement without serious consideration. Several years later, Song Zongqing (The Board Director of Wahaha Group) became experienced and felt being at a disadvantage in his agreement with Danone. Being unhappy about it, he had established a dozen of non-joint-venture companies behind Danone's back, using the Wahaha trademark. What was odd was that Danone did not say anything about it being aware of this.

These companies began to make profits, and had total capital of 5. 6 million and yearly profits of one billion. This time, Danone became unhappy because he thought he was the owner of Wahaha. Thus, Danone was forced to purchase the non-joint-venture companies of Wahaha's, and threatened to sue Song Zongqing on illegal using of the trademark.

Song had to go through years of lawsuits with Danone to fight for the control over the trademark.

In the end, Song Zongqing had won the case depending on the black-white contract, and got the trademark of Wahaha back from the French. But he had paid the price-he had won the case but lost his reputation.

So, for entrepreneurs doing financing, they need to take the issue of holdings into serious consideration.

Application

I. Which one should be the leading product?

Zhang Jun, from Chaozhou, had been in Shenzhen since 1985, running a store selling daily necessaries. After years of struggling, he had opened eight chain stores inside the customs. He wanted to expand his business outside the customs in 2009.

Zhang Jun knew very clear that the business of supermarkets depend on fast consuming products. Consumers had big demand of such products, and buy them often. Such products were easy to purchase. Beverages, in particular, took up a large percentage in the sales volume of the stores.

However, there was a disadvantage of selling beverages-the limited gross profit. So, Zhang Jun had decided to make his own "delicious" brand to save the cost. He found a factory to produce his products, which he could sell through his own channels.

The series of beverages included the following five categories-

1. Tea beverages-green tea, jasmine tea, ice black tea, and so on.
2. Cold tea beverages-heat-clearing tea, diet-tea, and so on.
3. Soybean milk beverages-black soybean milk, chocolate soybean milk, coconut soybean milk, and so on.
4. Syrup beverages-wheat syrup, corn pumpkin syrup, red bean syrup, and so on.
5. Juice beverages-orange juice, grape juice, lemon juice, vegetable juice, and so on.

Now, Zhang Jun wanted to choose one category as the priority of his product promotion. If you were his friend, which category would you suggest him to choose as the leading product? Please elaborate your opinion combining the current market demands.

II. How to build the selling-point of the goat milk?

On 8th December 2008, the author received a call my high school mate Li Jun. He said that he had transferred into the fast consuming product market to sell goat milk (liquid milk). He asked for my suggestion. The following are my conversation with him.

Assistant, "Let's first have a talk about the reason for you to enter this market."

Mr. Li, "The 'Melamine Milk Event' has made people change their face when talking about milk. The cow milk market is still in existence though there has been slight shrink. There is an urgent need for products to replace milk because people cannot give up on breakfast because of this event. Personally, I think this is a market opportunity for goat milk before the cow milk market gets back to its life."

Assistant, "Well, how is the quality your milk source and product?"

Mr. Li, "I have found an available factory to do the contract manufacturing for me."

Assistant, "As far as I know, there are already some people in this business. But, they could not enlarge the market, which may be because of the technology limitation on eliminating the unpleasant smell."

Mr. Li, "Don't worry about it. The factory I found has the top technology. "

Assistant, "Is your product registered? Are you planning on advertising on TV?"

Mr. Li, "The trademark has been settled. We are not planning on making advertisement. Instead, we would do promotion of free tasting at the gate of supermarket. "

Assistant, "How many people are you working with?"

Mr. Li, "I have myself, my wife, a former cow milk promoter in a mall, my elder brother, who knows people in the goat farm, my elder brother-in-law, who can drive, and a couple of other assistants. "

Assistant, "I don't know about the others, but I know that you used to sell feminine hygiene wash. . . "

According to the telephone record above, do you think that Mr. Li could have this market? And what's your reason? If you were a market inspector, how would you operate this business?

Chapter IV
Growth by leaps and bounds

Ctrip was not the discoverer and explorer of this market, but it survived by integrating the traditional industry through Internet technology. Surprisingly, Ctrip had soon become the leader in this industry just like a black horse. To understand how Ctrip could grow by leaps and bounds through the "winter" of Internet, we must first understand what its rivals had done wrong and what Ctrip had done right.

Quotations
Reflections on the business market 1-5

If you have a good sales achievement, you boss will be polite to you; more and more money will come to you, and your life will be enriched with meaningful things. But, I have to ask you, my brother, to just remember the sentence "What you can sell is your ability and what you cannot sell is your rubbish."

—reflection on Wu Hai's speech to motivate Ctrip Card promoter

Don't be afraid to be used because it's better than being useless. Understand this point because it works on everybody.

—reflection on Wu Hai's speech to motivate Ctrip Card promoter

All wolves would turn into sheep if they are lead by a sheep; all sheep will turn into wolves if they are lead by a wolf.

—reflection on WU Hai leading the Ctrip Card promoter

Do what others don't want to do and make the money that others don't want to make; do what others haven't done and make the money that others can't think of making; do what others can't do and make the money that others can't make.

—reflection on the promoters promoting the Ctrip Card

Do what others don't do; be good at what others do; be innovative on what others are good at.

—reflection on "the new way of promoting"

A fable
The chuck of the hen

Chicken eggs always sell better than duck eggs in the malls.

This is an inarguable fact which the duck couldn't understand. So, one day, the duck went to the hen.

The duck said, "Sister Hen, I am confused. Why do people say that your eggs are more nutritious when in fact the insiders of this industry all know that our eggs are the same in terms of nutrients? My eggs are bigger than yours! You tell me, why are people so ridiculous?"

The hen said, "Sister Duck, easy! Do you really want to know the truth?"

The duck answered, "I really want to know!"

The hen explained, "Well, what is the difference in our reactions after we lay our eggs?"

The duck was confused, "The difference? I'll go and look around quietly. Do you fly around in the yard?"

The hen said, "To fly around in the yard is not a good idea. I used to fly around in the yard once and was considered with pestilence by my owner. He had almost killed me!"

The duck got more confused, "Then what exactly is the difference?"

The hen continued, "The difference is that you are always so quite every time after you lay your eggs, but I would chuck to promote my product to show that my eggs are the best. That's the reason why chicken eggs sell better than duck eggs."

The duck asked surprised, "Ah! Doesn't the owner get annoyed by your chuck?"

The hen answered, "I don't chuck in front of the owner, but around the owner. As to which owner, you'd better choose the lady owner, because the gentleman owner would ignore you and the child owner would not be able to understand you."

The story of *The Chuck of the Hen* tells us-

1. Any product needs promotion.
2. The product needs the right targets to promote.
3. The product needs suitable promoting methods.

Text
Section Ⅰ What have the rivals done wrong?
The cause of the leading

Everybody thought that tourism was a perfect match for e-commerce because there were less attachments to the links of payment and delivery. Besides, there was large potential in China's tourism market. As the largest industry in the world, the tourism industry took 10% of the world's GDP. The number in China was 5%. However, this industry is growing twice as fast as China's GDP at the speed of 20% per year.

Therefore, many people aimed for this market and wanted to have a share in it. At the peak of the Internet's development, in January 2000, there were over one thousand tourism websites in the nation, including hundreds of tourism portal websites, nearly one hundred room reservation websites, and hundreds of websites invested by large-scale travel agencies.

During only a few years, there born over one thousand tourism websites in China. Did this phenomenon mean the flourish of this industry?

The result was that "it rose in a flash and in a flash it fell".

The year of 1998 was the year of e-commerce. The year of 2000 was the year of closing up. In the late half of 2000, China' tourism websites entered into a car-wash phase. Those who had sworn to become the grave diggers of the traditional travel agencies met with different destinies. Some tourism websites kept their smiles and gained power of the capital by cooperating with traditional forces; some tourism websites died in the washed Internet bubbles, and vanished from people's sight; some others adjusted and repositioned their business structure, and struggled to survive.

People became more clear-headed after the "winter" of the Internet. They realized that the Internet was a good stuff, but there were bubbles in it. Once, a CEO of a tourism website sighed, "The true Internet Economy should be a perfect combination of Internet technology and traditional economic models. It should be the development of traditional economy, rather than a simple Internet technology economy that goes against traditional business and modern enterprise model. "

What he said was indeed true and Ctrip had survived on the combination of Internet technology and traditional industry. What surprised all was that Ctrip had soon become the leader of this industry.

It was indeed surprising! Ctrip was not the discoverer and explorer of this industry. It was not the first tourism website. Before Ctrip, there was already China Travel Informaiton. com and Huaxia Travel. com; it was not the first Internet company to purchase a room reservation center. Before Ctrip's purchase of BizExpress and Modern Yuntong, Elong had purchased Baideqin. Plus, it did not have unique resources and advantages compared to Internet companies founded by traditional travel agencies like CYTS. com and Yigao Travel. com who had more powerful resources.

Tourism websites' unawareness of how to make money

Ctrip's rivals could be divided into four categories according to different positioning

1. Tour Portal websites-Huxia Travel. com, China Travel Information. com

2. Websites founded by traditional travel agencies —CYTS. com, Yigao Travel. com

3. Websites similar to Ctrip-Elong. com

4. Traditional hotel reservation centers-BizExpress, Golden Century (which still existed)

During the two years between 1999 and 2000, Ctrip. com was positioned as a portal website, so there were two competitive rivals —China Travel Information. com and Huxia

Travel. com.

China Travel Information. com was founded in June 1997 by Hua Qing. In November 1999, China Travel Information. com moved its headquarters from Wuhan to Bejing and Hua Qing formed the Beijing Business Travel Holiday Internet Technology Limited Company. It offered services including online ticket reservations, hotel room reservations, shopping, connecting travel agent companies to the Internet, and so on. It was said that it was a powerful website with abundant resources of as many as 40 thousand pieces of information. A regular user could look up for comprehensive information including resorts, tour tracks, hotels, travel agencies, shopping, entertainments and transportations across the country and the world.

Huxiatravel. com was a joint-venture company founded in October 1997 by China International Travel Agency, Guangdong XIntai Information Industry Limited Company and Huadakang Investment Holding Limited Company. It had rich upper-stream resources. According to an insider, there were over one thousand member agencies of Huaxiatravel. com.

Between the two websites, China Travel Information. com was founded the earliest and was jokingly named "the Huangpu Military School in tourism websites", having trained many talents for this industry. According to its Deputy Director Chu Siming, its Financial Inspector and Chief Art Designer were both working for others. The Online City was a piece of work of its Public Relations Department. The main strength in Ctrip's Marketing Department was borrowed from this company.

Would the senior leader of China Travel Information get mad about the company's talent loss? Unexpectedly, he was well-educated. He said to the public that it was normal for talents to flow from one company to another because it was a hard job to train such talents for so many new companies emerged in one year. Such flowing of human resources was necessary for the Internet to get somewhere. China Travel Information did not lose blood because of the talents' flowing from China Travel Information. There were limited amount of job positions in a company. Some people might leave being unable to adapt to the system while some others might leave because they could not get any chance at all. Necessary talent flowing could keep up the energy of a website as long as the cadre stayed.

Having trained many talents, how did they make money? Oddly, these two websites refused to publish the number of their income.

The Deputy Director of China Travel Information. com said, "Currently, the majority of our profits come from ticket reservation. The cash flow is considerable, which can be as high as millions of RMB every day. In terms of ticket reservation alone, China Travel Information was the best. The website could have the profit of 3% by selling one air ticket." When asked about the business volume every month, Chu Siming refused to answer.

The Marketing Manager of Huaxia. com introduced that Huaxia. com was focusing on B2B, which profited from two major parts-membership and commission. In addition, they were going to develop Internal Management Program for travel agencies. He had also admitted that they were not officially charging their members, honestly claiming that they were still in the stage of discovering and constructing.

In fact, at that time, Ctrip was only able to make ends meet, as well.

Why did these websites fail to make profits? Because at that time, tourism websites depended mainly on online ticket reservations and room reservations for income, aiming at white-collars from foreign business and large-scale enterprises. These people, rich and fond of traveling, used Internet regularly and were willing to be served by the modernized technology. However, this group of people could not support a website.

What should they do?

The market indeed existed! According to the data by China Travel Association, in 1999, the total income of China's tourism industry reached 239.9 billion RMB while the traditional travel agencies only took up 5% of the whole industry's income. This meant that there was plenty of room for tourism websites in the expanding China's tourism market.

But why were these companies still temporarily not making money? It probably had something to do with their marketing strategies.

Liang Jianzhang said that Ctrip was not simply a website, but a tourism enterprise that used to the Internet to reform the traditional tourist service model. The goal for Ctrip was not only to compete with other websites and traditional tourist companies, but also to lead in the industry.

However, the Public Relations Manager of Huaxia. com Zhang Shuo summarized that positioning of Huaxia. com was a friend of tourists and an assistant for tourist industry. He thought that tourism websites were more of a channel to connect the Internet to the traditional companies and clients than to replace traditional tourism companies.

The different ways of positioning lead to the different thoughts.

Liang Jianzhang thought, "There is no perfect product but perfect service. Service is the best market. Only by being more convenient than a supermarket, could an Internet company get more returning customers." Therefore, Liang Jianzhang copied the management system from Oracle to Ctrip and established a customer management system, in which there were customer profiles who had consumed here. At the same time, Liang had also built an employ assessment system based on the customers' feedbacks. According to this system, employees' salaries and promotions were affected by customers' evaluation.

The Public Relations Manager of Huaxia. com Zhang Shuo focused on the price relying on the sources from its upper steam. He said that the netizens could get 30%-70% discounts if they book rooms through Huaxia. com.

Facing with the suicidal low-price promoting methods of its competitive rivals, Ctrip had spread the word that despite Huaxia and China Travel Information's seniority, Ctrip had already surpassed them in terms of e-commerce. For Ctrip, its biggest rivals were not websites.

Chu Siming, of China Travel Information. com, heard this, and gave another expression, " Ctrip has investors no different from those of China Travel Information's-companies like IDG and Softbank. For those investors, they invested in two companies in the same field for insurance, because they could never exclude the possibility of reorganizing them. Therefore, Ctrip and China Travel Information were brothers rather than rivals. "

When the three websites were having fights that ended without any result, foreign investors came over. Tom. com layed their eyes on the top two websites Huaxia. com and China Travel Information. com, making them the strategic partners of Tom. com in China's Internet tourism industry.

Tom. com gave them attractive buying prices and they had reached initial agreements very soon. The chief directors of both website had even taken a photo together. Before the photo was developed, there came the China Travel Service (Hongkong) who stole China Travel Information. com from Tom. com in a lightening speed.

After China Travel Information. com was purchased by China Travel Service (Hongkong) , it began its calamitous life. First, its founder Hua Qing resigned. Then, it was purchased by Chinanet with a rumor price of 120 million RMB.

Thus, China Travel Information. com was in frequent share and human exchanges, developing slowly. After its merge with Chinanet. com, its management got into the stride. Chu Siming said, "The money in Chinanet's pocket is enough for twenty years' life. If we can get support from sucha portal website, we could have more time on the business. Once we get the internal relations sorted out, we are going to make profits soon. "

Whatever Chu Siming had said, the truth was that China Travel Information was purchased by others, meaning that it's dead and there was one less rival for Ctrip.

Oddly, speaking of being purchased, Huaxia. com was being delicate just like China Travel Information and did not admit its being purchased. The Spokesman of Huaxia. com said that it was a cooperative relationship between Huaxia. com and Tom. com. The two sides jointly invested in a travel company in Hongkong which offered English information for entering and exiting the port. Huaxia. com was considering introducing the French, Japanese, Korean and Complicated Chinese version of the website in the end of 1999 and the beginning of the year of 2000. Tom. com was a famous website, and Huaxia was only relying on its influence in abroad to go to the world.

Liang Jianzhang did not show his attitude, but Zhang Suyang from IDG urged them to continue on the negotiation. However, Ji Qi did not agree on any condition. He said, "Some bosses succeed because they don't bow to life; some bosses succeed because the bow to other people. The current situation is either that we get purchased, or that we purchase others. I think that the defense is offense, and that our only choice is to purchase others. "

Thus, the three large tourism portal websites had different lives when the "winter" of Internet came. Ctrip purchased two hotel reservation companies and transformed into a hotel reservation website; China Travel Information was purchased by Chinanet; Huaxia suffered a severe setback in the "winter".

The detours Elong had taken

Among all the Internet companies, Elong was a true rival to Ctrip.

Tang Yue was the founder of Elong. He had similar life experience with Shen Nanpeng- he was born in Nanjing, Jiangsu Province in 1971. His parents were professors in the university. He dropped out of school in his junior year from the Commercial School of Nanjing University in 1991. He passed the TOEFL test and was admitted by Minnesota Concordia University in the middle-west of America. He continued his bachelor's degree in commerce there.

His tuition fees were 14 thousand USD one year. The school offered him the scholarship of around 7 thousand USD, but he lack around 7 thousand USD a year. So, Tang Yue arrived in America two months ahead and planed on working part-time to make up for the rest of his tuition fees.

He arrived in Los Angeles in America with no one to pick him up. He was stuck at the airport. He was so helpless that he started talking to a young girl next to him. The more they chatted, the more the young girl had found that this twenty-year-old mediocre guy was independent and had affinity. Knowing his difficulty, the strange young girl decided to take him home with no other intentions.

At that moment, Tang Yue had only brought 200 USD with him, which was given by his mother. So, not too long after he got to the school from Los Angeles, he was doing part-time jobs.

Tang Yue's part-time work experience was worth mentioning. He was first working as an assistant for the chef in the school's canteen to make hamburgers. He did other chores, including cleaning the vegetables and washing dishes.

Later, Tang Yue decided to sell tickets in Disneyland. This was an uneasy job opportunity for Tang Yue. Disland had a university student program that they would choose one thousand students from hundreds of American universities, meaning that only one or two students got to be chosen to work in Disneyland in the summer. So the odd was small.

Tang Yue was the second student in his university being interviewed. After a series of confusing questions, he was asked by the interviewer, "Why do you want to work in Disneyland?"

Tang Yue thought for a second and told the interviewer a story, "When I was little, there was a little girl in Sichuan China who was in sick of leukaemia. Her biggest wish was to go to the Disneyland. At that time, there was a 'Dream Come True' program in the UN, through which she went to the Disneyland and fullfilled her dream. Not too long after she went back to China, she passed away. "

Tang Yue paused for a while, and said, "In fact, there are thousands of children suffering from diseases and hunger. They could never get the chance to come to America and have fun in the Disneyland. So, I want to build a Disneyland when I get back China to spread the culture of America. "

The interviewer heard his speech and smiled, "Come to work tomorrow!"

The two years of his student life went by quickly. In 1993, Tang Yue graduated from Concordia University and worked in the world's largest investment bank Merrill Lynch. He was in charge of researches on and sales of shares and stocks. Then, he had worked for one year in two other American investment companies.

Having been working in the venture investment companies for five or six years, Tang Yue had gradually realized that he could never belong to the mainstream society and influent the American society no matter how hard he tried. So, he decided to go back to China.

In May 1999, Tang Yue and three entrepreneurial partners founded Elong Company with the seed money of one million USD. In October that year, Elong. com was officially launched.

When Tang Yue first started on websites, he did not completely understand the Internet. Everybody said that Internet equaled to portal websites, so Tang Yue wanted to make the Chinese version of Yahoo. When he got back, he found that there were already Sohu. com, Sina. com and 163. com, and these companies were doing well. Thus, two months later, he decided to change the company's positioning to a city life website offering information on food, beverages, entertainment, shopping, accommodations and transportation in the cities.

To make Elong grow fast, Tang use the method of purchasing just like the Ctrip team.

In February 2000, Tang Yue purchased Xici. net, which was a famous community website in Nanjing with a large volume of flow every day. Xici. net qualified the standard to e-valuate an Internet company.

Two months later, Tang Yue purchased the room reservation center Baideqin.

Speaking of purchasing the Baideqin, it was quite dramatic. It was a small company next to Elong, which had only twenty staff members and serviced only through hotlines instead of on the Internet.

One day in January 2000, Tang Yue walked by Baideqin, and saw its employees making membership cards-Lohoo Card. On seeing this, Tang Yue realized that the tourism service of Baideqin had connection with the city life service of Elong. So he went to talk the person in charge of Baideqin and suggested that they should cooperate on a united promoting-Lohoo Cards for the users of Elong.

Through further understanding of this company, Tang Yue knew that the majority share-holder of Baideqin Chenyalin was losing faith in his company. He was planning on selling this company because it could only make profits of 80 thousand RMB. Tang Yue talked with Chen Yalin on the specific terms of the purchase. One of them wanted to buy the company, and the other one wanted to sell it. Soon, they reach the agreement at the purchasing price of 8 million RMB.

But, when Tang Yue talked to Chen Yalin about the purchase, Elong was not rich. The initial one million RMB had run out in January 2000.

How could Tang Yue make the purchase without enough money? Tang Yue wanted to find acquirers for Elong when he purchased Baideiqin. He told his idea to the three other founders, and they said, "Do what you want to do as long as we can make money."

Supported by his partners, this man, who was good at telling western mythologies to the oriental people and telling oriental stories to the Western, had soon found an acquirer. An A-merican Internet company Mail. com decided to purchase Elong with stocks in the price of 68 million USD on 14th March 2000.

After selling Elong to Mail. com, Tang Yue had the money to purchase Baideqin. In fact, purchasing Baideqin had done a great help to Elong. Many years later, Tang Yue ad-mitted that Elong could never enter the tourism industry without this purchase, and Elong could have broken without this purchase.

Before purchasing Baideqin, Tang Yue did not pay attention to business of this compa-ny, because Mail. com had already drawn a big pie for Elong.

Mail. com was the world's third largest provider of free email services. Because of this business, Mail. com was in possession of a lot of domain names. At that time China. com got listed in NASDAQ and had financed a large sum of money. Seeing this, Mail. com thought their domain names, such JAPAN and USA, could turn into Internet companies worthy of tens of millions.

Therefore, to develop and manage the large domain name resources, Mail. com had founded an incubated company for domain names. In the meanwhile, Mail. com formed a new company Asia. com as a subsidiary company to develop its business. Asia. com would build its subsidiary companies and offer B2B and C2C business in countries and regions a-round Asian centered by Elong. com, including Korea, Hongkong, Singapore and Thailand. Elong expanded its business in China from community-life service to all aspects of e-com-merce.

Tang Yue was intoxicated by this plan. He thought Asia. com could not only improve the brand recognition among the Asian consumers and commercial users, but could also build a bridge between enterprises and customers from all over the world and those in Asia.

However, one year later, Tang Yue had gradually come to realize that the super pie was actually a beautiful trap. Therefore, during the downhill of the Internet in May 2001, Tang Yue bought Elong back from Mail. com in the price of 1.5 million USD.

Unfortunately, when Tang Yue decided to transfer the business to hotel reservation service, Ctrip had already become the largest hotel distributor in China, supported by the team brought by Wu Hai and by the expansion in the Northern market by Wang Shengli.

Why did Elong lose to Ctrip? Tang Yue concluded, "We have to admit that Ctrip is the number one in the market, and that Elong is the number two. Ctrip had positioned its business on tourism industry from the beginning, so it is a pioneer in this industry. Besides, Ctrip is rich enough to get through the 'winter' of the Internet-the cash alone that Ctrip possessed were over 10 million USD. "

Failure of travel agencies to break the bottleneck

Elong took the detour, ending in losing to Ctrip. Then, how did those websites set up by traditional agencies perform? Were they more competitive because they had clear goals and abundant resources?

According to an authority survey, in 1999, China's tourist industry had the income of over 400 billion RMB, among which 10% were from tour groups and 90% were from independent commercial tourists and self-help family tourists. Independent travelling had become the mainstream in the development of tourist industry.

Faced with this result, Jiang Jianning, the chief of China's second largest travel agency China Youth Travel, started to work his brain. He said, "In China, the time has passed when travel agencies could make enormous profits. In the past, travel agencies depend on tourist groups, but now they are being replaced by personalized and scattered tour products. People no longer want to join the tour groups lead by a small flag, in which the time for using toilets is set. Travel agencies have introduced personalized tourism plans for customers, but nearly none of them would follow exactly what the plans say. They would revise the plans on their own. If travel agencies don't use the Internet technology and transform quickly into a time of personalized tourism, the tourism industry in China is going for a slow-motion suicide. "

Seeing this point, in June 2000, China Youth Travel Company decided to introduce venture investment to build a comprehensive tourism website CYTSonline. com. At the same time, it set up the chain stores of travel agency-China Youth Travel Service Chain Stores.

Later, China Youth Travel combined the China Youth Travel Chain Stores and CYTSonline. com together, resulting in the first real network of "mouse and concrete" in China.

Thus, the chain store across Beijing and the virtual websites together had formed a sales network-whether you were in front of a computer or in the chain stores on the streets, you were being served by of a unified network. For example, a customer in a chain store could enjoy the online services such as online ticket reservation and tourism information. He could also upload his demands through the virtual network to relative department of China Youth Travel, and the information would be gathered to the chain stores. In all, China Youth Travel set a goal to create the simplest and most effective tour plan through the interaction with the customer online and offline.

Jiang Jianning was quite confident with this idea. He said, "It is the real Internet network if one can enjoy the service online without using the Internet." Meanwhile, people inside the industry were having good expectation on this. They thought, "CYTSonline. com has broken the traditional business model of tourism. It does promoting using the platform of Internet. The travel agency plays a role of backstage, specified in business like market researches, product development, and reception. Thus, there born the new business model of tourist industry of the complementary combination of tourism websites and travel agencies."

However, it was not too long before people realized that this was a beautiful mistake. If the travel agency was running a tourism website, the resources it owned would become burdens rather than fortunes. The stronger a travel agency was, the paler its website seemed.

This fatal weakness was a result of the traditional structure of travel agencies. Such a large travel agency company as China Youth Travel had its business across the country with strength and abundant resources. But in terms of business operations, they were taken by its subsidiary agencies located across the country. Each of these agencies had their own pursuit of benefits, so they wouldn't be able to promote a business according to a same standard and for the same benefits. Therefore, the website was playing the damaging role.

In the end, CYTSonline. com did not end in the result as expected. In such a complicated industry with higher and higher demands on personalization as the tourism industry, the website can hardly provide any personalized service, but only some information.

The aborted Landlord Card

In the 400-billion-RMB tourism market, Jiang Jianning, the Chief of CYTSonline. com, was not the only one who wanted to make personalized tourism products with the help of Internet technology. Zhang Shengli was also hunger for the personalized tourism products because he had seen another market demand-the occupancy rate of tourism hotels and holiday villages maintained at 50% regularly, and the trend of independent tourists had become the mainstream in the development of the tourism industry. Therefore, Zhang Shengli had opened another new company-Beijing Xinlv. com Hotel and Holiday Village Investment Management company, and had introduced a new tourism product-Landlord Card. He wanted to provide tourists with personalized serviced through e-ecommerce.

The Xinlv. com was a joint-venture company invested by four companies including China Travel Joint Stock Company. It ran on the platform of the alliance of hotels and holiday villages, and in the model of time-share. This company sold tourism services as products.

Zhang Shengli had first copied the time-share model from abroad. Based on the situation in China, he had gathered plenty of hotels and holiday villages to form a benefit alliance. In this alliance, the original share holdings were not changed. It was just an Internet method to form a virtual business model of "the workshop of hotels lead by the main hotel Xinlv. com". Thus, all the hotels in this alliance could win over both the resources and the clients.

For tourists, the Landlord Card of Xinlv. com was like a card of the right to consume. That's to say, within the effective time (usually 5 years) and the spending limitation (3000-80,000 RMB) of the IC Card, a card holder could enjoy the consuming right and additional services in any of the hotels or holiday villages in the alliance. The clients could buy the card, make reservations for rooms and search for the spending on the e-commerce platform in the website of Xinlv. com. The card holders could also enjoy the lowest price for accommodation in the hotels and holiday villages that had work connection with Xinlv. com, and the price would remain the same for a while in order the keep the value of the Landlord Card.

So, Xinlv. com was like a grand hotel, and the hotels in its network were like the subsidiary departments. All the hotels and holiday villages shared the client resources and business equipments. Thus, all the hotels and holiday villages could share the scaled economic benefits brought by Internet business model. The clients got to choose from all the hotels and holiday villages, increasing the utility monetary cost rate for the card holders and enlarging the potential client sources for the alliance in return.

Besides, this virtual network business model of Xinlv. com, "the workshop of hotels lead by the main hotel Xinlv. com", prevented the increase of the cost in unit management after real hotels got expanded (uneconomical scale). Through the internal competition among the subsidiary hotels, the damage on the energy of a hotel from the monopoly of a grand hotel, such as "the grand hotels victimizing the customers", was eliminated.

Thirdly, through this business model, all the aliased hotels and holiday villages could readjust on their unoccupied rooms and sell them in ahead. Thus, Xinlv. com could negotiate with the hotels for its customers on the price, offering them the price lower than the price that any existing reservation centers could offer. With the preferential price, adaptive check-in time and region, and the selectable prices, it was easier for group and family consumers to control the travelling budget in ahead.

Thus, the Landlord Card could motivate the vacant capital for holiday villages and provide with tourists the most preferential price at the same time. Could this card become a fashion trend?

There must be a reason why Zhang Shengli promoted this Landlord Card so decisively.

He said to the journalist interviewing him, "In the recent two years, many big tourist enterprises in the domestic market had done exploration and practice in the aspect of network chain model and the group scale model, but the results were dissatisfying. The network business model could unify the brands, share resources and lower the cost, but the real network business requires that the member enterprises have reasonable geographical location, which means that they can not be in a centered region. At the same time, these enterprises should have innovative sales technology and scientific business management model. To solve this problem, these tourism enterprises had thought of many solutions. For example, some wanted to solve the geographical problem through merging, purchasing and capital exchange. But the negotiation were difficult, so there were many cases of failure. For instance, Oriental Guest House failed to purchase the Luoyang Hotel; Jinjiang Group failed in the capital exchange in alien land of its hotels in Shanghai. Even if some enterprises could solve the geographical problem, they can not link the subsidiary companies together to for the new competitiveness because they lacked innovative sales technology and scientific management. As a result, the over seven thousand hotels in the nation are still fighting solely. "

After series of analysis on cases of enterprise purchase and enterprise reorganize, and scientific analysis on the feature of tourism hotels, Zhang Shenli came to a conclusion that it was unrealistic to integrate hotels and holiday villages on a large scale by purchasing. The key was the whole new concept and business model. On one hand, he needed to explore the potential need in the market, and on the other, he needed to change the solitary business model of current hotels and holiday villages. Through changing the business model and improving the service quality, he could bring more convenient and preferential services to the consumers, as well as readjust the vacant resources in hotels and holiday villages.

Based on this thought, Zhang Shengli had decided to get involved as a third person between the hotels and holiday villages and the consumers, using the modern Internet technology and a brand new business model without changing the current ownership of the property in the hotels and holiday villages. Thus, he could for a network of the numerous hotels and holiday villages and the consumers, realizing the readjustment of the vacant resources in the hotels and holiday villages. He believed that this model could resume the vacant capital of the tourist hotels and improve the quality of the capital, realizing the true network of operation.

Zhang Shengli had sufficient reasons, but would the result come out as he expected?

Unfortunately, in the few months after 18th April 2000, when Landlord Card was launched , the reaction from the market was not so good. Many customers had found that in a short term, the hotel and holiday village sources provided by the Internet were far from their high requirements; when using the Landlord Card, there was problems of compatibility with traditional ways when settling the account; there were places needed to be improved in the technology services of the system.

Later, the practice in the market had proved that time-share holiday was not suitable for the China's market. The time-share tourism products, which was not luxury ones, had become luxury products as far as the current income standard of the Chinese residents was taking into consideration. Besides, the Leave with Payment system had not been widely implemented. Most family couldn't make sure which week they would use to travel in ahead, resulting in the failure of time-share travelling. What's more, the relative authorities had not given a clear definition on time-share travelling. If there was any dispute, the consumers couldn't get support from the law and would end in a passive situation.

Therefore, the Landlord Card baby was aborted before being brought up.

The failure to follow the time of the room reservation centers

Finally, let's take a look at the traditional room reservation centers.

Undeniably, Modern Yuntong and BizExpress were the first ones to discover the new market of hotel reservation. In 1997, they had already initiated the business model based on 800 Toll-Free Call Centers in China. In the following years, many small and large companies entered this market in a row. But these companies had all been faced with the same problem- it was hard for them to expand their business, thus, they were unable to grow fast enough. They were traditional enterprises which venture investor would not pay attention to, so they could not get the financial investment to enlarge their scales. Therefore, they could only run the small business and tried to make ends meet.

However, a few of them had realized the power of the Internet. For example, Modern Yuntong had also created a website called Futureyuntong. com in November 1999. But, several months later, Wang Shengli had found out that this website was not performing practically function at all. On one hand, Modern Yuntong did not have talents specialized in Internet to promote this website, and on the other hand, the company could not support the enormous expenses of a website on its own because of the small scale and singularity of products of the traditional reservation centers.

Upon realizing his shortcomings, Wang Shengli decided to merge with Ctrip. Among the other reservation centers, Modern Yuntong found a good enterprise to depend on. Some others struggled to fight for food against other big companies. Golden Century Commercial Travel. com was an example. Its boss Li Zizheng said to a journalist, "We are faced with challenges every day, and we are exploiting and creating every day. But, after these years' development, Golden Century has become the largest club of paid membership in the nation. We are keen on the life quality of high-end figures. We put in all of our energy to build the world's most influential platform of the intergrated life information, providing with our members the easy, preferential and dependable services including checking-in, reservation, and trade of hotels, air tickets, golfing, food and entertainment, travelling and holiday. We also have other additional services such as VIP channels in the airport, automobile assistant and financial insurance. We now have the leading call center in the nation and secretary senior client management teams. "

Li Zizheng had a vision for the future of his company. But, compared to the "BMW" Ctrip, the "tractor" Golden Century was far behind in development.

Why? Please read the next section!

Section II   What had Ctrip done right?

The competition on tour tracks.

One may wonder in which year the competition among tourism websites was the most intense and breath-taking. To be precise, the answer to this question was the time between 1999 and 2000.

In the end of April 2000, Elong announced its merge with Baideqin. The CEO of Elong Zhang Ligang said to the media, "This merge has helped Elong to make full use of Baideqin's original client resources and travel service network in and out of the country. We are planning on launching the Elong Card and Elong-LoHoo Card. We believe that with the development of our online business, the income of LoHoo's tourism services would increase on a large scale, reaching 100 million RMB by the end of the year.

In the beginning of June, CYTSonline. com was online over night. The spokesman for CYTSonline. com announce to the outside world that they were going to launch the English, Complicated Chinese, Korean and Japanese versions of CYTSonline. com in the latter half of the year. They would also start services targeting at major clients and B2B. This bluffing of CYTSonline. com had made the competition in the tourism e-commerce market more intense.

On 15th August, the Blue Dragonfly Olympic Digital Trip opened in Beijing. This was a large-scale event co-hosted by Chinese Internet Competition Organizing Committee and Huaxia Travel Internet Limited Company. The Deputy Chairman of the National Information Promotion Office opened the ceremony by clicking the mouse, also opening the combats between tourism websites.

In September, there were more exciting competitions.

Chinagc. com, the rising star among tourism websites had launched the National Day Preferential Cultural Trip in the Divine Land, including projects like double-flights and four-day trips to the Buddha Land in the Ocean Mount Putuo, Ningbo, Fenghuaxikou; single-flight and five-day trips to Yangzi Three Gorges, the Ghost City Fengdu and the Small Three Gorges on three-star ships (There is a poem line describing this tour track-"Enjoy the beautiful sceneries of the Three Gorges and travel in the Ghost City of Fengdu"); single-fight and five-day essential trips along the Jiujiang River to Jiujiang, Xunyanglou, Mount Lu, Mout Shizhong, Boyang Lake and the capital of china Jingde County.

The Tourism Channel of Sohu. com launched the event of "the Seven-day Trip guided by Sohu" relying on the advantage of being a portal website. It claimed that the dozens of golden tour tracks in and out of China could be reserved online.

Elong was not willing to stand falling behind, so it promised no rise in the price during the Naitonal Day holiday. VIP clients with accumulated points over than 10 thousand points could enjoy the regular price for members during the week from 1ˢᵗ October to 7ᵗʰ October.

Byecity. com said, "During this holiday, we have three series of more than 50 tour tracks out of China that cover the four continents of Europe, Asia, Africa and Australia. Those who have been living in the country for too long can say goodbye to the cities you are familiar with now."

Xoyo. com told people who planned on traveling during the National Day holiday that they had the set menus which were in real-time-connection with over one thousand hotels in a hundred cities in China. Their users could make reservations for rooms within half an hour withthe discount of as much as 30% off.

Sotrip. com liked to focus on less popular spots. During the National Day holiday, it promoted tour tracks to less popular spots such as Longmen and Hancheng. It had also promoted eco-friendly tour trips.

The two-month-old Toursmart. com. cn was not famous enough. So they introduced online activities of bidding for the rooms to attract travelling enthusiasts and Internet users, increasing the daily visiting record.

What was odd was that Ctrip, being competitive in online travel services, did not make any big moves in these competitions. What happened to Ctrip? What did it do?

Please read the following parts.

Ctrip's focus on room reservation

When every other tour companies strived to promote all kinds of tour tracks, Ctrip was busy promoting its hotel reservation business.

Ctrip had purchased the two reservation companies BizExpress and Modern Yuntong, and Modern Yuntong was the top ranking company among the room reservation companies. However, even withthe current achievements of these two companies, they could not support a "shark" enterprise like Ctrip. So, for Ctrip, they needed to work their brains on how to have a major breakthrough on the number of rooms reserved through their website.

The logic in hotel reservation was like this. Hotels could give larger discounts to reservation companies if they could bring more customers to the hotels; with larger discounts, reservation companies could attract more customers; hotel reservation companies could get more commissions from hotels if they could bring more guests.

When Ctrip first transformed itself from tour tracks to hotel reservation, it had signed agreements with over one thousand hotels over three months. But the agreements did not mean the actual business volume. During the three months, Ctrip had no more than one thousand room nights per month, which meant that Ctrip could only bring several guests to a hotel every month. Obviously, Ctrip was not so helpful to the hotels, which in return could not give Ctrip larger discounts.

There must be something wrong the promoting methods. Ctrip had burnt so much money on the advertisements, only ending in the heightened fame. But these advertisements had not "deceived" many clients to make room reservations. It seemed that Ctrip had to find other ways.

The four co-founders of Ctrip squeezed their heads but still could not find a solution. Wu Hai, on the other hand, had a unique strategy of his own. When Wu Hai joined Ctrip, he had said to Ji Qi, "This is not how you play the game of hotel reservation. You have to change all the methods you are using if you want to have a breakthrough on the number."

Then how did Wu Hai promote the hotel reservation business?

When he was in BizExpress, Wu Hai had tried every means to open the market of hotel reservation, but the results were not obvious.

Once, on a regular meeting on Monday, an employee told a story of selling the toothbrushes, "I have a friend who was an agent for an infamous brand of toothbrush. Because the brand was so infamous that the supermarkets would not stock them, neither would the small stores be willing to sell them. With no other choice, he had to apply the model of direct distribution. He hired a lot of direct salesmen and promoted his products door to door. This methods might have been inconspicuous, original and stupid, but through it, he had made over 30 million RMB."

Wu Hai agreed, "Ah! That makes sense. That's inspiring." Then, he asked, "Then, how should we do the promotion? Please speak your mind, will you?"

Some employee answered, "Hotel reservation is totally different from selling a toothbrush. There's nothing to learn from this story."

Wu Hai followed him, "Everybody, please express your opinion. Don't say something so frustrating yet, nor deny others' opinion. Please use your imagination and talk about our future freely."

Inspired by Wu Hai, they got interested. Like the Eight Immortals crossing the sea, each one showed his or her own prowess. They expressed odd ideas and colorful creativity.

One employee said, "Why don't we promote our services in the office buildings. We could give out the membership cards for free. Isn't this a method worth trying?"

A second employee said, "We could set a table on the streets or near the bus stations, and process the free membership cards for our potential clients. This is going to work."

A third employee said, "We'd better hand out our membership cards at the airports because the target clients are gathered there. This would be more effective. Personally, I think, our achievements will be shockingly good before too long."

A fourth employee said, "I think it would be more effective if we could promote our membership cards with the sales members from the hotels. This would be more trustworthy for our clients."

......

A good stuff-the Ctrip Card

Which method would work among the door-to-door service, processing membership on the streets, or selling at the airports? Wu Hai was uncertain. He was not sure whether it would work to hand out the membership cards in those places. He said, "Now that you have so many good suggestions, why don't you go and practice your own suggestions?"

Therefore, those employees who were willing to take the challenges went to distribute the membership cards.

As it turned out, the result was surprisingly good, especially at the airport. That employee handed out 500 cards in the first month and 3000 cards in the second month. After these cards were handed out, many people who got the cards and in need of hotel reservations would call the number on the card.

How many people called the hotline of BizExpress? Wu Hai was shocked by the result, not by the number of cards handed out, but by the inversion rate. The membership cards of BizExpress had the inversion rate as high as 30%, that's to say, among 100 tourists who got the cards, 30 of them would make reservations calls to BizExpress.

Handing out membership cards at the airports had indeed proved the existence of the demands in this market. Thus, Wu Hai decided to promote this method and required every card dispatch employee "work" at the airports. As a result, the reservation volume of BizExpress had grown far beyond the reasonable number they had expected.

Wu Hai had sighed afterwards, "The greatest truth is always simple. The truth lies only in sentence while the false lies in thousands of books. The simpler the idea is, the more helpful it is. Promotion is not so complicated. It's better to say that the idea of that employee helped me change this industry than to say that I changed the industry."

After Wu Hai left BizExpress, he had brought the entire team to Ctrip, including the unique strategy of handing out cards. At that time, the inversion rate decreased to the average of 10%, but Wu Hai thought that it was not the limit. Before Ctrip, many hotel reservation centers had applied membership cards in the market promotion, but they charged the cards for fee.

The following are two examples of room reservation centers, through which we could understand the features of tourist membership cards.

1. LoHoo Card

(1) The number of hotels-over one thousand hotels in over one hundred cities in the country

(2) Profiles need for membership-By filling in the application form on Elong. com, a user could get a number for the virtual card. Once the card has accumulated points over 3000, the user could get the real LoHoo Card. If a user wants to obtain the true card directly, he needs to pay 300 RMB.

(3) Reservation process-The room can be booked on the day. If there is no available room in the hotel, nor could the club arrange another room of the same class hotel with one hour, the user could get a free night in the hotel.

(4) Revise and reservation-If a client cancel off the check-in without notifying the club, his accumulated points will be decreased. If the client needs to revise the reservation, he also needs to notify the club in ahead.

(5) Price-20% to 70% discount

(6) Payment-Some hotels entrust the club with the payment. In other hotels, a client can pay at the front desk.

(7) Advantage and disadvantage-There are usually activities to draw prizes as feedbacks to the consumers. The fees for the card are high.

2. Golden Century Card

(1) The number of hotels-over one thousand hotels in the country; over 700 hotels in over one hundred countries and regions in the world.

(2) Profiles needed for membership-The card can be bought online. If a client has the Golden Tassel Card of the Bank of Agriculture, he could apply for the membership card in any branch networks. The card is sold at 398 RMB with the duration of three years.

(3) Reservation process-one day in ahead by phone call.

(4) Revise and reservation-Any revise should be notified to the company several hours in ahead. If a client doesn't check in the reserved room for three times, he will lose his membership and this card will be invalid.

(5) Price-30%-70% discounts in domestic hotels. If the price for members is higher than the price on the market or higher than 70% of the original price, the company would give the member a compensation twice of the margin.

(6) Payment-Customers pay for the rooms at the front desk.

(7) Advantage and disadvantage-When making the reservation, a member can use his cell phone number or his complete telephone number as the number of his membership card. It is troublesome to buy the card; there is a long period to wait for the card getting processed. (*Golden Card Project.* 2001:7)

At that time, all the room reservation centers, including BizExpress and the two companies mentioned above, charged their members for the membership fees. Most reservation centers had small scales with not too much sales volume each year, so by selling the membership cards, they could have actual earnings and seize the users.

However, there was a fatal shortcoming of charged membership cards-everybody like things for free, and nobody would like to pay hundreds for a small card. Charged membership cards had made some fortune for the reservation centers, but had limited the speed and width of their promotion.

So, Wu Hai decided to upgrade the methods of handing out the cards. He wanted to play the sales method to its limit.

What had he done?

The mad card dispatcher

Wu Hai decided to improve the chargeable membership cards into free cards-the salary of the card dispatchers consisted of a low base salary and high commission. The following are the specific salary system.

Base salary-800 RMB/month

Commission —3% of the consumption of the card holder (this was later improved with a limitation of three months)

Bonus-100 RMB for each new effective client

Requirement-the promoters need to draw a certain amount of membership cards from the company every month (these cards are all in a number unit), and work seven hours a day.

Later, on the motivation meeting for the Ctrip Card promoters, every one got a copy of this salary system. This new salary system was announced effective on that day.

At the beginning, some new card dispatchers did not get the sweets from promoting the cards, and they all thought that the effects would not be so impressive. They had such thoughts because they were unable to understand why they could get 100 RMB as the bonus for getting a new effective client. However, some old employees began to question this system because they were afraid that their salaries could surpass that of the managers'. They believed in their capabilities and the high salary brought by their capabilities.

As expected, two and three months later, these card dispatchers found that they could get three or four thousand RMB every month. Those who were capable would earn a salary as high as ten thousands per month.

With such thick packs of RMBs, the card dispatchers were out of doubts. They worked over time day and night. When the staff in the office building was off work, they would go to the streets on Wangfujing Boulevard in Beijing; on weekends, they would go search for clients in the Shanghai Bund. They were ousted by the securities in the office buildings, and driven out by the policemen at the airports, but they never backed down and they just kept rushing forward.

People would understand when Wu Hai wanted his card dispatchers to work over time. But they wondered if it was necessary to pay such high salary to such unimportant card dispatchers. People thought he was crazy.

Wu Hai had his reason-as an Internet company with support from venture capital, Ctrip was capable of dispatching membership cards on a large scale. By doing so, Ctrip could take over the market in a fast speed and gather more users, acquiring bigger volume of reservations and more commissions. This was like fishing-the current market was the fish in the coastal waters, where nobody was fishing. At this moment, they should seize the time to accumulate clients, or they would have to pay higher price to go fishing in the deep ocean when the market got more competitive.

Was the market really like what Wu Hai had described? Soon, the volume of room reservations had a geometric growth with the blue cards being dispatched to tourists by over one thousand dispatchers in the train stations, long-distance bus stations, airports and boarders in hundreds of cities across the country. Within only two or three months, the reservation volume had reached 20,000 room nights. By the end of 2001, the reservations had grown from hundreds of room nights to 100,000 room nights per month in 18 months.

In the middle of May 2000, a tour guide in Beijing led a tour group from Guangdong to of the outskirt of Beijing. Not too long after they got off the plane, a radio correspondent from Maoming in the group received a call. He had to rush to Yanji for a report. This correspondent asked the tour guide to help him book a ticket through the travel agency. But, at that time, the travel agency was off work. With no other choice, this tour guide called the hotline of Ctrip. com. Unexpectedly, Ctrip's server called back to inform them that there was a ticket available for the next morning. The tour guide gave the telephone number, name and the name of the hotel they were about to check in to the operator, who promised to deliver the ticket to the hotel before 7:30 that night. As it turned out, the correspondent received the ticket in the hotel before 7:30 that night. This correspondent never expected the Internet service to be so efficient. He thanked the tour guide again and again. Later, this tour guide was complimented by her leader in the travel agency.

There was another story about the CEO of Ctrip Liang Jianzhang. Once, his flight got delayed. Liang Jianzhang casually took some cards from a salesman of his company and began to hand them out. While he was handing out the cards, he put the card in one hand of a young man who was reading a magazine. This young man took the card over and shouted, "Ah? Aren't you the man on the cover of the magazine?" Confirmed twice, the young man said to Liang, "I admire you very much. It is really an honor for me to get a card handed by a business leader today. I'll treasure this card, and I'll be the most loyal client of Ctrip."

The miracle

Ctrip had created a miracle in the industry of hotel reservation-in 2001, it had the business volume of 500 million RMB in hotel reservation, and this number grew doubled in 2002. As a result, Ctrip became wealthy through this business because they could get commissions no less than 10% of prices from the hotel reservations made through Ctrip. com.

The company had been growing rapidly. The atmosphere on the group meeting was getting more and more active. The four co-founders were excited on the group meeting.

Liang Jianzhang said, "Hotel reservation is an industry with no ceilings, and we need to dig it deeper. Any ways, we have already become the leader of this industry."

Ji Qi said, "We have indeed dug a gold mine. But we have only arrived in Yan'an on the road of Long March. We need to go look for other gold mines."

"Yes. Among the series products of tourism, we need to make the other tourism products as good as hotel reservation." Fan Min suggested.

"What's the next project?" Liang Jianzhang made the voice. He had been working with Ji Qi on the position of CEO ever since the third round of financing. He was important when making decisive choices.

"What about air ticket reservations? This market contains profits no less than those in the market of hotel reservation." Ji Qi said.

"This is not an easy job! We have to apply for the distribution qualification for air ticket agency from CAAC. The process is complicated and time-consuming. It could probably take one or two years." Somebody interrupted.

Ji Qi said, "Apply for it? That won't work! The market doesn't allow us to waste so much time. We should use the same strategy as in the room reservation market-we purchase the well-performing ticket service companies." He paused for a second, and continued, "By the way, I have already found the perfect choice-Beijing Coast Ticket Service Company."

"That's a good company. It would give the doubled power for our market expansion if we could make purchase." A General Manger from a branch company said excitedly.

Just like he said, Beijing Coast Ticket Service Company was a well-developed company. It began its air ticket agent sales in 1995. In Beijing, they had had door-to-door ticket delivery service from early on. In 2002, Beijing Coast Ticket Service Company had the largest call center in Beijing.

In addition, the chief of Beijing Coast Ticket Service Company Ding Han was a specialist in air ticket reservation. He was strict on the training and management of his salesmen teams. After years of exploiting and reflecting, Beijing Coast Ticket Service Company had already formed perfect delivery system. Ding Han used the concentrated reservation-the company had founded a call center to process the reservations concentrated. If a tourist called in, the ticket agents would gather the ticket information of each flight. They would work on the results, make orders and produce group tickets. Then, the delivery team would deliver the tickets. In the peak, they could process more than 1.2 thousand tickets. On average, there were at least 800 tickets processed.

Faced with such a company, could Ctrip win over the negotiation with Ding Han? What do the Ctrip team have to offer to Ding Han?

The further success of purchasing Coast Ticket

Unexpectedly, this negotiation went on successfully because Ding Han had met with an obstacle which he could not get through.

People all knew that there were two major points deciding an outstanding air ticket agency-concentrated ticket reservation and delivery. Beijing Coast was quite familiar with the delivery. But it needed a company with larger volume of information to work with on concentrated reservation. Besides, the key problem was the regional restriction for Beijing Coast Ticket Service Company. It was no surprise that with the current scale of Coast Ticket Service, it would have nowhere else to go in Beijing.

Therefore, Ding Han wanted to build a national network starting from the major cities. This network was not limited to a certain place or on a certain level. But, Ding Han had soon realized that he would not be able to solve this problem in a short period of time if he had to build agencies one by one. In the meanwhile, there was a need of massive investment, including the capital, management, staff and so on.

Ding Han pondered on this question deeply.

Just at this moment, Ctrip came to the door.

Why did Ctrip wanted to work with Beijing Coast? It would be beneficial for both of them if they'd cooperate. Ctrip had a large amount of good clients who would also need service in air ticket reservation, which can be helped by Beijing Coast Ticket Service. Besides, Ctrip had an excellent technology service system and sales methods, which Ding Han lacked.

During their meeting, they had a great time talking with each other.

Ding Han said, "In terms of hard ware, we are in disadvantage. We would get pretty busy when we've received too many calls, so we need better equipments for our call center. Meanwhile, we are not sure about what kind of website to build if we want to exploit our business on the Internet, nor do we know how to manage the website. Plus, we need to enhance our sales methods."

Liang Jianzhang said, "The Internet technology you've mentioned is in our advantages. We have also exploited some good sales methods. You have the perfect products, services and connections with the suppliers, lacking probably only the combination of technology with sales and that of technology with resources. If we were to work together, we'd have a bright future."

It was indeed so. Ctrip had unique and effective sales methods. At that time, Ctrip did not have much money to advertise because advertisements paid back slowly and were expensive. They rented counters in major airports, near which there were the employees from Ctrip handing out membership cards and brochures.

Soon, Ctrip and Beijing Coast Ticket had reached an agreement. Later, they began to evaluate Beijing Coast Ticket Service Company.

Ji Qi said, "Chief Ji, in Ctrip's work with BizExpress and Modern Yuntong, we used shares in addition to cash. Let's do it so as well!"

Without too much cash, Ji Qi made Ding Han agree with his wonderful story.

Thus, in March 2000, Ctrip purchased Beijing Coast Ticket Service Company with millions of cash and parts of Ctrip's shares. Ding Han joined Ctrip and worked as the Deputy Director of Ctrip. com and the General Manager of the Beijing Branch.

After purchasing Beijing Coast Ticket Service Company, Ctrip located its air ticket reservation center in Shanghai, through which people across the country could make air ticket reservations. They had applied ERP to this whole ticket reservation system. Soon, Ctrip had become the largest air ticket and hotel room reservation center in the domestic market. By the end of 2002, Ctrip had reached the sales volume of 200 million RMB per month, taking up more than 50% of the market in the country.

Were they satisfied with the good performance of Ctrip? No, because there was another well-known way to make money, which was amazing. In this way, a person could become a billionaire over one night. So, let's read the next chapter *Listing and Monetizing*.

Summary

There are four questions related to this chapter.

I. The four principles of founding a team

A team (see p. 4-1) is a group formed by a small number of people. They have complementary skills. They depend on each and are responsible for each other for the same goal. They have a common standard.

From the above definition of a group, we can see that when forming an entrepreneurial team, there are four points that need to be considered.

1. Reasonable number of people
2. Complementary skills
3. A united goal
4. Responsibility

p. 4-1   the basic structure of a team

      team result personal growth team efficiency

      skills responsibility duty

      problematic human relation interactive small-numbered people the common in

      set goals

Here, let's focus on the first point. How many people should we invite to form an entrepreneurial team?

The definition of team has only given us a range-a small number of people. Then how small the number should be? Of course, no less than two, or else, they would not count as a team.

In previous entrepreneurial teams, there were some that had only two members. For example, the childhood partners of Hu Zhibiao and Chen Tiannan of Idall; the marriage couple of Li Guoqing and Yu Yufu of Dangdang. com. However, there were teams with other numbers of members-the Jiaotong University four-person team of Ctrip in Shanghai, the Fudan University five-person team of Fuxing in Shanghai, and the seven-person team of Huadi Fuel Cooker in Zhongshan. There were teams with more people-Alibaba in Hangzhou had 18 entrepreneurial partners, and they were called "the eighteen arhats".

Combining the labor divisions and successful cases, I think, the number of 3-5 is the most idealistic when the entrepreneurial team has just been founded. During the early stage, the team could meet with lot of unexpected problems. And the group effect of the team can't be performed because of the limited number of people. As to the "the eighteen arhats" of Alibaba, they were technically entrepreneurial partners rather a complementary entrepreneurial team. Ma Yun had once said to his entrepreneurial partners, "Currently, you can only be platoon leaders and company commanders. I'll find other people to fill in the position of military commanders. But you will one day become military commanders."

So, it is most easy to divide the job positions if a team consists of 3-5 people-one in charge of technology, one in marketing, one in management, one in financing, and so on. If a team has only two members, one would have to be in charge of technology, and the other in charge of marketing.

Then, let's look at the second point.

In fact, the second point is more important than the first one. There goes a saying like this, "A rival like a wolf is not fearful. A team partner like a pig is fearful." If your entrepreneurial partner is terrible, then you will not succeed in the market. We need people to give us aid, but not to give us leisure, speech or accessory. Besides, if you have succeeded in the market, you would feel imbalanced because your partner did not put in the effort equal to yours. Here is a classic case of such-the story of the two founders of Idall.

In 1994, Hu Zhibiao and his childhood friend Chen Tiannan opened a factory, in which they had put in 2000 RMB each. Hu and Chen had taken 45% of the shares each. Their village had provided them with the place to build the factory, so Yilong Village had taken up 10% of the shares of Idall Electrical Appliance.

Hu Zhibiao was a genius in marketing. He had invented the first suspense advertisement in China. In October 1995, Hu advertised for four days in a row on the expensive *Yangcheng Evening News*. In the first three advertorials, they read, "Idall······" On the fourth day, Hu Zhibiao exposed the identity of Idall. The advertorial read, "Idall —VCD".

Later, Hu Zhibiao had taught the advertisement industry a golden rule-build up the publicity first and then increase the popularity; hire the most popular celebrity to shoot the commercials, and then broadcast the commercials on the most powerful media.

Hu Zhibiao did so. He paid 4. 5 million RMB to Jacky Chen for the commercials, in which the line for Jacky Chen was, "Idall VCD, good Kongfu". And he chose to broadcast the commercials during the first 5 seconds after the weather report on CCTV.

Thus, Hu's talent in marketing helped Idall gain jaw-dropping achievements. In 1997, the sale volume of Idall rose drastically from 200 million in the previous year to 1. 6 billion RMB. When Hu Zhibiao flew to the Philips in Holland for investigation, he received the treatment of private jet and red carpet.

The successions of triumphs in the business market had made Hu Zhibiao's ambition begin to expand. He went for diversity and opened many new companies sequentially. However, he did not tell Chen Nantian about them when he made these big moves, let alone discussing with him.

This time, Chen Nantian was unhappy about it. He said, "It's like watching others dacing through the glass. " He could not bear this anymore. Thus, in March 1999, Chen Tiannan issued a lawyer statement on *Yangcheng Evening News*, "The new subsidiary companies of Idall have no relations with Guangdong Idall Appliance Limited Company. " Then, Chen Nantian had pulled the Yilong Village to his side and forced Hu Zhibiao to give up his positions of Board Director and General Manager.

Chen Tiannan's doing had lead to unexpected results. It was the slack of electrical apliances, and the commercials were stopped playing on CCTV. The lawyer's statement was like the blood for a predator. The journalists had not heard such exciting and booming news for a long time, so they all of them rushed to the headquarters of Idall in Zhongshan.

Hu Zhibiao could never have imagined that the journalists, who used to call him brother Biao and sing the praises of him, changed their faces and kicked Idall when it's down. These negative reports went out, and the suppliers and the dealers to whom Idall was in debt went to Idall to demand the payment of the debt. Some senior managers had also packed their bags and left.

Thus, the media had pushed Idall to the death. In August 1999, the Zhongshan Government launched an initial investigation on Idall's capital, and found Idall was insolvent. In December that year, Idall entered the bankruptcy proceeding.

Of course, among the reasons for Idall's bankruptcy, the operation of the capital was the most important one. Idall had a fragile financial system. Hu Zhibiao had no idea of the amount of money Idall possessed, neither did he know how much debts he was in. He usually mistook the cash for profits.

However, the trigger of Idall's bankruptcy was Chen Tiannan's lawyer's announcement. According to the story, one should be very cautious when choosing a team partner. This was a lesson taught by the two founders of Idall.

In this book, we can also find the evidence of the importance of complementary skills in building a top team. Let's compare the Ctrip team with the Elong team.

Both Ctrip and Elong had four co-founders. But differently, the four founders of Ctrip were famous, while Tang Yue was the only one with a reputation among the four team members of Elong. Why? This probably had something to do with the positioning when the team was first founded. Ji Qi had emphasized many times, "The name of our team is The Jiaotong University Four. Don't speak of us as somebody's entrepreneurial team." Besides, Ji Qi would always give compliments on his partners in front of the journalists. In an interview with *Internet Weekly*, Ji Qi said to the journalist, "Among the four founders, there is one who is very familiar with the venture investment and the capital market in abroad, who has spent two years in Wall Street, and has worked as the Board Director and General Manager of a foreign investment bank; there is one good at technology, who has programmed the data base and ERP soft ware for Oracle in America, and has years of experience working as a senior manager in foreign enterprises; there is one who has ten-year experience who has studies in Europe and has been a chief in a famous travel agency in the country ever since he came back. As to me, I am normal in capability. I am familiar with how to run a company in China, so I've pushed the company from zero to a successful phase."

Surprisingly, every Ctrip team member liked to talk in this way. Ji Qi was not the only one who gave compliments to his partners in front of the journalists, so would the other three. That's why they could be famous together.

But, speaking of the Elong team, people would know the name of Tang Yue and have no idea of the names of the three others or what their job divisions were. Tang Yue never mentioned their names on purpose in front of the media. And nothing about them could be found in any report.

Leaving the teams aside, Tang Yue was probably stronger than Shen Nanpeng if compared in terms of ability. He had once spread some brave words, "If needed, I could get a 10-million investment from the Wall Street in ten minutes, because I have wide connections with people." To prove this, he gave an example-in July 2004, he attended a meeting held by a friend in America. Over 100 people attended that meeting, among which were influential figures in all industries like Bill Gates, Warren Buffet, the Mayor of New York City Bloomberg and the Chief of CIA Tenet. They were invited to give a speech on the future development of China. At that time, many people had misunderstanding and prejudice against China, and they spoke of China as worthless. When it was Tang Yue's turn, he said, "The things Chinese people are pursuing are no different from those the American people are pursuing-education, medical care, fortune, happiness, freedom and so on." When Tang Yue finished his speech, all the Americans at present applauded, among which, there stood Yang Zhiyuan.

This was an example to prove Tang Yue's wide connections in America. However, this could not prove his amazing ability to finance the investment, because in the cold winter of Internet in 2001, Elong had only received investment of several million USD while Ctrip got over 10 million USD. However, this problem didn't lie in Tang Yue's personal ability. The Elong team was nothing compared to the Ctrip team even though Tang Yue is better than Shen Nanpeng. There was not a talent in marketing like Ji Qi, a talent in technology like Liang Jianzhang, or a talent specialized in tourism like Fan Min in the Elong team. No wonder that the venture investment companies preferred the Ctrip team.

As a whole, the Ctrip team is stronger than the Elong team. Without any doubt, Ctrip would become the leader in this business.

The third and fourth points had been discussed before.

II. The importance of sales promotion

The subject of Marketing has a history of only 100 years. However, it has developed very rapidly. There are new theories every two or three years. Take the theory of marketing combination as an example: before people could figure out 4P and 4C completely, there came 4R and 4V. Isn't it confusing?

This subject is not so mature like Management or Organizing Behavior-there are four set parts in Management, including planning, organizing, leading and controlling; the Organizing Behavior consists of three parts, individuals, groups and organizations. However, this is no common sense in Marketing yet. According to different professors, there are different marketing models.

Philip Kotler, the Father of Modern Marketing and a professor in the Kellogg Management Research Institute of Northwest University in America, has a theory that there are four major parts of Marketing-marketing process, understanding of the market, marketing combination and marketing extension. However, well-known professors in the country have their different ways to categorize Marketing. Professor Wang Houfen from Zhongnan University of Economics and Law thinks that there are five parts in Marketing-theory, value recognition, value creation, value transfer and value inspection. Based on the theories of Professor Lv Yilin from Renmin University of China, Professor Wang Houfen from Zhongnan University of Economics and Law, Professor Wu Xiaoyun from Nankai University and Professor Wang Fanghua from Shanghai Jiaotong University, I have come to a conclusion that there are six major parts in Marketing. (The following are my personal opinion. Different opinions are welcomed.)

1. The Introduction of Marketing. This is an introductive theory of Marketing, including the introduction on marketing and consumers behavior. This theory may contain introductions to the history of the subject, the concept of market, the types of market, the concept of market core, the concept of marketing, consumer's decisions of purchase, industries' decisions of purchase, deals' decisions of purchase, govern-

ments' decisions of purchase and so on.

2. The Prediction of Marketing. This is the theory on how to predict the size of a market, including management of the marketing information, analysis of the marketing environment, research on marketing, plans of marketing strategies, making marketing plans, and so on.

3. Distribution. Distribution focuses on how to sell more products, including production, price, channels, terminals, and so on.

4. Promotion. Promotion focuses on how to sell products faster, including advertisement, personal promotion, improvement on promotion, publicity, direct and indirect promotions, online promotion, and so on.

5. Control of the marketing. It is the control over the marketing activities, including the execution of marketing plans, audition on the marketing, evaluation on the achievements, moral assessment on marketing, and so on.

6. New marketing. This contains the new theories on marketing, including the theory of Customer Delivered Value, Global Marketing, cultural marketing, relationship marketing, cross marketing, experience marketing, green marketing, and so on.

Next, I'm going to talk about the means of sales promotion.

According the preview textbooks, there are four means of sales promotion-advertisement, publicity, salesman promotion and personal promotion. Advertising and publicizing are pulling strategies while salesman promotion and personal promotion are pushing strategies. Later, direct marketing and online promoting were added. Thus, we have six means of marketing. I'll introduce the first four means briefly.

Advertisement

Once, a rookie man in advertisement business asked a master, "How to make an advertisement and have a sensational effect?"

The master answered, "If you were a journalist and you saw a person was bitten by a dog. How would you report this to catch the readers' eyes?"

The rookie man replied, "I'd use a contrast. I would say that the man who was bitten has practiced Kongfu in Shaolin Temple, and he is well-built. But the dog is more violent and brutal. In result, the skinny dog had easily bitten the man, making him distorted beyond recognition…"

The master shook his head and said, "You could never write value news report in this thought."

The rookie man was surprised, "Master, how would you report it?"

The master answered, "Don't use too many words. Only one sentence would be enough-Today, a man bit a dog on the street."

This story tells us that if the lines in an advertisement are not wonderful enough, it will not be easy for the advertisement to attract people's attention. Some lines can be unforgettable, such as the advertisement for the fan, "Honestly, I blew my fame", or, the advertisement for the air-conditioner, "Men are not the only thing that can make women feel cold-hearted."

During the 1980s and 1990s, advertisements were the best means of marketing for enterprises. Let's read the entrepreneurial story of Liu Yonghao.

Liu Yonghao was once a teacher in a vocational school. After he began to run a business, he opened a chicken farm and a quail farm. He had made over 10 million RMB through the quail farm.

When he was cultivating the quails, he suddenly discovered that it was better to sell feed than to sell quails. He thought that the business of selling feed could be big if the cultivation of livestock became popular. Therefore, Liu Yonghao started to research on a popular brand of feed from Thailand "Zhengda". Three years later, Liu Yonghao had successfully developed Hope Feed. He immediately opened factories to manufacture the feed and put it on the market. Soon, his feed reached number one in Sichuan Province. Later, he had founded the Hope Group, and made it "the King of Feed" eventually.

Along the winding process, the Liu brothers had succeeded in one thing-they tried their best to sell the feed. Once, an owner of a feed company in Sichuan gave Liu Yonghao the following evaluation.

"First, Liu Yonghao is very smart. He had spotted the empty point in the market and moved faster than anybody else could. The so-called high technology was nonsense."

"Secondly, Liu Yonhao is quite smart. When other people were doing math on the cost and trying to improve the quality of their products, he had realized that promotion and channels were more important than the product itself. So, he spared no efforts in advertising."

"Thirdly, Liu Yonghao is always smart. When everybody else was advertising in the towns or in the cities, he had already begun advertising nationally."

In fact, they were selling the same thing. Why don't you try this method on a pig? Right now, only the pig knows the truth. No people would know it.

Personal Marketing

There are two types of personal marketing-telephone marketing and face-to-face marketing. Based on my experience, both the two types must fit two principles-the MAN principle and the Three Rights Principle.

The MAN principle means the Money, Authority and Need of the customers. If a customer does not find satisfaction in any one of the three points, he will not make the purchase. A customer would say to a salesman, "You product is very good, and the price is preferential. But I don't have any money in my pocket. What should I do?" A god can be helpless facing a customer like this.

The Three Rights Principle means that when you look for a client, you must look for the right person, speak the right words, and do the right thing. If you don't follow the three principles, your efforts will end in vain.

Here is an interesting case! It happened ten years ago.

Then, I had a friend who was promoting a special product. At 9 o'clock one morning, he knocked on the office door of a boss in the Shenzhen Huaqiangbei Saige office Building.

The boss asked, "What do you want?"

My friend asked him, "Boss, do you want to buy a cinerary casket? I am a salesman from Longgang Yongjiu Cemetery."

The boss got angry and shouted, "What the hell? Do you have any revenge against me? I haven't started my business today. Could you say something nice?"

My friend continued, "Boss, don't be angry. Actually, for every one of us, the things we have are temporary, including our houses and cars. What's permanent is this casket. This is a big issue for all of us, which we can't hide from…"

The boss got angrier, and interrupted, "Let me tell you. In Shenzhen, I have connections in black and white. If I want you dead, it will be as easy as killing an ant. If you don't leave right now, you will have to enjoy your product yourself."

Obviously, my friend broke the Three Rights principles. He could not sell his products, and had to change to the inspection job.

This story also tells us that promotion is not easy. It's not a job everybody can do, and only talents could do this job. Even if you are brave enough to jump in from the window after you have been thrown out of the door by your client, it would be a waste of emotion and time if you couldn't find the right person and speak the right words.

Improvement on Marketing

If you want to buy a big commodity, and the dealer tells you that there is no discount, will you feel good about it? You know very clear that the so-called discount is a trick. After all, the wool still comes from the sheep's fur.

So, the cover-up of the so-called discounts, lowering the price of a previously heightened price, is improvement on Marketing. Of course, this is not how it is defined in text books.

How many marketing strategies are there? They are listed below.

1. Discount. This is a direct marketing strategy, which is normal but widely used by
   dealers.

I still remember that a couple of days before the opening day of a furniture store, they published advertisements on Shenzhen Evening News several days in a row. According to the advertisement, a chair was sold at 8 RMB and an office table was sold at 80 RMB. There, a homeboy of mine took the first bus there and rushed in the store as soon as it opened. He said he wanted the exact chair and table on the advertisement.

However, the salesman said, "The piece of furniture you want has been sold out. "

He was very surprised, and asked, "What? Sold out? I am the first customer today!"

The salesman smiled, " I am really sorry about that! Our internal employees have bought them out. Actually, the qualities of those are not so good. You might as well take a look at these tables and chairs over here. They are of good quality and reasonable prices. "

My friend had to take the second bus home.

Actually, there are many cases like this in real life. When the new store of Guomei was doing a promotion, some old ladies queued from 3 o'clock in the morning to buy the TV on sale. However, the queue was long, but only two TV sets were sold.

Such cases proved that deals would use some "smart" strategies on promotion if needed. They also proved the saying on the business market, "I'm not afraid that you won't buy my products. I am afraid that you won't come to my store. Only the buyers could be wrong. Never could a seller be wrong. "

2. Coupons. This is a common method of improvement on the promotion, and also a universal strategy in food and beverage industry. I believe that everybody has received coupons from McDonald and KFC.

But, here, I want to talk about the coupons of a clothing brand in Shenzhen-Valentino. There is something special about the coupons. On the coupon, there is a spot where a customer could scratch for prizes. On the coupon, there are the requirement for the prize and a series of prizes. The requirement is that a customer could only get the prize on condition that he buys a suit worthy of more 800 RMB. The prizes are-A whole set of stereo of a famous brand and a super DVD machine for the first prize; a whole set of stereo for the second prize. Even the fifth prize was considerable-380 RMB in cash.

In fact, every coupon was printed in the first prize. There was never one coupon printed with the fifth prize. The purpose was to stimulate the purchase of the customers.

3. Accumulated points. This is a strategy aimed at seasonal products. For example, this is widely used in the beverage industry. Jianlibao had once use this strategy—when a customer pull the ring off, which read the character "jian", he could win a certain prize; if he could collect the three characters of "jian", "li", and "bao", he could win the first prize.

Speaking of accumulated points, I have a friend who has some personal experiences. He likes to smoke the Jianpai cigarette. Once, the Jianpai cigarette was doing a promotion. The manufacturer required that any customer who could accumulate 200 empty cigarette boxes would win a tour entrance ticket in abroad for free.

With every effort, he had accumulated 193 empty boxes. Thus, he decided to buy seven packs of Jianpai cigarette. He pulled all the cigarettes out, emptied the boxes, and gathered them together. Then, he lifted the bed board because he used to throw the empty boxes under the bed board every time he finished one box.

When he lifted the bed board, he was surprised to find that there was no box under there.

At this moment, his girlfriend came and said, "Are you looking for you empty boxes? Yesterday, I threw all of them out. You hid them under here, and they attracted lots of cockroaches. It's so annoying!"

Therefore, accumulated-point is a good promotion strategy. For many reasons, customers could not get the prize.

4. Returns. This is a strategy better than discount. Even if you could offer a customer a 50% discount, he would not feel the satisfaction. However, if you say to your customer that he could get 50 RMB returned in cash if he buys products more than 100 RMB, he would feel that he has earned something.

I still remember that on the opening day of Dongmen Maoye in Shenzhen, there was a POP advertisement that read, "50 RMB returned if you buy 100 RMB". As a result, it was a crazy scene inside the building. Even policemen had come to maintain order. A female colleague of mine went there and got outside with bear foot. There were so many people that her shoes were lost among the crowd.

Nowadays, Maoye is still doing promoting activities like "220 RMB coupon returned if you buy 200 RMB". But, the scene was no longer what it was. Maybe it was because Maoye was the first one to do such promoting activities.

5. Additional Payment. This is a strategy that has been tried so many times. For example, if you buy some things, you can take some certain products if you pay a certain sum of money in addition.

In Shenzhen, there was a dealer of red wine. He came from Hubei to Shenzhen when he was 15 years old. He had already made a fortune using this method.

Here is how he operated. Once, the Renrenle shopping center opened near the Guanwai Xiujing Jiangnan Community. During the first few days, the employee of the red wine dealer shouted at the entrance of the shopping mall, "For 10 RMB plus the receipt, you can buy the red wine worthy of 35 RMB."

Many aunts and uncles really believed the red wine was worthy of 35 RMB, and they bought it in a hurry.

In fact, the cost of the red wine was 5 RMB per bottle, and the receipt was just an excuse.

6. Competition. This strategy could only be effective for the big events. Mengniu spon-

sored the competition of Super Gril. This is a convincing case which I won't elaborate.

7. Samples for free.

8. Drawing prizes.

9. DM magazine.

10. VIP card.

I won't elaborate for the limitation of the length of the content.

Publicity

The common ways in companies' publicity are news conferences, sponsorship, exhibitions, symposiums and product forums.

Among Chinese companies, the Jiaduobao Group is probably the best at publicity. Jiaduobao Group had an excellent line in its advertisement, "Drink Wanglaoji if you are afraid of heat." However, its publicity was more outstanding comparatively.

After the Wenchuan Earthquake on 12th May 2008, Duojiabao had donated 100 million RMB. There are techniques in making donations-either be the fastest one, or the most one. On the long list of the donators, we can remember those who had donated 17 or 18 million RMB. Therefore, it had an obvious effect thought Duojiabao had donated dozens of million RMB more. Later, there was some discussion on the Internet, "Make Wanglaoji disappear from the shelves! Force it out!" However, the netizens got enthusiastic about it, and expressed, "From now on, I'll cook with Wanglaoji." Some others said, "Donate 100 million RMB if you want to donate; Drink Wanglaoji if you want to drink." Thus, the brand of Wanglaoji had become a black horse in 2008. Some authorities predicted that by 2009, the sales volume of Wanglaoji would surpass 12 billion RMBs, leaving the two "colas" (Coca Cola and Pepsi) far behind.

After reviewing the book of *Marketing*, let's go back to our case. Ctrip had used all of the four types of promoting strategies mention above.

Advertisement-in 1999, Ctrip had built a light-box board at the Beijing Airport which cost one million RMB a year. This light-box board had increased the clicking rate and improved the reputation of Ctrip. However, "there is only thunder, but no rain." It didn't bring many clients to Ctrip.

Publicity-in April 2000, Ctrip had worked with CAAC to host the first stewardess competition in the civil aviation industry-Shanghai International Stewardess Century Elegancy Competition. Ctrip was the only online media to broadcast this competition. It had provided with the netizens a virtual community to witness the elegancy of the stewardess. They could vote for their favorite stewardess. However, this event got normal feedbacks, being not able to obtain the predicted effect.

· Personal Promotion-in the beginning of 2000, a salesman from Ctrip went to a splendid hotel and knocked on the door of the manager. He said, "I am a salesman from Ctrip.com. We are hoping to work with you on hotel room reservation." Unfortunately, most managers wouldn't let him finish and wanted to ouster him.

Improvement on promotion-it is also called business promotion. There are various kinds of promoting strategies as mentioned before. Ctrip had chosen the VIP Card, which was one of them. In March 2003, Ctrip began dispatching the membership cards with the leading of its Deputy Director Wu Hai. This time, Ctrip had a practical breakthrough. 18 months later, with the efforts of over one thousand card dispatchers, the reservation volume of Ctrip grew from hundreds of room nights per month to 100 thousand room nights per month.

Ctrip had use all four of the basic promotion strategies. As it turned out, the improvement on promotion brought the most amazing result, while the three strategies of advertisement, publicity and personal promotion were far from what they had expected.

Seeing this result, people may wonder whether the three strategies of advertisement, publicity and personal promotion are out-dated. Do they not apply in today's industry?

The answer is no.

The reasons why the three strategies didn't perform to their best are as below.

There are two situations when launching an advertisement. If you want to launch an advertisement to build the fame of your company, you need to put in as much investment as possible in a short term. If you want to launch an advertisement to maintain the fame of your company, you need to put in the investment gradually in a long term. Somebody once said, "If you want to launch an advertisement to build the fame on CCTV, any amount of money less than 16 million RMB could be waste." Therefore, without too much money, the advertisements Ctrip had launched was already performing to their ultimate limits if they could have any effect in promoting Ctrip. They shouldn't expect the effects like "advertisements in the sky that rain money to the ground".

As to the publicity, this could only be effective during the growing and mature stage of a product. Initiating the publicity promotion during the introductive stage would not have good effect. Thus, the stewardess competition held by Ctrip could only increase the clicking rate of the website.

Besides, the model of personal promotion needs to work with advertisements if a company wants to achieve the effects quickly. When the tanks are dropping bombs in the front, the foot soldiers should clean the ground in the behind. It would take a long period of time if a company depends only on personal promotion. Thus, when Ctrip realized it, they took the measure of purchasing quickly to shorten the cycle of nurturing a market and exploiting the models.

What's more, the Ctrip Membership Card needs to be mentioned. At that time, when other companies all charged their membership cards, Ctrip decided to hand out the cards for free, which shows the stronger points than other companies. In addition, they had introduced high efficiency salary. Thus, with the combination of a good model and encouragement, the effects of the promotion were outstanding. This has also proved the saying about competition in the market, "Do what others don't do; be good at what others do; be innovative on what others are good at."

Those who are innovative would always win the markets, and those who copies would hardly gain ideal achievement. When the model of card dispatch became a universal model in the hotel reservation industry, its effect had become less and less obvious with the transfer rate of only 3%-5%.

Application

I. Where and how to hand them out?

Wang Yong was a technician in a famous foreign cosmetic company, who had been researching on skin-care products. Through 10 years of efforts, he had finally developed a product which could remove the freckles.

The documents for cosmetics could be easily applied for. So, after ODM, Wang Yong's freckle-removing product was on the market. He didn't spend too much money on the advertisements, and he was confident with his product. Therefore, he decided to promote his product by handing out free samples.

Now, if you were his Product Manager, would you agree with his promotion strategy? If you do, where and how would you hand out the free samples?

II. Which distribution and promotion method to choose?

Chen Qiang was a Chief Agent in Guangdong of a famous ion bottle brand in the country. This bottle he was selling was amazing-when you pull in some regular drinking water in the bottle, the acid water would change into alkaline water, which could be tested by a PH testing bar on spot. Meanwhile, this bottle was beautifully shaped and is classical. However, the retail price was a little high. The cheapest one, a personal set, would cost 499 RMB. The "silver bottle" and "golden bottle" for gift would cost 1688 RMB and 2688 RMB separately.

Chen Qiang dealt this product with 30% of the price. Now that we have known that the manufacturer had already put in a large amount of advertisement on CCTV, which distribution and promotion method would you choose if you were Chen Qiang? Please express your opinion.

Chapter V   Listing and Monetizing

Everyone who has founded an enterprise holds a dream of strengthening and enlarging his enterprise, and more than 80% of these entrepreneurs plan to get their companies listed and Ctrip was no exception. Through the game of NASDAQ, a game of fortune-maker, the senior management staff of Ctrip had monetized 200 million. The reason why Ctrip could lead the second wave of listing and had successfully monetized so much was that Shen Nanpeng was an expert in playing with capital. What was more important was the they had grabbed the opportunity in the market earlier than anybody else.

Quotations
Reflections on the business market 1-5
Your thoughts make your way; your horizons make your boundary; your attitude makes your altitude; your position makes your status; your pattern makes your outcome; your brain makes your pocket.

—reflection on Ctrip's listing

If you are a genius, it would show; if you are a talent, it would show; if you are a fool, it would show.

—reflection on the Ctrip team's success in listing

Life is like a gambling game. One should not gamble on his life. But if necessary, one should take the risk and win.

—reflection on the Ctrip team's entrepreneurial story

If someone appreciates you, it means you are lucky; if nobody appreciate you, it's you fate; as a friend, I wish you all the best!

—to all the entrepreneurs

I can't pull myself out of my dream, yet I struggle in reality. I am a fly on the glass-the future is bright, but I just haven't found the way out.

—encouragement to myself

A fable
The ideal of the eagle
On a stormy and raining night, an eagle had fought against the storm and rain for an en-

tire evening. In the end, it was injured and fell onto the ground.

At this moment, a sparrow came along and asked how the eagle got hurt in concern. The sparrow advised the eagle in sincere words, "Brother, why did you fly so high? I don't see the benefit it could bring to you, but the many risks that come along with it. Look at us. We sparrows have lived under the roof for generations. The wind can't blow us , nor could the rain fall on us. What a free life! What a stable life! You might as well come and live with us. I can guarantee you a carefree life. What do you say?"

The eagle replied, "Brother, thank you for kindness. I am an eagle, so I must have the ideal of the eagle. I can't give up on my goal as soon as I face some setbacks. I can't give up on my pursuit only for the interest in front of me. It's your ideal life to live under the roof. But for me, it is the true happiness to fly high in the sky and look down at the world. There are risks to take, but this is exactly the happiness that can't be described in words. "

The sparrow felt incredible. It shook its head and took a glance at the eagle, "You are being so impractical. You are chasing after the imaginary and invisible things. Aren't you asking forthe suffer for yourself?"

Before too long, the eagle's wound had healed up. It flew back to sky happily.

Later, something unexpected happed. The poor sparrow was wet by a stormy rain. It couldn't fly back its nest, ending in becoming a "toy" to a child.

This story tells us-

1. Your attitude makes your altitude; your pattern makes your outcome.

2. One who settles for a small fortune can't gain great achievements.

3. There is only relative risk, but no absolute safty. What you have to do is to make yourself impeccably strong.

Text

Section I   Liang Jianzhang's efforts on internal improvement
The work shift scheme for the leaders

In the first half of 2000, Ji Qi and Liang Jianzhang had been the joint CEOs for half a year. In the latter half of 2000, Ji Qi changed to being the Chief Director and Liang Jianzhang remained being the CEO.

This job transfer was quite democratic, which Wu Hai had witness in person.

In March 2000, Wu Hai joined the Ctrip team when Liang Jianzhang was still the CTO. Once during a chat, Wu Hai mentioned, "I don't think the structure of Ctrip is reasonable. "

Liang Jianzhang said, "You should come over!" Then, Liang Jianzhang gave a pile of files to Wu Hai. In Wu's eyes, Liang Jianzhang was a classic technician.

From then onwards, these two would gather together to exchange their ideas on tourism websites. Wu Hai had gradually realized that Liang Jianzhang was not simply just a technician. He was serious at work, and was good at learning at the same time. He had never been in the hotel reservation industry before, but he found what others couldn't see from his own angel with his own professional background.

Just like this, Wu Hai was conquered by Liang Jianzhang's specialist techniques and strategic way o f thinking. Later, when asked about the choice for CEO between Liang Jianzhang and Ji Qi by the board, Wu Hai gave his vote to Liang without any hesitation.

Wu Hai said, "Ji Qi is a man with vigor and pioneering spirit without whom the other three team members might dare not to start this company. However, Ji Qi is rough on management, and he is not able to be exquisite on many things. Now that Ctrip has got on the right track and has been moving forward steadily, Liang Jianzhang could bring Ctrip further forward. "

Ji Qi also admitted on this point. In one of his speeches, he said, "My historical duty was the entrepreneurship, financing and purchasing. Now that I'm done with my duty, I need to transfer my power to the right person. Liang Jianzhang is a exquisite and rational leader. His management ability is stronger than mine because he knows how to manage a modern enterprise. I am an excellent entrepreneur, but not an excellent manger. I am impatient with things. I will lose interest in the things that I have already known the outcomes. "

After Liang Jianzhang became the CEO, he didn't let all the people down. He knew about authorization and trusting.

Wu Hai had a deep understanding of this. Ever afternoon, Liang Jianzhang would come to his desk with a bag on his back and ask Wu Hai, "Any thing?"

Wu Hai would say, "Nothing. "

"If there's nothing, I'll leave. " Then, Liang Jianzhang would walk out of the office from Ctrip.

This was how Liang Jianzhang trusted his work partner. So, as a CEO, he never worked extra time. Why not? Liang Jianzhang explained, "When a company is mature enough, what matters to its CEO is not how many things he does, but how many things he does right. "

Liang Jianzhang had indeed done many things right, among which the first one before anything he had done was about the service technology.

When being interviewed by *China Economy Times*, Liang Jianzhang had concluded, "There is one word that can be used to best describe the profit model of Ctrip-margins, which means the margins of our business of selling air tickets and making reservations for hotel rooms. Ctrip has been trying whole-heartedly to build our own core competitiveness so that we could gain more margins. There are only four key points in Ctrip's core competitiveness. The first one is the scale. Ctrip is in its own control of advanced Internet resources and the largest call center in the industry, realizing the large-scaledly concentrated processing. The second one is the technology. When the scale is enlarged to a certain point, we need to develop application systems such as the customer relation management system, the call queuing system, the order processing system, e-map inquiry system. ... The third one is the processing. With the scale and technology that are already in our command, Ctrip decided to break through the traditional workshop mode. Through the systemized and processed design, the whole process can be optimized. Through reasonable job shifting and assembly lines, the mistakes could be minimized, and the each procedure could be more efficient, resulting in the best service quality on a large scale. The last one is the concept. Ctrip pays great attention to the strengthening of servants' concept. We do relative training on our employees on a regular basis. There is only one-hundred-percent satisfying service, but no one-hundred-percent satisfying product. "

The leading of technology

Over all these years, Ctrip had been a leader in the industry. Some people might wonder how Ctrip could maintain its leading position and leave the others to be only imitators, followers and challengers far behind in such a competitive industry.

Now looking back at it, the reason was that Ctrip was competitively strong in technology. In other words, Ctrip's technology, at that time, was outstanding in the whole industry. Someone in the industry once gave Ctrip the following credit, "It was always being imitated, but has never been surpassed. "

But, what Ctrip had been through on the way of pursuing the perfection in service technology couldn't be concluded in one sentence. The Deputy Director of Ctrip. com Ms. Sun Maohua had witnessed the growth of Ctrip's call center herself.

In July 1995, Sun Maohua graduated from the Hotel Management in Shanghai Jiaotong University. She had been in the hotel industry. She started as clerk at the front desk doing some paper work, and then she was promoted as the department manager. She had been in charge of deparments such as the switchboard unit, reservation department and front desk.

In February 2000, she saw the Ctrip was hiring people through the Internet. She mailed her CV and was employed by Ctrip. At that time, Ctrip was in need of large numbers of talents, and Ctrip's HR arranged her to be in charge of the management of call center.

In the very beginning, there were only two telephone sets for the hotline and three employees in the call center. And they were unoccupied sometimes and enjoyed the leisure work. Later, with the development of the company and rise of its business volume, the call center expanded into five telephone sets for the hotlines and a dozen employees. But, the problems appeared itself-how to improve the work efficiency of the employees? How to guarantee the quality of their service? However, for Sun Maohua, she had no concept of the call center, who only knew how to pick up the calls and place orders.

Not too long afterwards, Ctrip had established the call center with 24 boarded seats. At the same time, with the help of digital technology, Ctrip had formed principles and management regulations of the departments step by step. Then, through the study of some English books on call center management and practice in the work, Sun Maohua had finally understood the concept of call center, the meaning of service level and its calculating procedure. She had also understood how to predict the volume of phone calls and how to arrange the staff. She stopped worrying about not being able to make a call. She could see the performance of the call center more rationally and more scientifically, and could know how to improve the call center.

Then, in August 2000, Ctrip's call center had developed with an amzing speed. It had developed from a reservation department with only 24 seats and dozens of employees into a call center with 2400 seats and over 4000 employees in five departments that were in charge of hotel reservation, ticket reservation, holiday, service and commercial tourism. The scale and employee number were believed to grow much more.

Ctrip must have commanded top ranking technology so that they could grow so fast and so powerfully. Now, let's take a specific look at the e-commerce application system Ctrip had issued.

The first one was the E-TEL (the reservation telephone hot line). This was an integrated system of call center and online reservation. Of course, this was not simply the traditional phone shopping, nor a simple combination of phone shopping and the Internet. This was a unification done by modern technology.

It processed like this. When a customer called in, he would hear the navigation, "Hello. Welcome to Ctrip. com! For hotel services, please press 1; for domestic flights, please press 2; for international flights, please press 3; for tourism and travelling, please press 4; for customer service, please press 5; to hear this again, please press the #button. "

The moment when the customer heard the beautiful voice of the navigator, the system would have already detected the caller's status. If he was a long-time cooperative partner with Ctrip, his call would be automatically transferred to the major-client seats, and the call would be picked up by specialists. If he was a new member or a stranger, his call would be automatically transferred to the computer system for recorded inquiry and reply. Customers could make relative reservations according to the guide from the navigator. The reservation system was specifically divided-some were in charge of hotel reservations and some were in charge of ticket reservation. Besides, the specialists in charge of ticket reservation might not know about the hotel reservation because the two categories had their own separate operation systems.

The second one was the CTMS (Commercial Travel Management System). This was the first Commercial Travel Management System in our country.

On 25th July 2000, Ctrip. com hosted the 2000 Commercial Travel Management Forum in Beijing Kunlun Hotel. Over 40 representitives from famous enterprises in and out of China attended this forum, and they were all foundational managers of business travel management departments. On the meeting, Ctrip. com had constructive discussions with the attendants on how to improve business travel management as well as on how to control the cost.

Liang Jianzhang said, "Today's market is becoming more and more competitive. Effective control on the cost could play an important role in enhancing the competitiveness of a company. Some companies have realized the importance of effective control over the business travel expenses, and have taken measures to control the expense on business trips and their relative expenses, but they couldn't manage it comprehensively as an important part of the company's business activities. The reason was that the business travel system couldn't guarantee the employee's efficiency on travel and couldn't be guaranteed on execution. At the same time, it could not provide the decision makers with management reports regarding to the situation in business travel management or the usage of different resources, through which they could find the most effective way to manage business travel. "

Liang Jianzhang continued, "This time, Ctrip has launched the Commercial Travel Management System to provide the clients with control in cost of business travel and to provide with managers an executable solution. According to investigation performed by some authorities in abroad, business travel and its relative expenses are the second largest controllable cost other than salary. Some big foreign enterprises, such as IBM, Motorola, Siemens, Ericcson, and ABB, spend over 100 million RMB averagely on business travel every year. But their business travel management system could control the cost effectively, playing a crucial part in enhancing the enterprises' competitiveness. The managers could use this system to analyze all kinds of data. For example, analysis on average loan and average usage of money; analysis on occupancy of hotels and the purchasing power of the company itself; analysis on the expenses of a certain department; analysis on the construction of travel expense of the company or a certain department. "

From the above, we could see that CTMS was a soft ware made especially and customized for enterprises. Through promotion of the soft ware to the enterprises, Ctrip had enhanced the loyalty of its enterprise clients, and expanded its percentage to a considerable scale in the B2B market.

At that time, Ctrip had devoted half of its technicians into the development of the soft ware. Liang Jianzhang believed that by developing in ahead, they could take the B2B market a step ahead than anybody else. Once the companies had accepted this soft ware, they would not give it up so easily for other similar systems considering the cost for the transformation.

If the CTMS was for the convenience of Ctrip's clients, then the reservation service system was for the convenience of Ctrip itself.

Some people may wonder, "Is Ctrip's reservation system fully developed? If a hotel plays a trick on Ctrip and declaires that the client didn't check in, what could Ctrip do to handl the situation? If the clients lie and make reservations without checking in, what would Ctrip do this time?"

Now let's take a look at Ctrip. com's reservation procedure using the hotel reservation as an example.

Step one, log on the website using the user name and password of the seated specialist on the homepage. (Every telephone operator had a set ID of himself.) When a call comes in, the operator would check on the status of the caller-Is this client a domestic one or a foreign one? Next, the operator would require clients to give their expectance on reservation of the city, check-in and check-out date, the client's requirements on the class, price, or location of the hotels. If a client wants to make the reservation of a certain hotel, the operator would only need to type in the name of it directly.

Step two, click on "search" and there would appear the interface of "search results on hotels". This window will offer recommended hotels and city exhibitions.

Step three, click on the " × " or " — " to close the pop-up windows, and then enter the reservation interface to search for and recommend hotels to the clients. Click on the "region/ map search" on the left of the page, and select the region of the hotel to search for it; you can also type the name in the "search for place"; you can search more specifically using the map. Click on the name of the hotel, there appears the specific information of the introduction, address, telephone, and price of the hotel. But the price on this page is usually the price at the front desk on that day. If you want to know about the price in a week, you can click on the "price in this week".

Step four, if the client approves of this hotel, you can choose the room type, and you should notify the client if there is breakfast available. Then, confirm the check-in and check-out date with your client.

Step five, click on "start to make reservation" and enter the page to fill in the reservation form. Type the client's information in proper order into the form. Use the client's real name, cell phone number and telephone number in the box of "contact". Then notify the client tactfully that because of the shortage of rooms, the client's credit card information will be need for guarantee, including the accurate name, credit card number, the ID number of the card holder and check whether the card is used by the holder himself.

Step six, confirm the order with the client, and send the confirmed order to the hotel and double-checkwith the hotel on the reservation.

In this reservation procedure, there were two problems. The first one was that if a client had made the reservation, but failed to check in, what should Ctrip do? Therefore, the credit card guarantee was more secure than the cancling on the reservation if a client didn't check in before 18:00. The other problem was that if a client arrived at a hotel and provided effective certificates, but still couldn't check in, what should Ctrip do? Wang Shengli had met with this problem before. At that time, the reservation system was not entirely connected with hotels, and they could only use telephones and faxes. Later, they used computers to control the fax, and with the confirmation of the head of shift, the fax could be sent to hotels no less than a minute. In addition, Wang Shengli had set up an alarming system. If there were only one or two rooms left available in a hotel, the system would set on its alarm.

Of course, the best strategy was the joint of the systems, greatly reducing the time and personnel cost on confirmation of the reservation orders and improving the efficiency on reservation. This would be saved for the following chapters.

The top-ranking service

If Ctrip's reservation procedure could be described as irreproachable, then its requirements on the service quality should be described as successive refinement. The following are Ctrip's training material on service expressions.

1. Requirements on answering a call

When answering a call, you should place the phonemic about 1cm below your lip. Smile during your service, and make the clients hear your smile and feel your passion.

2. Opening speech

Hello! I am very glad to serve you!

3. Silent call

(1) It is probably because that the client is unaware that the phone is already connected while he is waiting to be connected. You should keep your smile and say, "Hello! This is × × × × Customer Service Center. You are on the line now. How may I help you?"

(2) Wait for 3 seconds, and repeat yourself, "Hello! You have been successfully connected. Can you hear me now, please?"

(3) If there is still no response from the client, there is probably something wrong with the phone machine. Tell the client patiently, "Excuse me! I can't hear you on the phone. Please try again on another phone. Thank you for your call. Goodbye!" Wait for 2 seconds for your clinet to hang up first, and then hang up.

4. Unclear voice

(1) You should adjust the volume of your phone immediately. If it's already the biggest volume but you still can't hear the client clearly, smile and remind your client, "Excuse me, but I can't hear your voice clearly. Could you please speak louder?"

(2) If you still can't hear his voice clearly, repeat the above in a gentle and mild voice.

(3) If you really can't hear the voice clearly, you should ask for the client's forgiveness, "Excuse me, your voice is too small. Could you change your phone and call again, please? Thank you for your call. Goodbye!" Hold the call for two more seconds and then

hang up.

(4) If the client suggests that your voice is too small, you should pull the phonemic closer to your mouth and slightly lift your voice up so that the client can hear you clearly. Then ask the client, "How can I help you?" If your voice is loud enough, but the client can't hear you, you could ask the client to change a phone and call again. Don't raise your voice anymore because it would affect the other phone operators. Say to your client, "I am sorry but I am being as loudest as I could. If you still can't hear me clearly, could you change a phone and call again, please?"

(5) When a client is on the loudspeaker (some clients like to use the loudspeaker), and you can't hear him clearly, you can tell him gently, "Excuse me, but I can't hear you clearly. Would you pick up the phone and use the speaker, please?"

5. Being unable to hear the client clearly or understand him

(1) If you can't hear the client clearly, and was only unclear about certain words, you can confirm with him, "Did you mean⋯, please?" Or you can ask him, "Are you saying ⋯?" If you can't get his whole sentence, you should consult him, "Excuse, could you repeat, please? Thank you. "

(2) If a client is unable to understand what you are saying, you should instantly find out the reason. If you are using too many terminologies, you should explain to your client more lucidly by using daily language, "Excuse me, but maybe I wasn't being clear. Should I explain it to you again, please?" If the terminology wasn't the reason, and the client is unclear about the related technology, you could explain it to the client patiently in another way if necessary. Don't make a client feel that you disdain explaining to him or laugh at his ignorance. If a client misunderstood the business, you should correct him tactfully, "Excuse me, but maybe I wasn't being clear. What I was saying was that ⋯" Don't use forceful words such as "no" or "wrong". If a client can't understand mandarin and requires you to speak in dialect, you may be allowed to speak in dialect under this circumstance.

6. Requirements during the explanation

(1) Give response at the right time when you are listening to a client, and use words such as "yes" and "right" to show him that you are listening. Don't make a client feel like he is talking to himself.

(2) When a client paused, CSR (Customer Service Representative) could say, "Sir/Miss, please go on. I'm listening. "

(3) If a client is concerned that you may not understand him, you should say, "I've got you r point. Please go on. "

(4) When there is no voice from the phone during the CSR's explanation, you should say, "Sir/Miss, can you hear me, please?"

(5) When a client is finished with a question, don't hang up immediately. You should

ask, "Is there anything I can help you, please?"

(6) If a client expresses his thanks for your service, you should say, "You are welcome. This is my pleasure. "

(7) When a client is being unclear expressing about his question, you should ask him with instructive questions, "Do you mean···?"

(8) If you realize what you have explained to your client was wrong, you should apologize to your client and receive the critics sincerely. Don't argue with him irrationally. You should say, "I am truly sorry about my explanation earlier. It is···"

(9) If you didn't give your client a complete explanation, you should tell your client sincerely, "I am truly sorry, but I've got some things to add to what I've just said ···"

7. The pause during the search for information

(1) When you can't give a confirmed answer to a client's question, you should say, "Please hold on. I'll check it for you. "

(2) When a client thinks you are slow when he holds on to wait for your answer, you should say, "Sorry for the inconvenience. I'll handle your problem right away. Could you hold on for a little while, please? Thank you!"

(3) When you continue the talk after the pause, you should say, "Thank you for your patience!"

(4) If you can't give a confirmed answer to a client's question, you should keep a record of his full name, telephone number for contact. You should say, "Sir/Miss, we need to consult relative departments for you question. I'm afraid this will take a long-period of time. Please leave your phone number and I will call you back when I get a confirmed answer, will you? Thank you!"

(5) After confirming the phone number of your client, you should ask, "Can I contact you anytime, please?"

8. Needing for the profiles of a client

(1) When you need the client's name and telephone number to issue the ticket, you shouldn't ask him directly, "Please give me your name and telephone number. " You should ask, "Who is going to take the flight, please?" Or you should ask, "What's your telephone number, please?"

(2) You should confirm with the client after he gives you the information, and ask, "Please check. The name is ···, and the telephone number is ···, right?"

(3) When you check the the name of a client to input into the computer, try to speak in the complimentary sense rather than in the derogatory sense. Besides, when you exemplify the names of celebrities, try to use the positive figures rather than the negative figures. For instance, the character of "Li", you should ask, "The 'Li' as in 'Li Shiming'?" Don't ask, "The 'Li' as in 'Li Lianying'?" Don't make mistakes like these-"The 'Xiong' as in

'Gouxiong (a coward)'?" "The 'Pan' as in 'Pan Jinlian (a woman convicted with adultery in a Chinese fiction)'?"

9. When the client's requirement reaches out of the clarity of your work

(1) You should wait for the client to finish his expression patiently. Don't interrupt your client.

(2) You should explain the reason to your client and express your sorrow. Meanwhile, you should suggest another solution or volunteer to help him find one, "Excuse me, Mr. / Miss ××, but this is beyond my work clarity. I can't help you with this, but I will notify your problem to my superior departments. What do you think of this?" Don't say something like, "I can't help you."

(3) If a client put forward an unreasonable requirement, you should explain to him patiently and ask for his forgiveness, "Excuse me, Mr. / Miss ××, But I really can't help you with this. Your requirement is beyond the service of ××××. Please forgive us!"

(4) If there are some clients being impolite, try to manage your temper. Don't argue with your client even if you are on the right side. Ask for your superior manager for help if necessary.

(5) If a client apologizes for his impoliteness, you should receive his apology generously, "It's OK! Is there anything else that I can help you with, please?"

10. Clients refuses to hang up when he is finished with his questions

(1) If you are sure that a client is finished with his questions, you could remind him tactfully, "Excuse me, Mr. / Miss ××, if you don't have any further questions, please call 95160 the next time. Thanks for your cooperation! Goodbye!"

(4) If a client is making a harassment call, you should remind him calmly, "Excuse me, do you have any questions with regard to our business?" If a client still doesn't have any questions on the business, you can take the harassment call as a silent call and say, "Excuse me! I can't hear you on the phone. Please try again on another phone set. Thank you for your call. Goodbye!" Wait for 2 seconds, and then hang up.

11. Refusal of a client's invitation

(1) If a client invite you on a date out of good will, you should thank him first, and then ask for his understanding, "Thank you for your invitation and recognition on my job, but I can't accept your invitation. I hope you can continue to support us. Thank you!"

(2) If a client asks for your name, you should explain to him tactfully, "I'm sorry, Mr. / Miss ××, but we only have employee number when we are at work. My employee number is …"

12. End of the call

(1) If you confirmed that a client has no further questions on reservation or search, you should end the call like this, "Thank you for you call! Goodbye!"

(2) If you confirmed that a client has no further questions when he has ordered the ticket, you should end the call like this, "Have a good trip! Thank you for your call! Goodbye!" Clients will be happy to receive your wish.

(3) If a client's ticket can't be ordered, you should end the call like this, "Please call if you have any need next time. We'd be glad to provide you with our service. Thank you for your call. Goodbye!"

Striving for perfection

There is no best one, but always a better one. This was Liang Jianzhang's pursuit of service quality management and process management.

Why did he had so a requirement? It originated from his experience.

When Liang Jianzhang was still in America, he liked to go to the bookshops. But, sometimes he couldn't find the book he wanted. So, he had to look for the books in the online bookshop Amazon. com.

This time, on Amazon. com there were hundreds of thousands of books for the customers to search and there were different ways to search for the books. A book could be identified by searching its category, the sales board, the author's name, the book of the name, and so on.

When a book was found, there were introduction to it and book review from experts and readers, which could help the readers in selecting a book.

What's most incredible was that on Amazon. com, customers could make reservations of books which stopped publishing and books that were to be published. As soon as Amazon. com got hold of such a book, they would mail it to the customer.

Liang Jianzhang thought this was awesome, so he picked a book he wanted. Surprisingly, when he booked the book, Amazon had also suggested him that customers who had bought this book had also bought the following books. Liang followed Amazon's suggestion, and found the other relative books. Thus, within several minutes, Liang Jianzhang had found several good books, which was more efficient than the traditional way of shopping in the bookshops.

In addition, after Liang had put in his credit card password, address and email, Amazon. com had memorized his personal information. From then on, he only had to put in a user name if wanted to buy a book.

What had also impressed Liang Jianzhang were the links of Amazon. com.

On many websites, there were the links to Amazon. com. At first, Liang had thought them to be advertisements of Amazon. com on that page. Later, Liang Jianzhang had figured out that this was a way to cooperate with Amazon. com. If a client entered the Amazon. com through the link and purchase books, the profits would be shared by both websites. Through this means, Amazon actually found itself many distributors online.

The interaction and convenience of Amazon. com had enlightened Liang Jianzhang. He thought, "Websites should be like Amazon. com, or else the advantage can't be realized. "

During his days in America, Liang Jianzhang had visited Wall-Mart. That day, he had seriously observed the computer system and management model in a branch store of Wall-Mart. To his surprise, the company put the whole process flow into the database in the computers, including the job instructions to each job position, responsibility, and limitations, all of which were clearly regulated. If these documents were to be printed, they would be as thick as several books. As it turned out, Wall-Mart depended on the information facilities to link its branch stores across the world.

Amazon. com had enlightened Liang Jianzhang on interaction and convenience. Wall-Mart had helped Liang Jianzhang recognized the process management. Thus, during the cold winter for the Internet in 2000, Liang Jianzhang put in great efforts on backstage management. He applied management systems on Ctrip including customer service system, customer relation management, stock management system and accounting system, especially the EPR and Six6.

Are ERP and Six6 really so amazing? The following are the basic knowledge about these two management systems.

ERP is short for Enterprise Resource Planning. It is a new-generation integrated management information system developed from MRP (Material Resource Planning). Its core is the supply chain management. It has great influence on improving enterprise business process and enhancing the core competitiveness of enterprises. The planning systems in the ERP system includes main production planning, material demand planning, capacity planning, purchase planning, sales executive planning, profit planning, financial budget and human resource planning. In addition, these planning function and value control function have been integrated into the supply chain system.

How about the Six6? The Greek alphabet 6 is a statistic unit used to measure the standard errors in total. Since it was introduced to the manufacture industry, it has been used to indicate the deficiency of products. The bigger the number of 6is, the less error or deficiency a product has. 66is a goal which meant that during the whole process and in all the results, 99. 99966% are perfect, that's to say, among one million things, only 3. 4 things are defected.

From the above, we can see that both ERP and Six6 are the management tools in manufacturing enterprises. Could they apply to a service enterprise like Ctrip?

Unexpectedly, Liang Jianzhang said, "We should serve like a manufacturer. "

Many people doubted this saying because they had never heard of service industry applying these two management tools, especially the Six6. Besides, services couldn't be qualified. The regular process of Six6 was to demarcate, measure, analyze, improve and control.

How to measure the service?

Solutions were always more than problems. Liang Jianzhang decided to divide the process of service into small links like the manufacture process.

Take the call center as an example. All the seated employees were like the workers on the manufacturing line. The phones were their manufacture tools. The information and time of hotels were their manufacture materials. The services they provided to their customers were the products. Thus, the links of the room reservation process were divided.

1. Asking about the relative information about the customers.
2. Searching for and recommending hotels to the customers.
3. Confirming the reservation demands with the customers.
4. Typing in the customers' information.
5. Issuing the order.

After the process was drafted, Liang Jianzhang and Sun Maohua had a random inspection to see how much time was needed for the whole process. They measured the time of the seated employee's call from different angles-the amount of time he needed to issue a new order, to revise the order, and to cancel the order; the amount of time needed by a new employee, and by an experienced employee. Upon series of measuring and summarizes, Liang Jianzhang had discovered that the average time for the whole process were 240 seconds.

After he had measured the length of the calls, he wondered to how long he should reduce the time of the calls.

Sun Maohua said, "Let's set the ideal time to 200 seconds!"

Liang Jianzhang agreed. Thus, they began to record the calls. After they had found an ideal record of the call, Sun Maohua divided the record into bytes to observe the time taken by a byte and the link which wasted most time, through which he could compress the number of words used in the link that cost most time.

After continuous testing and correction, they wrote a teaching material on the requirements and instructions on each link. They used it as the evaluation standard, which was directly connected with the seated employees' salaries.

Later, Liang Jianzhang had found that with the application of Six6, their customer server had reduced their time to 180 seconds, lower than the 200 seconds set previously. By reducing the time from 240 seconds to 180 seconds, the time saved could be used to provide the customers with experience of higher level service, and the cost was greatly reduced. By saving one minute in every call, dozens of thousands of RMBs were saved every month, counting the telephone expense and manual expense.

Section II   The recovery of the Internet

The Internet company saved by text messages.

The outside world had changed dramatically when Liang Jianzhang was working on the internal improvement of his company —internal business process regulation and quality management enhancement.

Between the two years of 2001 and 2003, the fate of Internet companies had a 180 degree change because the cold winter for Internet was over.

When the wave of Internet came, the CEOs of Internet companies focused only on how to increase the clicking rate of their companies. They never thought about making money out of Internet. After the Internet bubbles bursted, they had to start thinking about the survival problem for their own companies.

How did they save themselves?

In August 2001, the largest domestic e-mail server Sina. com announced a piece of news which caused intense reaction from the netizens-it reduced the capacity of its free e-mails from 50MB to 5MB.

In the afterwards, the Executive Deputy Director of Sina explained that they had only reduced the capacity of free e-mails to balance the budget of Sina, modifiying Sina jinto a more competitive company to survive in the environment. To maintain the previous e-mail system, Sina had to spend over 30 million RMB on 30 servers every year. If they could deduct 90% of the capacity of the each e-mail account, they could save 20 million to 40 million RMB every year. Besides, the proceeds of Internet companies were mainly from the advertisements, and Sina was no exception. However, proceeds from advertisements of Sina were over 90% of its total proceeds, which was an unsafe proportion. Therefore, Sina hoped to have some breakthrough on the expansion of its business such as personal home, personal homepage, online photo album and VIP e-mail.

Sina thought the charged e-mails could save its future while Netease. com had found another gold mine.

In 2000, the number of Chinese phone users had reached 100 million. 14 months later, this number had doubled and increased into 200 million. At this time, Guangdong China Mobile had launched a value-added service-Monternet. This service was invented for China Mobile to compete with its rival China Unicom, however, it had unexpectedly saved the whole Internet industry of China.

Monternet worked with Internet companies by charging the phone users and shared the profits by 20% and 80% —the telecommunication server got the 20% and the Internet content server got the 80%. This plan had solved the problem of charging fees theoretically for the Internet companies, who were having a headache trying to charge the enormous amount of users.

When Guangdong China Mobile launched this business, not many Internet companies thought it was a good one. However, there was one person who thought this was a good opportunity to revive his company. He was Ding Lei.

At that time, Ding Lei was desperate and was leading a miserable life. On 30th June 2000, Netease. com was officially listed on NASDAQ with an opening price of 15. 3 USD. When the market closed, the price dropped to 12. 125 USD, which was lower than the issued price. The price of Netease. com had been dropping ever since until the exchanges of its stocks were stopped.

Therefore, Ding Lei decided to sell Netease and start a new business. In the Shenzhen Wuzhou Hotel, Ding Lei told his idea to the owner of Bubukao Duan Yongping, Duan advised him not to do that.

Duan Yongping said, "You already have a company now. Why do you want to start all over? The price of your company's stock is so low and the buyer offered so low a price, so it's not the right time. Don't forget that whoever laughs best, laughs last. Shirley had once said, 'When the winter is here, will the spring be far?' Hold on for a little longer!"

Duan Yongping had supported him both spiritually and 0financially. Duan had bought Netease. com's shares from the secondary market in a large amount with a price lower than one dollar. To his surprise, after February 2007, the price rose to 20 USD. Duan Yongping's investment was increased a hundred times, and he had thus gained the name of "Duanffett". Of course, I can save the story for later.

After Ding Lei had regained his confidence, fortune fell upon him-the Monternet mentioned above. Ding thought that he could only earn several fens from a text message, but the number would be considerable if he could earn one RMB from every client every month. Thus, Ding Lei entered the wireless value-added service using his enormous client resources and the platform of China Mobile.

As a result, Ding Lei walked out the shadow brought by the advertisements on portal website. In Netease. com's annual report, he wrote, "The major increase of Netease's income in 2002 is from the wireless value-added service, especially the text message products and services through telephones offered by us. In the past two years, the business of text message has grown greatly and Netease. com has benefited from our early move. " This was indeed true because in 2002, text messages had helped Netease. com gain 161 million RMB, taking up of 69. 4% of the total income.

Ding Lei had succeeded. The other Internet companies swarmed to the business because they had smelled the money. In 2002, Zhang Chaoyang had also focused on text messages and promoting new games. As a result, the business of text message had brought him extraordinary achievements. In the meanwhile, Ma Huateng, an old friend of Ding Lei who also had enormous client resources but could not make money out of them, also made a perfect turn through the text messages. Sina. com was the latest one to open the text message service, but it was doing well on it because of its scale and popularity.

The popularity of online games

If the cooperation with Monternet had helped Ding Lei made a perfect turn, then the cooperation with Stone Age had strengthened Ding Lei like a tiger mounted with a pair of wings.

In 2001, the rapid growth of online games took many Internet companies by surprise. This was a market grew almost overnight. Those who dared to try the first tomato had begun to profit. The online game *Lord of the King* had registered members of half a million. At its peak, there were 160 thousand people online at the same time. The sales volume of the 18-RMB month cards was over 100 thousand. *The Smiling Proud Wonderer-Loyalty to the Country* also had registered members of 1.5 million and paid members of over 50 thousand. This game grew steadily with daily registered members of 10 thousand and paid members of 500. The *Stone Age* which cooperated with Ding Lei had an amazing sales achievement. They had sold half-a-million sets of one-month-free account and a soft ware cost 20 RMB.

In this year, in the investment market, the stocks of technology companies were weak because of the economic recession in America. However, the stocks of online game companies kept on rising. The market value of game soft ware such as Activision, THQ, The 3DO and Midway Games had doubled or even tripled. It was because that paid online games had been widely accepted.

In China, according to the latest statistics of CNNIC, 20% of the 26.9 million users selected the "game and entertainment" as their commonly used function of the Internet. There were over half a million paid game player in the domestic market, and the number would rich one million by the end of 2001. A big market was presented in front of the Internet Companies.

At this time, text messages and online games were both in Ding Lei's vision. But in his opinion, in a country full of pirate products and knockoff goods, the online games were a better project to attract money.

Therefore, Ding Lei decided to enter this market.

Ding Lei went to the bookshops to buy books on Marketing. He did researches in the web café and second-classand third-class cities. He needed to figure out a product that fitted the demand of the China's market.

Then, Ding Lei decided to work with *Stone Age*. Seeing that Sony and EA in America had developed a graphic online game, Ding Lei wanted to deal the game. "Waters flow by regardless of shatter's wills". He got denied.

Ding Lei had to use 300 thousand USD to buy the first open graphic MUD engine in the country-Guangzhou Tianxia Technology Limited Company. He use the develop team of this company as the core, and developed the most successful online game in the history of Chinese online games-the series of *Westward Journey Online*. Different from other companies who were dealing Korean and American games, Netease owned the intellectual right of this game.

When *Westward Journey Online* was first online, the product manager asked Ding Lei how to set the price-3 jiaos or 4 jiaos for one hour? Ding Lei wasn't sure about it so he went to ask Duan Yongping for help. Duan Yongping told him, "Of course 4 jiaos. Why would they care for the extra one jiao when they are already playing and paying for the game?" Ding Lei used to do researches in webcafes. He had also thought so, "They are willing to spend 2 RMB per hour. The extra one jiao is a piece of cake for them."

With the magnificent business in text messages and online games and the up-rise of the Internet commercials business, the good time was back for Ding Lei. In 2003, Netease had become the favorite of NASDAQ. On 10th that October, the share price of Netease reached the historical high point of 70. 27 USD, which was 108 times higher than that when it was at its low. The famous Bloomberg News gave Netease such a review, "It could become the number one stock in NASDAQ in terms of growing."

Actually, Ding Lei wasn't the only one who had found this enormous market. There another person who needed to be described in specific and his name's Chen Tianqiao.

In 2001, the owner of the Actoz Company of Korea came to China with an online game *Legend*, wanting to find an Internet server to promote this game. He found Chen Tianqiao, who agreed immediately. Shengda decided to buy the sole dealership of *Legend* in China with half a million USD.

Holding the contract with Actoz in his hand, Chen Tianqiao started his series of activities to "gain the valuable things". He first contacted server manufacturers like Langchao and Dell, and told them politely that they were running a Korean online game and that wanted to apply for use of their server for two months. The manufacturers were astounded by the contract in English. They agreed without consideration because they thought this young man could be a potential major client.

Then, in the same way, Chen Tianqiao "deceived" China Telecom with the contract of servers, "Langchao and Dell would offer us the servers. But we still need a wide broadband to support our running." China Telecom had agreed immediately and provided him with a period of free broadband. Thus, Shengda made through the two-month testing period.

However, Chen Tianhua wasn't leading a good life at that time. The company was lacking money, scale development, and relative experience. What surprised Chen Tianqiao more was that *Legend* wasn't a first-class online game in Korea and had only ranked only the eighth. People in the industry all thought *Legend* was a second-class game.

Finally, Chen Tianqiao had come up with a good solution. On one hand, he enhanced the services. He created many personalized services in the country and set up a call center. On the other hand, he signed agreements with web cafes in the domestic cities, especially in the town cities. The web cafes sold the point cards of the game as distributors, and they would gain commissions. Shengda had signed agreements with over 250 thousand web cafes.

Just like this, the one who had the terminal had the world. In only half a year, Legend, the game not so popular in Korea, became the favourite of the market. They became rich so quickly that many experienced employees in the company would wake up in the morning and ask each other with this opening line, "My brother, is this real?"

Thus, Shengda had entered the fast-growing period. According to statistics, Shengda had the income of 160 million RMB in 2001.

Section III   Ctrip's successful listing
Which company gets listed first?

Of course, the two mentiond above were not the only ones doing the text message business, nor are Netease and Shengda the only ones who made a fortune from online games. "From thhe leaves we can tell the coming of the fall. " However, these were clues that the Internet industry was recovering and that the whole industry was coming out the difficulty.

I still remember that during the two years from 1999 to 2000, there were many companies that planned to get listed in the United States because they had seen that Netease, Sina, and Sohu had gained millions of USD from their investors. Unfortunately, in the following days, the banquet of the Internet was suddenly overed. Therefore, the Internet entrepreneurs in China had to hide their dreams for IPO temporarily.

But this was when Ctrip was working on its third round of financing. Some investor once asked Shen Nanpeng, "Is Ctrip planning on listing after the financing right now? If not now, when are you planning on doing so?" Shen Nanpeng answered, "It might not be a good thing to go for listing at such early stage. The issued price in America is normally between 10 and 30 USD. If the share price falls to low, the imagining room left for the investors as a listed company would be empty, and it would be hard for the company to get another round of financing in the public market. This practical situation would be worse than not being listed. However, a company shouldn't get listed too late or it would lose the market opportunity. So, the best time for listing is when Ctrip is mature in business and stable in income, and when the Internet industry has recovered. "

When the time reached 2002, the Internet industry had once again become flourishing. There was no doubt of the listing in NASDAQ of the Chinese enterprises. But, which company would lead the second wave of listing?

Among the circle of Internet business, people thought some companies was preparing for listing-Tencent, Ctrip, Baidu, Elong, Shengda and Alibaba. Among these, Shengda, Tencent and Alibaba were the loudest, and they cried and shouted for getting listed.

In the office of Ctrip, the co-founders began to make their dreams.

Ji Qi said to Shen Nanpeng, "My brother, I'm done with my historical duty. Back then, I promised Liant Jianzhang that I would start this company, and I have done that. I have also taken part in the three rounds of financing. Now it's your turn!"

Liang Jianzhang followed, "Yes, brother. I have built the structure of management system-the EPR, the Six6 and the personal balanced point cards. Now the relay stick is passed into your hands. If you couldn't accomplish the duty, our efforts we had made would end up in vain. "

Ji Qi said, "I heard that Shengda was planning on listing in 2004. What about us?"

Shen Nanpeng answered, "My brothers, please set your mind at rest. I'll take care of it and I'll make the move when necessary. But I believe that we would be the first one in this round of listing. "

Liang Jianzhang was shocked, "What? The first one? Last time I checked, it is already the latter half of 2003, and people are still in the threat of SARS. "

"We would need only three months. " Liang Jianzhang smiled and said, "In the Kongfu novels, there are three kinds of sword players. The first kind is a sword player who has a sword in his hand but doesn't have a sword in his mind, so he would kill people at random selection. The second kind is a sword player who a sword in his hands and a sword in his mind, but he is powerless to kill. The third kind is a sword player who has no sword in his hands but a sword in his mind, so he could performe a leaf as a sword. I am the third kind. Wait and see. You will see what profession is in three months. "

Liang Jianzhang responded, "OK! My heart is at a rest if you are in charge. "

Who could tell the best story?

A couple of month earlier, the epidemic disease of SARS broke out in China. Zhen Nanyan, the current General Manager of Ctrip's China Region, had experienced it. He said to a journalist, "During the epidemic of SARS, the whole industry received unprecedented attack. Many companies were cutting staff numbers to reduce cost, and some companies even closed. Guangdong is a heavily damaged area by SARS, and the business volume was dropping. But Ctrip didn't cut off any employee. Instead, we were doing job-sharing training during the few months. Fortunately, the panic got away quickly and we made through it. "

As soon as the SARS passed, Shen Nanpeng set off on his work. He knew very clear that "an opportunity knocks once".

Between Hongkong and the NASDAQ in America, where should he get Ctrip listed? There were many opportunities for Ctrip as a Chinese enterprise. However, the market in America was more advanced and had bigger capital capacity. So Shen Nanpeng chose America.

There were four listed tourism companies in America. As to the model of "Internet +

Call Center", it was a little strange to the American people. However, in 2003, the American investors had already known the profits brought by the text messages in Netease, Sina and Sohu. Shengda, who was more prepared for the listing at the same time as Ctrip, began telling its "legend of the web cafes" to the Americans.

Here is a story of how Tang Jun, the owner of Shengda, "decieved" the investors on the Wall Street. Shengda was listed a few months later than Ctrip, but this story happened after Ctrip was listed.

The first thing Tang Jun did after he became the Chief Director of Shengda was to get listed in NASDAQ. Shengda was one of the concept stocks from China preparing to be listed. There was not a previous example of online game companies being listed. The stock exchange environment back then was terrible, so it's safe to say that Shengda was going on the contrary of the market trend.

One day, Tang Jun entered the office of an investor in London, who had asked him directly, "Yesterday, concept stocks all dropped 15%. Why do I want to buy your company?" Tang Jun replied, "Because the good quality of our shares." To his surprise, the investor smoked a piece of cigar and ignored Tang Jun.

The investor took Tang Jun for granted like a person who "does not take the rural govener seriously". Tang Jun calmed down, and continued, "We have a space of improvement to be heightened. In the future, you can earn 200%, 300%..."

The investor still kept his silence. Tang Jun asked suddenly, "Do you believe in Gates?"

The investor answered, "I do."

Tang Jun kept on asking, "Do you know who Gates believes in?"

The investor was surprised, "Who?"

Tang Jun smiled, "Gates believes in me."

"What a load of nonsense!" The investor felt incredible about Tang Jun's speech.

"I am the only one in the history of Microsoft who has gained the life-time honorable Chief Director, which proves that Gates believes in me."

The investor thought for a while, "Yes. That's logical."

"Gates believes in me, so you should believe in me too." Tang Jun smiled again.

"Why would I believe in you?"

"It's easy. I gave up on the options of 5 million USD to take part in the gambling of 30 million USD in Shengda."

"Is it possible that you are wrong?" The investor was shocked because the number of 5 million USD was a quite large one to Americans.

In the end, the American was persuaded by Tang Jun. Tang Jun told this story to many people, and pulled a lot of people onto his boat. Finally, he sold the shares out. On a roadshow, Shengda had financed 800 million USD.

On 13th May 2004, Shengda got listed, which brought a wave of domestic online games being listed and changed the whole structure of the industry.

Finished with the story in 2004, I would like to bring you readers back to December 2003.

After SARS was gone, Ctrip had chosen Merrill Lynch Securities as its main dealer. On the other hand, out of concerns for safty, Ctrip had hired four investment banks as assistant dealers including CLSA and China Bank International. There was only one goal for Ctrip-to head toward the NASDAQ.

Shen Nanpeng and the main dealer Merrill Lynch went to Hongkong, and Singapore and London were the following destinations. Their focus was the America. He had roadshows in Boston, New York in the east of America, and Los Angles and Denver in the east of America. In addition, they held a telephone meeting for an entire afternoon with the investors in San Diego.

The Merrill Lynch Securities representative who went on the roadshow with Shen Nanpeng was Wang Zhongke, the Board Director of the Investment Bank Department of Merrill Lynch Securities's Asian Region. He had witnessed this process. On their busiest day, they had ten conferences with investors in a row, being both nervous and excited. Shen Nanpeng was very professional because he could give answers to questions without even being asked, which made Wang Zhongke felt incredible. Shen Nanpeng could give the answers about the industry and all kinds of figures without checking any documents. Shen Nanpeng, who had the eight-year work experience in Citibank, Deutsche Bank and Lehman Brothers, knew very clear what kind of story the market wanted.

Why? Because whenever Shen Nanpeng met with investors and analysis experts in New York, Singapore and Hongkong, he would first show them the2003 annual report of Ctrip.

Shen Nanpeng told the investors, "You can see very clearly on our profit-and-loss report about the gross increase rate, gross interest and profits. The expenditure of our capital was small. We had limited non-cash projects. We use margin instead of total for accounting. Until now, our profit-and-loss reports are very simple. "

Then, Shen Nanpeng would start telling them the legendary story of "Call Center Plus E-commerce".

What kind of company was Ctrip? In nature, it was a tourism service company. But it was different from traditional travel agencies because the latter ones had limitations on technology while the previous ones provided their services through technology —Internet and its call center. In America, call centers had brought revolutionary change and replaced real-life shops. This revolution took place in the 1980s. But in the 1990, call centers were replaced by e-commerce. But in China, call centers were not falling behind. On the contrary, they were as new as the Internet. In China this phased was jumped over. Call centers and Internet appeared at the same time.

Another question was that did call centers cost much? Actually, they didn't. In China, where labor cost little, it was easy to find cheap operators. In Shanghai where labor cost high, the money needed to hire an operator would be no more than 3000 RMB, which was one tenth of the price in America. So, in such a the labor environment in China, running a call center was efficient. Our call centers could offer us higher profits.

In addition, the advantage of call centers was obvious. In China, there lacked greatly the basis for e-commerce. There weren't many credit card users. Those who had credit cards wouldn't user cards online, which caused problems for the paying process on the Internet. Meanwhile, 50% of the reservation calls were made one day before the trip or on the day. Those who usually used credit cards to make room reservations would have problems when they didn't have access to the Internet.

The wave of listing brought by Ctrip

Actually, after series of financial scandals, the examination system in America became more and more strict. Investors were cautious about Chinese companies that wanted to be listed in NASDAQ. However, Shen Nanpeng could offer clear reports and he had keen insight. Meanwhile, with the development of China's economy, especially with that of the Chinese tourism industry, these investors were interested in the development of tourist industry. Not too long after the opening of the roadshow, the great demands of the investors were activated, especially those international and regional funds which was called the "authentic orders" because they could be depended on. Thus, Merrill Lynch Securities had decided to heighten the originally planned price gap from 14-16 USD to 16-18 USD. The eve of its official exchange day, Merrill Lynch Securities set on the final price to the increased 18 USD.

At 10:45a. m. Eastern Time in America on the 9th December 2003 (11:45 p. m. in Beijing), Ctrip was officially listed on NASDAQ. Ctrip had become another listed Chinese company after Sina, Netease and Sohu.

This time, Ctrip issued 4.2 million shares of American Depository Receipts at the price of 18 USD per share, taking up 28% of its expanded shares. On the first day, it opened at 24 USD, and rose to 37.35 USD. It ended with the price of 33.94 USD, growing 88.6%.

The price was raised at the last minute, but the pursuit from the investors had helped Ctrip gain 10 times extra purchases. Unintentionally, Ctrip had become the leader of the Chinese companies in the second wave of listing. Seven senior management staff including the four co-founders and three other senior managers took 23.65% of its shares. Carlyle, the largest shareholder of Ctrip, gained profits of 9.22 million USD and 18.30% of its shares. IDG had invested 1.6 million USD in the three rounds of financing, and on the listing day, it earned 37 million USD.

The thing worth enormous mentioning the most was that the difference of Ctrip's listing between those of the three portal websites. Apart from the 2.7 million new shares, Ctrip was also selling 1.5 million company's internal shares. The management staff sold their internal shares. If the financing was 75.6 million USD, then they had monetized 27.21 million USD, which was over 200 million RMB. The percentage of the shares sold by the five senior managers among the shares issued this time were-12.68% of the CFO Shen Nanpeng; 2.75% of the Deputy Director Wang Shengli; 2.02% of the Executive Deputy Director Fan Min. The other two senior managers Gabriel Li and Robert Stain didn't sell their shares. By the way, these weren't the money written on the paper, but real money. The senior managers of Sina, Netease and Sohu could only experience the pleasure of monetizing two years later when China's Internet industry recovered.

Apart gaining from monetizing, the senior managers of Ctrip had also earned increased "money written on the paper" with the rise of the share price. The shares held by the seven senior managers after the issue took 23.65% of the total shares, of which Sheng Nanpeng still held 7.60% and Liang Jianzhang held 6.24%. If measure by the market price 2.72 USD, Shen and Liang were in possessof over 20 million USD and 17 million USD separately.

Leaving the money in their account aside, the problem was how were the senior managers going to spend so much cash?

To reveal the mystery, please read the next chapter Birth of Home Inn.

Summary

In this chapter, there are these following important problems.

I. Roles of the team

Shakespeare once said, "All the world is a stage and all the men and women merely players. What matters is for everyone to play his role right." Once a Chinese performing artist also had a similar saying, "There is no small role but a small actor." This means that whatever environment you are in, you need to be clear about the role you are playing. Of course, the role here needs to be put into a team. A famous team coach had advocated, "The individual should obey the role. The action should surpass the goal." Then, how should we understand the concept of role? It can be explained by the following four aspects.

1. Role perception. In a certain circumstance, you know how to perform. Meanwhile, the perception and understanding of the performance.
2. Role recognition. After understanding the role you are performing, you need to keep your attitude balanced with your behavior.
3. Role expectation. How others think you should perform your role, meaning others expectation on you.

4. Role conflict. You are performing one role, and you realize that you are not suitable for this role.

Here, what we care the most about is the role conflict. The aim of a team is the perfect match between individuals, not perfect individuals. Of course, here the perfect match doesn't necessarily mean the match of the strong points. Sometimes, if the shortcomings are well used, they can also turn into a perfect match. The following two stories can prove this point.

In Qing Dynasty, there was a military General called Yang Shizhai. Once in a battle, he met with a problem that made his head ache. Among the limited numbers of soldiers, there were three war-disabled ones-a mute, a cripple and a blind. What should he do? After thinking about it for some time, he decided to send the mute as a messenger because the secret letter could not be caught if this mute was captured. He sent the cripple to watch the battery because he could only stay in the field rather than leave the battery and run for his life. He sent the blind to ambush in the frontline because he had good ears that could hear the move of the enemy, which was the best at detecting the enemy. As a result, the team lead by Yang Shizhai had a triumph in this battle.

Coincidentally, there was a similar story in recent history. A new factory director came to a factory in the south. He found that the Section Chief of Marketing was very cautious; the Office Director was picky on everything; and the Section Chief of Manufacturing was always exaggerating...

The new Factory Director had finally realized why the factory was on the edge of being broke. Therefore, he decided to have a reform of the personnel. He positioned the one who was picky as the Section Chief of Quality Supervision; he positioned the one who was cautious as the Section Chief of Manufacture Safety Supervision; he positioned the one who was calculating as the Checker of Stocking; he positioned the one who liked to spread rumors as the Information Deliver; he positioned the one who were exaggerating as the Section Chief of Promotion... Thus, through his "promotion", these people who used to be looked down upon had become key persons, and they felt very proud of themselves. When they worked on these positions, their shortcomings became their strong points. Each one of them performed their separate functions, leading to the flourish of every field of work. Therefore, lead by this new Factory Director, the factory was given a new life.

The above story was about the positioning of a role. However, in a team, there is more than one role. A perfect and great team consists of many roles. How many roles are needed? The British Dr. Bellbin had reached a conclusion through 20-year researches on over one thousand teams-there are nine roles (see p. 5-1) in a perfect team. The following are the nine roles.

1. The messenger. People of such kind are very sensitive to the outside world. They are

curious about everything, and are aware of the changes in the outside; they don't like to stay home, and play outside; they are born with talent to communicate. They are outgoing, passionate. They like to have parties and make friends.

2. The inventor. People of such kind have new concepts, wild thoughts and rich imagination. They are impulsive. Their thoughts are always extreme and unrealistic. They don't like to be restrained, nor are they punctilious. They are not punctual and obeying. They are not good at dealing with people. Other people would see them as sick and freaks.

3. The specialist. People of such kind are authorities in a certain field. They are smug and narcissistic. They love their careers and are proud of their specialties. Their job is to maintain a standard, avoiding it to be decreased.

4. The doer. People of such kind work their fingers to their bones. They believe that hard work would pay off. They are good at planning, principles and self-controlling. They are loyal and sacrifice their personal interests for the companies'. They are tireless and see responsibility as the priority.

5. The promoter. People of such kind are purpose-driven. They are efficient at work. They are highly passionate with their work and feel strong sense of satisfaction. They believe that solutions are more than questions. They find solutions for the goal and find excuses for the failure. They are outgoing and like to challenge and argue with others. They are usually self-centered and can't understand each other. Their reactions on setbacks and difficulties are strong. They don't like to be thrown white blanket on their enthusiasm.

6. The coordinator. People of such kind are charming and can guide a group of people with different skills and personalities to a same goal. They would appear mature, confident and reliable. They are subjective and have no prejudice. They can find everybody's advantage during interpersonal communication, and make use of them during the pursuit of the goal. They have good self-control ability and can stay calm. They are hardly emotional and merely lose their temper.

7. The inspector. People of such kind are cold-blooded. They are serious and rarely smile. They lack the emotional cells, so they hardly praise their subordinates, which doesn't means they disapprove them. They are hardly emotional, and they like to keep distance from other people. They don't act on a moment of heat in the head, nor are they easily excited. They like to look for the errors with a strong sense of critics.

8. The perfectionist. People of such kind pay great attention to details, and pursue perfection and prominence. They are determined that there is no best but better. They can be initiative and self-motivated on work without the stimulations from the out-

side. They never fight the war they are uncertain of. They have high standard on work and on their subordinates. Whoever works with them would be tired to death.

9. The "glue". People of suck kind are refined and cultivated. They are good at dealing with people. They are intelligent. They care about, understand, sympathize, and support others. They deal with matters flexibly. They could always blend themselves into groups. They can adapt themselves to other people's thoughts and ideas, and the surroundings. They would not give opinions that are against other people. They are cooperative and believe in the important of peace. They care about anybody's suggestions, and the influence of his behavior on other people.

p. 5-1   Nine team roles of Belbin

type content features

(1) The messenger outgoing, curious, good at social
(2) The inventor creative, have lots of ideas, being oneself
(3) The specialist narcissistic, main standard, introvert
(4) The doer highly loyal, serious at work, obey principles
(5) The promoter challenge others, passionate, react strongly
(6) The coordinator unemotional, reliable, fair
(7) The inspector calm headed, picky, critical
(8) The perfectionist hard working, responsible, strive to improve
(9) The "glue" mild, accept suggestion, cooperative

After Dr. Belbin put forward the nine roles in teams, he had placed them in orders. In a team, these people present themselves in this order. The messenger offers the latest information. The inventor put forward his new thoughts. The specialist offers technology support. The doer starts to make plans. The promoter wants to execute the plans. The coordinator wants to choose the right person. The inspector starts to throw the white blanket. In the end perfectionist picks on the problems. The glue smoothen the members.

Of course, the model theory of nine roles team put forward by Dr. Belbin is only an ideal. In real life, such teams can never be found. If such teams can be found, they might not succeed because they are too perfect. Meanwhile, a competitive team don't need all of nine roles, but they would need at least nine members. However, among the nine members, a messenger, a doer, an inspector and a "glue" are indispensable. In addition, a member can play several roles at the same time. For example, a doer and a promoter, a coordinator and a "glue", and a perfectionist and an inspector can be in one member.

Now, let's take a look at the Ctrip team in real life. They were only four persons. If we want to apply the model theory of team roles onto them, could the nine roles be found?

We have unexpectedly found that a team member was carrying several roles. Liang Jianzhang was the messenger and specialist of the team; Ji Qi was the doer and promoter of the team. We have also found that a role could be embodied by two members. Ji Qi and Fan Min were playing the role of the inventor together while Ji Qi and Shen Nanpeng were playing the role of the promoter together.

Everybody knows that the perfection of the value of the team could be realized through combinations and that every role must be good at different fields. Looking back the development of Ctrip, their cooperation was flawless on the entrepreneurial road. Liang Jianzhang, who had lived in America for years, put forward the plan to enter the Internet industry first. Ji Qi and Liang Jianzhang made the decision to set their goal on tourist industry. With Shen Nanpeng and Fan Min joining the team, their entrepreneurship began. However, at that time, Ji Qi was the only one who was doing the work and the other three were just working part-time. Later, after the first and second round of financing, the other three founders devoted themselves into this business. Then they were faced with the transformation of the company. They transferred their business into hotel reservation and purchased reservation companies. Up until here, Ji Qi had made the greatest contribution. That's why Wu Hai had sighed, "Without Ji Qi, the other three founders might not dare to operate this company, let alone succeed."

After the latter half of 2000, Ji Qi gave his position of Ctip's CEO to Liang Jianzhang. Then, Liang Jianzhang had the ability to make the full use of his specialty to the limit. The website was developed under his leadership, and he had also developed the customer management system, call waiting system, order process system and e-map search system. The most incredible thing he had done was that he had introduced the EPR, Six 6system to the management system. The construction of such systems had done a great help to Shen Nanpeng for the listing.

After the recovery of the Internet industry, many Chinese Internet companies were preparing for listing. However, to many people's surprise, Ctrip was the first one to be listed in the second round. The speed of Ctrip's listing made many insiders of this industry applaud. What had made others admire them more was that with Shen Nanpeng's understanding of the game rules in NASDAQ, he had not only got Ctrip listed but also helped the senior managers monetize ASAP. CEOs of the previously listed companies had no idea about this move.

After Ctrip was listed, history had pushed Fan Min to the front stage, which will be elaborated later.

In all, the team members of Ctrip were running a 400 meter relay. The first runner was Ji Qi, the second Liang Jianzhang, the third Shen Nanpeng and the fourth Fan Min.

II. The wings on creation by technology

According to a survey, every entrepreneur has dreamt about enlarging and strengthening his company. 80% of them plan to get their companies listed. Why do they dream about this? Nowadays, the global economy is going for unification. People admire that the international capital giants could command the market. When a company gets listed, the founder would become a billionaire over night, which gets people carried away. Therefore, listing has become an irresistible temptation to domestic entrepreneurs.

Here, I'd like to cut in with a story of the unsuccessful listing.

In 1994, the Yansheng Hubao lotion made by Feilong Company was selling well in the coutry. The founder of this company, Jiang Wei, began to plan on making his company listed in Hongkong. At that time, many distributors owned Feilong money. But, Jiang Wei had his way. Under his command, the profits on the books were as high as 200 million RMB.

Jiang Wei went to Hongkong excitedly. But he was integrated by the lawyer in Hongkong unexpectedly, which made him speechless.

"The profits on the books are pointless. In Hongkong, any debts older than eight months are considered dead debts. " The lawyer kept asking, "What's your yearly cost on technology development?"

He clenched his teeth, and said, "Probably 20 million RMB. "

The lawyer said, "Mr. Jiang, you must be joking! With so little investment, how could you support the 2 billion sales volume in 5 years?"

Jiang Wei couldn't give him an answer immediately. The Hongkong lawyer kept asking him several questions, to most of which Jiang Wei could give no answers. Jiang Wei had realized that the method used in the domestic could no long work in the international capital cosmopolitan Hongkong.

Later, the Hongkong lawyer had give Feilong a diagnosis, "It has no trustworthy long term development plan, nor high technological products. Its capital is solid and low. There are flaws in its financial management. "

The conclusions on the diagnosis were shocking. But the operation for listing was still on. On 23th March 1995, Feilong Group had finally got approval letter for listing on The Stock Exchange of Hong Kong. However, at this moment, Jiang Wei made a decision to everybody's surprise-he gave up on listing. Thus, after six months' torture and 18 million expenses, Jiang Wei flew back to Shenyang with a pile of financial reports and assessment reports.

From Jiang Wei, we can see some problems that need to be considered.

"Am I qualified for listing?" "What's purpose for listing?" "Does my company have to go for listing?" "Will my company have a wonderful journey after the listing?" "How should I avoid deficit after getting listed or stopped exchange?"

Here, I want to tell you that there are good and bad in listing. The good aspect is that the problem of capital could be solved, talents could be saved and they would be more passionate. After getting listed, the market will force you run your company under regulation. The company would be more famous, and the brand effect would be more obvious. However, after getting listed, it would be dangerous like "dancing with a pair of golden cuffs because your company would lose its privacy. Your company would be under the supervision of the public and your rival companies, which is obviously a disadvantage. In addition, the manager would be limited because all the major decisions would have to go through the board, or maybe even all shareholders. Plus, once your company is listed, the public would have the right to purchase the shares. The company owner could be changed in any minute if a major buyer purchases enough shares. "

But the Ctrip team introduced in this book is a professional team. In February 2004, two months after Ctrip's listing, Sheng Nanpeng spoke on the China Entrepreneur Forum in Yabuli, "Ctrip is a company with premeditation. The story of Ctrip is no different from those of Sina and Sohu. The only difference was that the company was built with premeditation. We have planned to gain support from venture investment and to be listed on NASDAQ in three or four years. Our business model is similar to that of some famous companies in America. We designed our route clearly, and along the way to the success, there weren't too many surprises. "

Do you think Shen Nanpeng's speech is powerful? This is a team different from others, and no wonder Shi Mingchun, the partner of Softbank China, would say, "This is a once-in-a-lifetime team. "

Applications

I . Why wasn't Huawei listed?

Huawei Technology Limited Company is a private technology company with its employees as shareholders which manufactures telecommunication equipments. It was founded in 1988 and headquartered in Longgang Region of Shenzhen, Guangdong. Huawei's mainly produced exchange, transfer, wireless and data telecommunication products. They provide Internet applications, service and resolutions to clients all over the world in the telecommunication field. Huawei has set up research institute in America, India, Sweden, Russia and China' Beijing, Shanghai and Nanjing with more than 80 thousand, 43% of them are doing research. By the time of June 2008, Huawei had applied for over 29666 patens, being the company with the most patents for years in a row. Huawei has set up over 100 branches across the globe. Its sales and internet service network covers the world. Now, Huawei's products and resolutions are applied in over 100 countries across the world and in 36 top 50 operators.

In 2008, the company kept growing steadily and healthily. The global sales volume reached 23. 3 billion USD and grew 46% compared with that of the previous years. The income from the global market took up 75% of it. According to reports from abroad, with such income, Huawei could surpass Beidian and become the fifth largest telecommunication equipment seller in 2008.

Seeing such glorious development history, many people couldn't help wondering, "Why didn't such good a company go for listing in all these years?"

Ⅱ. How to achieve seamless joints?

Li Jun is an Internet Constructor with over ten years experience and is currently a Internet Technology Supervisor in a famous private company. He is tired of the nine-to-five work and decids to start his own business in the hotel reservation industry. He positions his business at the convenient hotels in the regional markets and plans to connect the single hotels into a virtual chain hotel.

What has made Li Jun's head ache was how to tie his website to the reservation business of the hotels so that it will be both saving and convenient for the customers when they make reservations.

Appendix I   Teaching Materials of team management

In this chapter, we used PPTs how to manage a team briefly and directly. The contents are practical, clear at a glance. They will help you command the essence of team management.

Special subject training course

Teaming Materials on Team management black eye

There is no perfect man, but a perfect team.

—the author

Notes-the purpose of forming a team is to perform the function of 1 +1 >2. So I have emphasized from the beginning that there is no perfect men, but perfect teams.

Life journey petrol station

Outline

Chapter Ⅰ   Theory on team

Chapter Ⅱ   Formation of a team

Chapter Ⅲ   Leader of a team

Chapter Ⅳ   Team spirit

Chapter Ⅴ   Team promotion

Notes-there are five chapters in this material. In the first chapter, it contains understanding of a team, including the concept and type. From the second to the fourth chapter, they contain analysis on a team to analyze the growth of a team. In the fifth chapter, it contains the comprehension of a team and discussion on the secret to build a powerful team.

Chapter Ⅰ   Theory on team
Section one The meaning of team
Section two Teams and groups
Section three Types of teams
Notes-In this chapter, first the definition of team is give. Then, there are analyses on the difference between teams and groups. Finally, there is introduction to the most effective type of team.

Section one The meaning of team
1. The meaning of team
A team is a group formed by several people with complementary skills who depend on each other and are responsible for each other to achieve the same goals.
Reasonable numbers of people
Complementary skills
Same goals
Responsibility
Notes-this definition was introduced by Katezenbach and Smith in 1993, which is the most widely approved in the industry. It emphasize on the complementary skills and same goals.

Section one The meaning of team
2. Structure of team
(1) Skills
(2) Responsibility
(3) Duty
team result personal growth team efficiency
skills responsibility duty
problematic human relation interactive small-numbered people the common in set goals
Notes-this structure was brought about by Katezenbach and Smith. And it was so extracted from the three elements of skills, responsibility and duty from the definition of team. But they emphasized on the interactive and common features of team members, that's to say, men of totally different principles can't not work together.

Section one The meaning of team

3. The elements of a team

(1) Purpose

(2) People

(3) Place

(4) Power

(5) Plan

Note-the author of this book can't find out who brought out the theory of 5P. However, this theory is very important because it emphasizes the important of the team members' self-positioning, which implies that if the self-positioning of the members are not clear, they would have conflicts with other team members easily.

Section one The meaning of team

3. The elements of a team

(1) Purpose-without a purpose, the existence of the team is invaluable

(2) People-people are the core elements of a team

(3) Place-including the place of the team and person

(4) Power-the special rights in the organization of a team

(5) Plan-the specific procedure of realizing the goal

Notes-this the specific explaination of the 5P Theory

Section one The meaning of team

4. The efficiency model of team

(1) Team environment-the salary system, communication system, and the leadership

(2) Team design-the features, scale, formation of a team

(3) Team process-development, principles, roles, and the cohensive force of a team

(4) Team efficiency-realization of the team goal, satisfaction of team members demands, and maintaining of team's survival

Notes-this theory was brought about by M. A. West, C. S. Borrill and K. L. Unsworth in 2000. This is a comprehensive model, which indicates that the team efficiency is related to the team environment, the design when the team is founded and the development of the team.

Section two Teams and groups

organization Contents	groups	teams
1. Leader	set leaders	Share of the leading rights
2. Purpose	The same as organizations	Can be produced
3. Cooperation	Mediocre or negative	The most positive
4. Responsibility	Personal responsible	Responsible for each other
5. Skills	random	Complementary
6. result	Personal products	Group results

Notes-from the above form, we can see that the advantages of the formation of teams over the traditional groups from six aspects.

Section three Types of teams

1. Problem-solving

This type of team focuses on solving problems. For example, they focus on how to improve product quality, increase production rate and improve work environment.

2. Self-managing

This type of team is usually form by 3 to 10 persons. The team members or the work achievements were connected with each other. Or they work on jobs that depend on each other.

Notes-the first type is the most common and basic one. The second type emphasize on the cooperation.

Section three Types of teams

3. Cross-functioning

This type of team is formed by employees from the same class but in different fields. They work for on project.

4. Network virtual teams

This type of team has scattered members connected through computer technology to realize the same goal.

Notes-in the third type, every member play multiple roles at the same time. The fourth type has only made its appearance recently.

Chapter II Formation of a team

Section one the meaning of formation of a team

Section two the channels of formation of a team

Section three behavior transition of a team

Section four phases in the development of a team

Notes-the chapter focus on the development of a team. Many team collapse before finishing its duties. What's reason? Please read the following analysis.

Section one the meaning of formation of a team

1. The features of an ideal talent

(1) Xing —Compatibility.

(2) Ge-strong physical build and easy-going character

(3) Qi-ambition, brilliance and luck

(4) Neng-capability of thinking, doing, speaking and writing

Notes-every boss likes such employees and he is look for such employees. Unfornately, in real life, they can never be found.

Section one the meaning of formation of a team

2. The division of real-life employees

(1) Type AB-good at management

(2) Type A-good at finance

(3) Type B-good at market

(4) Type O-good at being a boss

red cell antigen A

red cell antigen B

Notes-this is a talent formula summarized by the author from work. It emphasize that "there is no perfect gold, nor perfect talents", and it also explains that organization is most important in a efficient team.

Section one the meaning of formation of a team

2. The division of real-life employees

(1) Type O-good at being a boss. The O-type people are characterized as being predictive. They like to make plans in ahead and make use of the sources they have.

(2) Type A-good at finance. The A-type people are characterized as being cautious and sensitive to numbers. They have excellent at analyzing and want to do everything perfectly.

(3) Type B-good at market. The B-type people are characterized as being outgoing and passionate. They are energetic and impulsive. They like jobs of challenge.

(4) Type AB-good at management. The AB-type people are characterized as being cool and humble. They also stay neutral and have special viewpoint. They do their work rationally.

Notes-the four types of talents are specifically analyzed to provide managers with specific theoretical instruction.

Section one the meaning of formation of a team

3. The reasons to advocate on team

(1) The call from the times

(2) Requirement on oneself

4. Personal benefits from the team

(1) The work load is reduced

(2) The responsibility is shared

(3) The return and appreciation are shared

(4) The sense of self-value is enhanced

(5) All members could feel satisfied

Notes-here the reasons for the popularity of teams and the benefits brought to persons from teams are analyzed.

Section two the channels of formation of a team

1. Method of personal relations

Eric Berne had put forward that people have three sense states-Parent, Adult and Child. Meanwhile, he had created the analysis method of PAC.

2. Method of character definition

Belbin had introduced in 1981 that there are eight important characters in a team, which number later increased to nine.

Notes-the first theory means that people work together because of their personal relations. The second theory indicates that a perfect could be founded because the characters have been set.

Section two the channels of formation of a team

3. Method of value

West M. A put ward that there are five aspects to pay attention to achieve mutual understanding, which are the direction of the direction on team construction. They are separately motivated value, capability, mutual understanding and future potential.

4. Method of mission direction

Katzenbach & Smith emphasize that there are eight basic rules to construct an efficient team. Make plans according the emergency of the situation. Choose team members according to skills. Pay attention to the first assembly. Make some behavior principles. Have several emergent missions. Test new members with new information. Spend as much time together as possible. Acknowledge the result with compliment.

Notes-the third theory is that people would get together if they share same value. The fourth theory means that a team needs to be founded because missions have to be accomplished.

Section three behavior transition of a team

1. a group
2. a false team
3. a potential team
4. a true team
5. an efficient team

a team behavioral curve

team characteristic

job efficiency

Notes-when a team is first founded, it is not a true team. The team members need to adapt to each other to make an efficient team. This theory was introduced by Katzenbach and Smith in 1993.

Section four phases in the development of a team

1 the foundation period
2 the unrest period
3 the stabilized period
4 the high production period
5 the adjustment period

Notes-this theory was introduced by B. W. Tuckman and M. A. C. Jensen in 2001. It reveals that in the development of a team, it is hard go forward but easy to go back.

Section four Phases in the development of a team

1. Behavior feature of team members in the foundation period.
(1) excited and nervous
(2) high expectations, anxious, confused and insecure
(3) give themselves placement and to carefully try out their placement on others

2. Behavior feature of team members in the unrest period.
(1) find the reality different from their expectations
(2) tension arises between the members
(3) begin to complain about their leaders
(4) begin to feel frustrated and emotionally hit

Notes-here the classic behavior features of the team members during the foundation period and the unrest in the development

Section four Phases in the development of a team

3. Behavior feature of team members in the stabilized period.

(1) begin to trust and accept other members

(2) begin to focus on other matters

(3) skills get improved

(4) standard and routine will be built

4. Behavior feature of team members in the high production period

(1) become confident, have a good command of various techniques

(2) share their view and gained knowledge with each other

(3) have the sense of mission and honor

Notes —here the classic behavior features of the team members during the stabilized period and the high production in the development

Section four Phases in the development of a team

5. Behavior feature of team members in the adjustment period

(1) Team dismissed

(2) Team rested

(3) Team readjusted

Notes-here explains the direction of a team during the adjustment period in the development

Chapter Ⅲ   Leader of a team

Section one The styles of leaders

Section two The goal of teams

Section three The decisions of teams

Section four The conflict of teams

Section Five The communication of teams

Section Sxi The motivation of teams

Notes-when a team has been founded, how to make it develop healthily? How to achieve the team goals better? These are discussed in the following points.

Section one The styles of leaders

1. Two styles of leaders

(1) Care about business

(2) Care about people

2. The theory of leader styles

(1) The incapable style

(2) The caring style

(3) The mediocre style

(4) The duty-driven style

(5) The team-driven style

Notes-teams need leaders, however, leaders are usually taken in turns by members. Of course, not every team member could have the chance to become leaders.

Section one The styles of leaders

2. The theory of leader styles

(1) The incapable style-they care nothing about business or people, but only themselves.

(2) The caring style-they care nothing about business, but people. They are good at activating the atmosphere.

(3) The mediocre style-they care about both business and people. But they have low requirements and don't want to tire themselves.

(4) The duty-driven style-they want to achievements but not people. They don't care about the life or death of other people, and only want to increase the achievements.

(5) The team-driven style —they care both about production and people. They could bring high profits to the company and make employees feel satisfying.

Notes-here, the five types of leaders' management style are explained specifically.

Section two The goal of teams

1. The principle of making the team goal —SMART

(1) Specific

(2) Measurable

(3) Acceptable

(4) Realistic

(5) Timed

Notes-there are principles in making team goals.

Section two The goal of teams

2. Avoidance of traps of goals

(1) Don't set your goals too high.

(2) Don't underestimate your team.

(3) Don't use too many words.

(4) Let all team members know the goal.

Notes-after the team goals are made, the four details mentioned above are very important.

Section three The decisions of teams

1. Process of decision making

(1) Recognition of problems

(2) Set of the goals

(3) Draft of the plans

(4) Selection of plans

(5) Execution of plans

(6) Assessment of results

2. Methods of decision making

(1) Brain Storm

(2) Delphi

Notes-how to realize the goals once they are set? Here goes the decision making methods and results.

Section four The conflict of teams

1. Model of trust

(1) Trust based on psychology based on the intimidation, the trust is gained through the worries for punishment

(2) Trust based on knowledge based on the capability, the trust is gained through the professional performance

(3) Trust based on status based on the value, the trust is gained through the high status

Potential trust level

Three foundations of trust in a team

Notes-it's not easy to make others believe in oneself. Because it needs reasons. The model of trust discusses this problem specifically.

Section four The conflict of teams

2. Conflict management

(1) Problem-solving

(2) Avoiding

(3) Forcing

(4) Making recessions

（5）mediocre

decisive

cooperative

motivated by personal interest

motivated by the opposite's interest

Notes-it is said that trust starts from conflicts. If the conflicts are dealt with well, trust would begin.

Section Five The communication of teams

1. three principles of communication

（1）Emphasize on the importance of communication.

（2）Listen positively when communicating.

（3）Express opinions on business but not one people.

2. The theory of Communication Window

（1）Open zone

（2）Hidden zone

（3）Blind zone

（4）Unknown zone

Notes-in communication, people are afraid of unsuccessful communication the most. So, to understand others, one must understand himself. This was introduced by an American Psychologist JoeLufthe and HarryIngam in 1969. Joe-Harry window is short for the name of the theory.

Section Five The communication of teams

2. The theory of Communication Window

（1）Open zone-the information you and other people all know about. e. g. your name, sex, place of work.

（2）Blind zone-the information you don't know, about which others know. e. g. you weakness, week point and bad habits.

（3）Hidden zone-the information you know about, which others don't know. e. g. your privacy, conspiracy and secrets.

（4）Unknown zone-the information unknown to both yourself and other people. e. g. the unleashed news of you winning a prize or a promotion.

Notes-these are the four zones of Joe-Harry's theory.

Section Five The communication of teams

3. Application of communication window

(1) Open zone

A. Feature. If a person has a big open zone, he is a easygoing and good at relations. Such people could win others' trust.

B. Analysis. If one could make his open big, it means that he is balanced between speaking and asking. He pays attention to expressing and is good at looking for feedbacks.

C. Suggestion. To make the open zone bigger, one need to speak more and introduced oneself to others initiatively. He should ask more about the suggestion and feedback from other people, and try to understand and trust each other.

Notes-the above are the features and application of the open zone in Joe-Harry's Communication Window theory.

Section Five The communication of teams

3. Application of communication window

(2) Blind zone

A. Feature. If a person has a big blind zone, it means that he cares little about trifles and is exaggerating. People are annoyed by such people.

B. Analysis. If the blind zone is too big, it means that he speaks and asks too much without checking others' feedbacks.

C. Suggetion. To make the blind zone smaller, the Chinese ancients had a saying that goes, "One who knows himself is wise." By speaking too much, it would be easier for others to know about oneself. By asking too much, one can see his shaow in other people.

Notes —

Section Five The communication of teams

3. Application of communication window

(3) Hidden zone

A. Features. If a person has a big hidden zone, it means that he seals him off and is mysterious. Other people have low trust in him.

B. Analysis. If one has a big hidden zone, it means that he asks too much and speaks little. He is not good at speaking to others about his information, or is willing to do so.

C. Suggestion. To make the hidden zone smaller, one should expose his hidden zone when asking other people, avoiding other's protection against and dislike of him.

Notes —the above are the features and application of the hidden zone in Joe-Harry's Communication Window theory.

Section Five The communication of teams

4. Application of communication window

(4) Unknown zone

A. Features. If a person has a big unknown zone, it means that he has totally closed himself. People would care little about such people.

B. Analysis. If one has a big unknown zone, it means that he doesn't ask others about their understanding of himself, nor would he introduce himself to others initiatively.

C. Suggestion. To make the unknown zone smaller, one should let others know about himself by introducing himself, and tell them about his personality, specialty in order to be eliminated from soeity.

Notes —the above are the features and application of the unknown zone in Joe-Harry's Communication Window theory.

Section Sxi The motivation of teams

1. The reasons that motivate the team morale.

(1) The acceptance of the team goal

(2) The distribution of the interest

(3) The harmony inside the team

(4) The transportation of information

Notes-here the specific reasons that affect team morale are analyzed.

Section Sxi The motivation of teams

2. The cohesiveness of a team

(1) The similarities between team members

(2) The scale of the team

(3) The influence from team members

(4) The progress of the team's success

(5) The appropriate difficulty of challenge

(6) Competition and challenge from the outside

Notes-the cohesiveness is the pre-condition of increased team morale.

Chapter Ⅳ   Team Spirit

Section one A general introduction of team spirit

Section two The roles of the team members

Section three The cooperation between team members

Notes-In this chapter, the forming of the team spirit is introduced. How should team members go along and work with each other? Is there any good suggestion or method? Please read the following part.

Section one A general introduction of team spirit

1. The concept of team spirit

Team spirit is the mutual centered thoughts and state of mind shared by a group of people.

2. The content of team spirit

(1) The cohesiveness

(2) The awareness of team cooperation

(3) The high team morale

Notes-here, the generous description about the definition and content of team spirit are given.

Section one A general introduction of team spirit

3. Attitude of team members

(1) They share the same value and goal.

(2) They fight for a result without sparing any effort.

(3) One's contribution can't be replaced by another one's.

Notes-attitude is altitude. Horizons make boundaries. Attitude is very important.

Section two The roles of the team members

1. Concept of role

(1) Role perception. In a certain circumstance, you know how to perform. Meanwhile, the perception and understanding of the performance.

(2) Role recognition. After understanding the role you are performing, you need to keep your attitude balanced with your behavior.

(3) Role expectation. How others think you should perform your role, meaning others expectation on you.

(4) Role conflict. You are performing one role, and you realize that you are not suitable for this role.

Notes-this is excellent theory on roles. The conflicts always lie in the conflicts between roles. It was introduced by Steven P. Robins.

Section two The roles of the team members

2. Types of roles

The Belbin Nine Team Roles

Types content	features
(1) The messenger	outgoing , sensitive, curious, good at social
(2) The inventor	Creative, have many ideas, being oneself
(3) The specialist	Narcissistic, maintain a standard, inward going
(4) The doer	Loyal, serious at work, obey rules
(5) The promoter	Challenge others, passionate, strong in reaction
(6) The coordinator	Emotionally stable, trust worthy, fair to people
(7) The inspector	Calm headed, picky, critical
(8) The perfectionist	Bury one's head into work, responsible, pursue the perfection
(9) The "glue"	Mild, accept of advice, highly cooperative

Notes-how many roles should an ideal team have? Dr. Belbin from Cambrige has explained that there are nine different roles in a team.

Section two The roles of the team members

2. Roles of team members

(1) The messenger. People of such kind are very sensitive to the outside world. They are curious about everything, and are aware of the changes in the outside; they don't like to stay home, and play outside; they are born with talent to communicate. They are outgoing, passionate. They like to have parties and make friends.

(2) The inventor. People of such kind have new concepts, wild thought and rich imagination. They are impulsive. Their thoughts are always extreme and unrealistic. They don't like to be restrained, nor are they punctilious. They are not punctual and obeying. They are not good at dealing with people. Other people would see them as sick and freaks.

Notes-the above are the specific analysis on the messenger and the inventor.

Section two The roles of the team members

2. Roles of team members

(3) The specialist. People of such kind are authorities in a certain field. They are smug and narcissistic. They love their careers and are proud of their specialties. Their job is to maintain a standard, avoiding it to be decreased.

(4) The doer. People of such kind work their fingers to the bone. They believe that hard work would pay off. They are good at planning, principles and self-controlling. They are loyal and sacrifice their personal interests for the companies'. They are tireless and see responsibility as the priority.

Notes-the above are the specific analysis on the specialist and the doer.

Section two The roles of the team members

2. Roles of team members

(5) The promoter. People of such kind are purpose-driven. They are efficient at work. They are highly passionate with their work and feel strong sense of satisfaction. They believe that solutions are more than questions. They find solutions for the goal and find excuses for the failure. They are outgoing and like to challenge and argue with others. They are usually self-centered and can't understand each other. Their reactions on setbacks and difficulties are strong. They don't like to be thrown white blanket on their enthusiasm.

(6) The coordinator. People of such kind are charming and can guide a group of people with different skills and personalities to a same goal. They look mature, confident and reliable. They are subjective and have no prejudice. They can find everybody's advantage during inter-personal communication, and make use of them during the pursuit of the goal. They have good self-control ability and can stay calm. They are hardly emotional and merely lose their temper.

Notes-the above are the specific analysis on the promoter and the coodinator.

Section two The roles of the team members

2. Roles of team members

(7) The inspector. People of such kind are cold-blooded. They are serious and rarely smile. They lack the emotional cells, so they hardly praise their subordinates. This does not necessarily mean his disapprove of them. They are hardly emotional, and they like to keep distance from other people. They don't act on a moment of heat in the head, nor are they easily excited. They like to look for the errors with a strong sense of critics.

Notes-the above are the specific analysis on the inspector

Section two The roles of the team members

2. Roles of team members

(8) The perfectionist. People of such kind pay great attention to details, and pursue perfection and prominence. They are determined that there is no best but better. They can be initiative and self-motivated on work without the stimulations from the outside. They never fight the war they are uncertain of. They have high standard on work and on their subordinates. Whoever works with them would be tired to death.

Notes-the above are the specific analysis on the perfectionist.

Section two The roles of the team members

2. Roles of team members

(9) The "glue". People of suck kind are refined and cultivated. They are good at deal-

ing with people. They are understanding. They care about, understand, sympathize, and support others. They deal with matters flexibly. They could always blend themselves into groups. They can adapt themselves into other people's thoughts and ideas, and the surroundings. They would not give opinions that are against other people. They are cooperative and believe in the important of peace. They care about anybody's suggestions, and the influence of his behavior on other people.

Notes-the above are the specific analysis on the "glue".

Section two The roles of the team members

3. Order of the roles

(1) The messenger offers the latest information.

(2) The inventor put forward his new thoughts.

(3) The specialist offers technology support.

(4) The doer starts to make plans.

(5) The promoter wants to execute the plans.

(6) The coordinator wants to choose the right person.

(7) The inspector starts to throw the white blanket.

(8) The perfectionist picks on the problems. The glue smoothen the members.

Notes-the above are the order of the nine roles.

Section Section three The cooperation between team members

1. Relations between team members

(1) $1 + 1 > 2$ Team members share mutual appreciation, mutual trust, mutual understanding and mutual cooperation. (cooperative relationship in the mature period)

(2) $1 + 1 = 2$ Team members share mutual respect, mutual exploration, and mutual adaption. The relationship is not deep. (cooperative relationship in the early period)

(3) $2 > 1 + 1 > 0$ Team members share mutual suspicions, mutual restriction and guard against each other. (competitive relationship in the early period)

Notes-after analysis on the relations between team members, there came 5 cooperation results. The first one is the best. The second one is what every team has to go through.

Section Section three The cooperation between team members

1. Relations between team members

(4) $1 + 1 = 0$ Team members expose and have a grudge against each other. (competitive relationship in the mature period)

(5) $1 + 1 < 0$ Team members exclude and fight with each other. (dog-eat-dog relationship)

Notes-if team members have the above two relations, it means the two of them are against each other.

Section Section three The cooperation between team members

2. Cooperation means of team members

(1) To play Go. Consider the overall picture, and sacrifice some pieces for the whole.

(2) To play bridge. Cooperate with the opposite to fight fiercely with another two rivals.

(3) To play Majiang. Fight alone, and watch over the previous player and the next player.

Notes-according to three different entertainments, there are different ways for cooperation between people.

Section Section three The cooperation between team members

3. Two results of cooperation

(1) "Two heads are better than one. "

(2) "Everybody's business is nobody's business. "

4. Enlightenment from classic teams

(1) The tragedy of the Shuihu Team

(2) The triumph of the West-journey Team

Company Director Tang Seng

CEO Sun Wukong

HR manager Zhu Bajie

Logistic manager Sha Seng

Notes-based on two of the four classical Chinese literature, here are two different teams and their development. In the West-journey team, everybody has shortcomings, but they have succeeded. In the Shuihu team, everybody is outstanding, however, they ends up in failure. This proves the importance of team goal.

Section Section three The cooperation between team members

5. Cultivating the cooperation ability

(1) Look for others' positive qualities

(2) Trust and put hope in others

(3) Check on the shortcomings of one's own

(4) Try efforts to gain support from others

(5) Stay humble forever

Notes-you have to recognize the opposite so that he could recognize you. This is the precondition for cultivating the cooperation ability.

Chapter V   Team promotion

Section one Team culture

Section two Leaning teams

Notes-in this chapter, it emphasize that a team could depend it permanency on culture. The learning teams have the strongest vitality.

Section one Team culture

1. Introduction to team culture

(1) Introduction to team culture

It is a meaning shared system by all the team members. It makes the organization special and different from other teams

Notes-first, here is a definition of team culture.

Section one Team culture

1. Introduction to team culture

(2) The iceberg model of team culture

Stories and legendaries

Ceremonies and celebrations

Language

Symbols

Symbols

Language

Ceremonies and celebrations

Stories and legendaries

Faith

Value

Presumption

Notes-this is the iceberg model of team culture. It tells us that the foundations of culture are presumption, faith and value.

Section one Team culture

2. The effect of team culture

(1) Orientation

(2) Rule

(3) Cohesiveness

(4) Coordination

(5) Education

(6) Encouragement

(7) Radiation

(8) Stability

Notes-here introduced are the effects of team culture

Section two Leaning teams

1. Model of learning ability

(1) Motivation-goal

(2) Persistence-will

(3) Ability-knowledge and practice

model of learning ability

ability goal will Learning

could learn can be learned should be learned

Notes-this is a model of learning ability which shows that there are three dimensions in learning, motivation, persistence and ability.

Section two Leaning teams

2. Model of team learning motivation

(1) Gradual study

(2) Sudden understanding

(3) Nirvana

(4) Reborn

team power personal behavior future prospect

Notes-this is a model of team learning ability summarized by the author. There are two kinds of personal behabior, gradual study and sudden understanding. There are also two kinds of team power, nirvana and reborn.

Thank you!

Notes-that's the end of Team Management.

Appendix II Answers to application questions

You must be eager to know the answers to the application questions in the text. The most wonderful always comes last. We'll reveal the answers in this part.

Chapter I   A Reverie Team

I . Is he an ideal partner?

In his first experience of entrepreneur, Hun Hun had some disagreement with his business partner and then left the team.

One day, Hun Hun met a friend on the Internet, who was 40 years old and was just back from abroad. Hun Hun was feeling depressed and wanted someone to talk to, so he started chatting with him. The more they chatted, they more common interests they found they had. Then, Hun Hun talked to this "Hai Gui" (a person back from abroad with educational or work experience) about his idea.

Hun hun said, "I want to make knockoff laptops. What do you think about this idea?"

Hai Gui said, "Good! We can form a partnership. I have the business platform. "

Hun Hun asked, "Do you?"

Hai Gui answered, "Hehe! I am the Chief Consultant for Beijing University Students Entrepreneur Alliance, which I could use as a platform to promote the knockoff laptops. In the meantime, we could do OEM and make our own brand. If we make use of this platform and promote our product in universities in Beijing successful, we can copy this model to other big cities around the country. "

Hun Hun kept asking, "Do you have control over this platform?"

Hai Gui responded, "Of course. We can also promote related marketing on own laptops and gain profits from advertisement. "

According to the above chatting records, would you work with Hai Gui if you were Hun Hun? Please specify your reason!

Answer.

There were two problems involved in this question. First, he needed to choose the right entrepreneurial partner. Second, he needed to choose the right entrepreneurial project.

Let's talk about the how to find an entrepreneurial partner? There is a saying goes like, "In the entrepreneurship, the most dangerous is not a project, but the partner. " A rival like a wolf is nothing to be afraid of, but a team partner like a pig can be frightening. So, choosing the right person is the precondition to do the right thing.

There are several ways to meet entrepreneurial partners. First, they can be found from human relations. For example, they can be found from your relatives, places, and occasional relations. Secondly, they can be found from role placement. Such relations are usually formed in the unit organizations. Thirdly, they can be found through mutual value. Such relation can be helpful to the stability of a team. Fourthly, they can be found through assignments, which happen in companies or groups.

Now let's look back at the meeting of Hun Hun and Hai GUI. It's hard to find out that their entrepreneurial partnership was formed through occasional relations. Of course, they shared mutual value so they felt more and more approving of each other during the talks. However, when choosing a partner, there are three principles needed to be taken into consideration-skill complementary, mutual goal and responsibility for each other. Thus, Hun Hun and Hai Gui could only divide their job like this-Hun Hun was responsible for product development and Hai Gui marketing. Hun Hun was in charge of market expansion, but as to the possibility of Hai Gui in charge of product development, it was really small. Because Hai Gui had already said that he could find platforms for the promotion.

Now that the job division is done, we could analyze whether their promotions was executable according to their conversation. Hai Gui said that knockoff laptops could be produced in OEM, and promoted on university campuses. Then they could find distributors to sell them nationwide. At the same time, they wanted to do related sales on their knockoff laptops and charge for advertisements.

The last sentence sounds unreasonable. From that, we can see that Hai Gui's mind wasn't on the knockoff laptops, so, they didn't share the mutual goal from the beginning.

Besides, let's talk about the future prospect of knockoff laptops. Why did knockoff laptops get so much attention from the industry? This obviously was related to the market demands. The popularity of Internet had promoted the consumption of PCs. Many student and families hoped to use laptops for study and surfing the Internet. But they didn't have high requirements on the performance of them. Any laptops that could function would be OK. And they also demanded that the price was low. Therefore, these customers were in need of ULPCs. Accordingly, before Intel had launched the Atom Processor, the most positive prediction on the global sales volume of ULPCs was 5 million. But the actual sales volume had surpassed the prediction of Intel.

However, the reality was that many customers came to ask about knockoff laptops, only a few of whom would actually buy one. Customers were happy but worried about knockoff laptops even though they could offer one-year quality guarantee. Under this circumstance, Intel had followed and launched cheaper CPU, wiping out the 200 RMB profit of a knockoff laptop.

Therefore, this was still an immature market. Zong Qinghou produced the nutrient drink of Wahaha for children in those years, and he had once said, "Rush into the market, make money and get out of it in ahead before it gets regulated." This saying fit Hun Hun's project.

In all, this was not a long-term market. Hun Hun and Hai Gui were not perfect partners.

Ⅱ. Who would you choose?

In the end of 1997, a time when the stock market was flourishing, the author was approached by an inspector from a securities company in Shenzhen. They requested me to design a paper test for a job interview. They specifically requested-

3. They are interviewing for the position of a Customer Manager, which required the reading ability equalling to a high-school graduate.

4. This should be a test of the interviewee's awareness on investment. And it should allow interviewees to give different answers based on their different awareness.

That evening, the author sent an email to the inspector including the test and key to the test. It read like this,

Test

One brought 100 RMB to a Shiduo shop. He bought a commodity at 25 RMB, which had a prime cost of 20 RMB. The shop owner didn't have enough change, so he took the 100 RMB to the shop next door to make some change.

Half an hour later, the shop owner from next door came and said the note was a counterfeit one. The shop owner had to give him another 100 RMB note.

How much had the shop owner lost? Please give a specific answer.

Choices for the answer

D. 195 RMB

E. 95 RMB

F. 100 RMB

The next day, the inspector had over 70 test papers return during the first round of the interview. But the answers varied from one another, and were beyond the choices given-there were answers like 225, 205, 200, 195, 100, 95⋯ Some interviewees even wrote answers that read, "The answer is however much you think he had lost."

The author didn't specify the reasons for the three choices. The inspector was totally confused by all the answers he had got.

If you were the inspector, what would you think of the efficiency and credibility of this test? If you approved of this test, which answer would you choose? Please tell me your reason.

Answer

There was limitation on the test-to test on the readers' reading ability of high school graduates and their investment awareness. So, there was two knowledge points designed in the test-a fake note and cost.

If the interviewee chose the A type answer, e. g. 225 RMB, 200 RMB, and 195 RMB, it means that he was fooled by the fake note. Actually, the one-hundred-RMB note was still the note wherever it had been. It couldn't turn into 200 RMB, or 300 RMB. Besides, some interviewees might think like this, "In such a test, the bigger the number of the answer is, the more possible that it is the answer." So, some people chose 225 RMB. In fact, the fake note was used to test if a client manager's head was still clear after rounds of capital transferring.

In addition, the condition of the cost of 20 RMB was added into the test. Here, it was designed to test if a client manager has the sense of opportunity cost when he is making investment suggestions to their clients. Thus, the expected answer was 100 RMB-100-(25-20) + (25-20) =100 RMB.

Of course, from the angle of mathematics, the standard answer is 95 RMB. However, in most interview tests produced by HR managers, the tests were more of logical thinking than mathematical ability. So, if you ever run into such test, think more from the philosophical angle rather than the mathematical one.

Chapter Ⅱ   Enterprising and Financing

Ⅰ. Should I enter the market of cactus drinks?

In the afternoon of 19th January, 2009, a former colleague of mine flew from Hainan to Shenzhen to discuss something with me.

At eight o'clock, we met in the North Huaqiang Shangdao Café.

"Zhang Chao, it's been six years. You must be doing pretty good, aren't you?" I said directly.

"Heihei! My former leader, honestly, I'm doing so so. I have at present opened a beverage factory in Hainan, which is specialized in producing cactus drinks."

"Cactus juice? This is new to me!" I was quite surprised.

"Yes, I wanted to take the road nobody else dared to take. You know that in the market of mineral water, there are Robust and Nongfu Spring; in the market of tea beverage, there are Uni-president and Master Kong; in the market of soda, there are Coca Cola and Pepsi; in the market of herbal tea, there are Wanglaoji and Guangdong Herbal Tea; in the market of energy drinks, there are Red Bull and Jianlibao… There is currently no famous brand in the market of cactus drinks."

"That' a good idea! But, I wonder what the market positioning of the product is. That's to say, what's your appeal to the customers?"

"We have a great product with a special taste and delicate fragrance. It's good for your skin and stomach. It helps to diminish inflammation, to reduce blood sugar and to reduce blood fat. If well promoted, this product will have a prominent future in the market."

"Yes. I've meant to mention the promotion-why would customers want to drink this?

You should know that this is a new product. There are already similar products in the current market. But no company could really build up this market. " I said seriously.

"So, I came to you! Would you please join our team? We'll give you the job position of Market Inspector if you are willing to join our team. "

"Would you be willing to burn money on the advertisement?"

"Our boss is a billionaire and is confident in this product. He is a local resident in Hainan, and had contracted thousands of mu's land to grow cactus. "

......

According to the above conversation, do you think there is a prominent market for his cactus drinks? If there is one, then how to construct the selling-point of this product?

Answer

Actually, there had been people doing this business, but they couldn't work it out. Many manufacturers had introduced the Opuntia Milpa Alta, an eatable cactus from Mexico, and researched successfully drinks out of it. On their advertisements, they read, "This drink is made out of cactus juice, and maintains the trace elements, amino acid, vitamin, calcium, and flavonoids of the cactus juice. The calcium contained in cactus pills is three times of that in milk. Therefore, the ordinary fruit juice is nothing compared to the nutrition in the cactus beverage and its health-care function. It is also times better than milk in terms of calcium. "

The above paragraph was the selling point of their beverage. But, is this selling point aimed for the empty spot in the market? It needs to be discussed further. According to specialist, cactus has many functions. Cactus juice can improve metabolism and immunity, it can also provide medical function for gastritis, colitis, diabetes mellitus, hyperlipidemia, high blood pressure, gallstones and urinary stone. But, among so many functions, which should we choose as the function to promote? Must the product positioned as a function drink? Currently, there are manufacturers who think that cactus is anti-radiation. Faced with so many selling points, we could understand why the cactus drinks haven't been made popular yet. There were so many selling points that the customers didn't know what to choose and who to believe.

Looking back at when Jiaduobao Group were promoting their green tea drinks, they chose "extraction from the tea leaves" as the selling point. They spent dozens of millions on the advertisement, only to gain the sales of ten or twenty million RMB, so that had to close this business. Later, the cold tea market was fingered by Jiaduobao. It rent the brand of Wanglaoji from Guangdong Pharmaceutical Company and became to produce cold tea drinks. This time, they hired a special consultation company to make the promotion for them. The company thought that the product of Wanglaoji shouldn't be position on the concept of clearing heat. If so, the target would be small, after all, this was a publicized product. They should position their selling point on "Drink Wanglaoji if you are afraid of excessive internal heat." Thus, a drink with prevention function was born. Wanglaoji has been popular ever since. In 2008, its sales volume was 12 billion RMB, surpassing Coca Cola and becoming the number one in the industry.

According to Wanglaoji's successful experience, let's have discussion on the market positioning of the cactus, that's to say, the selling point of this product.

If we position the cactus as a product that can prevent gastritis, stones and high blood pressure, it would be inappropriate. Because in many customers' mind, there is not such function and they couldn't accept that. The market would be small even if customers could accept the concept from the boom advertisements. So, we need to start from the aspects that customers are familiar with. For example, everybody knows that cactus is drought resistance, and has a strong life.

Why do we start from here? Because this could be the trigger of a booming market. We would wonder why a cactus could survive such harsh environment. It is because of a substance in its body-Cactin, which could balance the metabolism to sustain the healthy growth of the cactus. Meanwhile, the substance is good for human body. It could improve the internal environment of human body, balancing the body liquid. Thus, we have found the selling point of cactus drinks. And the functions of prevention against high cholesterol and high blood pressure were derived from here.

II. How much share should an one-hundred-million RMB investment take up?

I have a friend from Chaozhou who had fought for his business in Shenzhen for twenty years, owning eight inns. The current situation is that he invests around 5 million RMB in each inn every year. And 7 inns are profiting, earning 200 to 300 thousand RMB per month. The seventh one was opened one year ago and is still in a deficit, losing 4 to 5 thousand RMB each month.

This friend began to have some ideas when he saw the chain hotels are developing rapidly in these years. He hired a management consultation company to give his inns a unified name. He had also spent 150 thousand RMB on a VI brochure.

Soon, a venture investor had an eye on his company, offering 100 million RMB to hold 70% of the share.

The question is-is the percentage of shares reasonable? If not, then what do you think the percentage should be?

Answer

Here involves the question that venture investor would perform evaluation on the target companies. How much did this company worth? First, let's look at the financial report. If it was a listed company, this report would be accurate. If it was not a listed company, the financial management might be messy, so the investors would restore the report.

According to the summarize of Dr. Slite, there are seven deceitful tricks, including the prerecording of the incomes, recording of the incomes with problem, recording of false income, putting forward or afterward the current expense, transferring the current incomes to the future, transferring the future incomes as the special expense to the current.

After the restoration of the company's capital, we could use the following methods to perform evaluations on them.

Method 1 —Value basis, which means the net assets on the account and general checkup on assets. This method is subjective, but, enterprises who wanted venture investment wouldn't accept this method. So, we'll have to consider other methods.

Method 2—parameter estimation. In this method, replacement cost method and P/E estimation method are commonly used methods. But, the most commonly used method is P/E estimation method, in which the reference value is multiplied by a number to gain the value of the company.

For example, if a counterpart company has been listed. We set its P/E as the reference, now the target company has net profits 10 times than that of the listed company. Thus, the target company can be evaluated 10 times of this listed company. However, there is a weak point in this method-what if there no listed company in the same industry? The P/E of the counterpart company would have to be replaced by P/E estimated by experience.

Apart from the two methods mentioned above, there are the discounted cash flow and venture capital pricing. However, these methods could be only taken as references. In real life, there is Valuation Adjustment Mechanism.

Now, let's look back at the application test, the Chaozhou person had already invest 40 million RMB in (500 * 8 =4000). Without counting the profits in, if the venture investor put in 100 million RMB, he would take up 71% (1/1.4), which is slightly more than he wanted to take up (70%). But, this was unreasonable. After all, venture investors were not the shareholders.

To explain this, we could take Ctrip's financing experience as a reference. Ctrip had the initial capital of one million RMB. During the first round of financing of half a million USD, the investor IDG took up only 20% of the shares. During the second round of financing of 4.5 million USD, the five venture banks including Softbank took up only 30% of the shares. During the third round of financing of 8 million USD, the investor Carlyle took up only 30% of the shares. From this example, we can see that, there are several rounds of financing of an enterprise. The later an investor come, the more money he would invest in, and the less percentage he would take up.

To draw a conclusion, the Chaozhou person wanted to receive the 100 million RMB private fund, and if the percentage was between 20% and 30%, it would be acceptable. If the percentage was too high, it would do no good to the enterprise's growth. Because after all, this was the first time to receive investment capital.

Chapter Ⅲ   Transformation and Purchase
Ⅰ. Which one should be the leading product?

Zhang Jun, from Chaozhou, had been in Shenzhen since 1985, running a store selling daily necessaries. After years of struggling, he had opened eight chain stores inside the pass. He wanted to expand his business outside the pass in 2009.

Zhang Jun knew very clear that the business of supermarkets depend on fast consuming products. Consumers had big demand of such products, and buy them often. Such products were easy to purchase. Beverages, in particular, took up a large percentage in the sales volume of the stores.

However, there was a disadvantage of selling beverages-the limited gross profit. So, Zhang Jun had decided t made his own "delicious" brand to save the cost. He found a factory to produce his products, which he could sell through his own channels.

The series of beverages included the following five categories-

6. Tea beverages-green tea, jasmine flower tea, ice black tea, and so on.

7. Cold tea beverages-heat-clearing tea, diet-tea, and so on.

8. Soybean milk beverages-black soybean milk, chocolate soybean milk, coconut soybean milk, and so on.

9. Syrup beverages-wheat syrup, corn pumpkin syrup, red bean syrup, and so on.

10. Juice beverages-orange juice, grape juice, lemon juice, vegetable juice, and so on.

Now, Zhang Jun wanted to choose one category as the priority of his product promotion. If you were his friend, which category would you suggest him to choose as the leading product? Please elaborate combining the current market demands.

Answer

Strategically, Zhang Jun had chosen the backward integration, which meant that the distributor extended towards the upper stream of the industry chain to the fields of the suppliers'.

But, from the present situation, it would not work out if Zhang Jun wanted to expand his own brand using only his own channels, and without other promotions. The born of a brand depends on the large sum of money spent on advertisements. With the ability and will to do so, his purpose should not be "making the situation", but "by the situation". He should manufacture whatever sold well at that time. Thus, when the companies were having the "chicken", he could at least enjoy the "chicken innards" or "chicken soup". Then, a-mong the five categories of products, which kind of drinks would be the most popular drinks recently? Now, let's have a specific analysis.

Let's start with the history of beverage.

In China, the earliest popular drinks were carbonated beverage, especially the Coca Co-la and Pepsi from America. Coca Cola was good at telling stories. It was said that it was o-riginally a granule on cold. Through an unintentional mistake, the pharmacist made the cold medicine into a drink. But, the formula of Coca Cola never went public. It was hidden in the basement and locked by 13 parent keys. Only by the appearance of all the 13 people, could they obtain the formula. If a lie is repeated over one thousand times, it becomes a truth. Therefore, Coca Cola has been popular for over 100 years with this story.

In the late 1990, the market was taken by mineral water. I remember that the series ad-vertisements of Jingtian water were everywhere, especially on the Dongmen Walking Street in Shenzhen, on which advertisements cost a lot. The advertisements of Jingtian were hang-ing on the lamps on both sides of the street, including Jingtian mineral water, Jingtian puri-fied water, Jingtian space water and Jingtian super purified water … there only lacked the Jingtian tap water. Later, the green tea from Taiwan entered the market of China Mainland. Through years of fighting, Chef Kang and Uni-president got their feet steady in China. Lat-er, Jiaduobao had also invented a green tea beverage, saying that they use the low-tempera-ture extraction to produce the drink. In the end, it ended with failure and was forced to de-velop new products-Wanglaoji. This also proves that one mountain can't bear two tigers, unless of one them is female and the other one male. It is safe to say that after fierce compe-tition, only one or two could survive among the drinks of the same kind.

At this time, the market of juice was activated. In those years, Huiyuan Juice and Mr. Juice could be seen everywhere. As to function drinks, there were Red Bull and others mak-ing their appearance at the approximately the same time. At the same time, there were soy bean milk drinks and milk drinks.

After Huiyuan promoted the juice drinks, the demand of the market had pushed many factories into this industry. Carbonated drinks were restricted to children in America, so Co-ca Cola started to promote the brand of Meizhiyuan and its first juice drink Guolicheng. Next, Pepsi had also launched Guobinfen serial products.

The juice of Guolicheng could be seen by bear eyes, so it had run far ahead of Huiyuan juice, who was the leader in the juice drinks. In 2008, Coca Cola had almost purchased Huiyuan. By the way, juice milk went into people's eyes around this time.

Before too long, Guolicheng had taken half of the market of orange juice. Therefore, Pepsi just woke up and invented Chunguole almost overnight. Currently, Chunguole is sell-ing well. Besides, Meizhiyuan has developed four products. And Meizhiyuan C lemon is selling pretty well.

In conlusion, it is not hard to see that the green tea market had already been taken by Chef Kang and Uni-president. The market of syrup couldn't be enlarged. That's to say, the best choice for Zhang Jun was the juice market, specially the lemon juice, which was more prospective. If he had to take the seasonal problem into consideration, he could chose soy bean milk as a backup plan.

II. How to build the selling-point of the goat milk?

On 8th December 2008, the author received a call my high school mate Li Jun. He said that he had transferred into the fast consuming product market to sell goat milk (liquid milk). He asked for my suggestion. The following are my conversation with him.

Assistant, "Let's first talk about the reason for you to enter this market. "

Mr. Li, "The 'Melamine Milk Event' has made people change their face when talking about milk. The cow milk market is in existence, though there has been slight shrinkage. There is an urgent need for products to replace milk because people can't give up on breakfast because of this event. Personally, I think this is a market opportunity for goat milk before the cow milk market gets back to its life. "

Assistant, "Well, how is the quality your milk source and product?"

Mr. Li, "I have found an available factory to do the contract manufacturing for me. "

Assistant, "As far as I know, there are already some people in this business. But, they couldn't enlarge the market, which may be because of the technology limitation on eliminating the smell. "

Mr. Li, "Don't worry about it. The factory I found has the top technology. "

Assistant, "Is your product registered? Are you planning on advertising on TV?"

Mr. Li, "The trademark has been settled. We are not planning on making advertisement. Instead, we would do promotion of free tasting at the gate of supermarket. "

Assistant, "How many people are you working with?"

Mr. Li, "I have myself, my wife, a former cow milk promoter in a mall, my second brother, who knows people in the goat farm, my elder brother-in-law, who can drive, and a couple of other assistants. "

Assistant, "I don't know about the others, but I know that you used to sell feminine hygiene wash. . . "

According to the telephone record above, do you think that Mr. Li could have this market? And what's your reason? If you were a market inspector, how would you operate?

Answer

For a new product, there eight steps in its development and they are finding of creation, selection of creation, formation of product concept, planning of sales strategy, commercial analysis, product research and development, trial sales, and scaled production. Actually, a-mong the eight steps, the most important are the formation of the concept and market analysis. The following are a few key points.

1. Formation of the concept

According to the research result, most people never drank any goat milk. The reason was that some people thought that goat milk had the smell of mutton, which was not good. Some others thought that milk contained high quality nutrition and that they were used to milk so they didn't want to try on goat milk.

In fact, it is very hard to change customer's habits. A market needs long-time cultivation and caring. Once, a brand of instant noodle wanted to enter the Taiwan market, but couldn't get the market open. So, he had to send the instant noodle to children in the kindergarten. Those children were growing teeth and thought the instant noodle was delicious. Thus, he had finally made it to market. The owner of the company later said to the journalist, "In China, football needs to be trained from children, and the market needs to found from children too."

Now let's turn back to the analysis on goat milk. To give a concept to this product, we need to start from the empty points of nutrition without breaking the basic theory of Nutriology. So we have to hit the lining balls. From the Western Medication's angle, cow milk is better than goat milk because of the smaller molecular which can be more easily absorbed. But, from the Chinese Medication's angle, in terms of nutrition, goat milk contains more nutrition than cow milk because goat milk is mild and provides more nutrition.

In conclusion, the concept and selling point must be obtained from the Chinese medication. And the trademark could be a name like "Happy Goat".

2. Specific division of market

With the concept formed, now let's start with the specific division of market.

There are many standards to divide markets specifically, geology factor, population factor, psychology factor and behavior factor, to name a few. Here, we use age as a division standard in the population factor. We have three age-gaps as our target group to select from.

First, in China, the populations are aging, and the number of senior citizens multiplies every year. In the meantime, most of the aged citizens in the cities have stable income and save-ups. They have strong sense in health care, thus they provide infinite business opportunities to manufacturers. But, if the aged people are set as the target market, there will be difficulties in the promotion because they are usually less accepting to new things. However, otherwise, this is also an opportunity because once we are accepted by them, they'll show high loyalty to us.

Secondly, goat milk could be the best substitute for infants' milk product. More and more mothers are reluctant to feed their infants because they want to keep their figures or for other reasons, which bring a big market for goat milk as long as the product and technology are reliable. The goat milk would definitely win the trust from those young mothers.

Thirdly, teenagers are better customers of goat milk. They are accepting of new things and are the main body of consumption. However, they are picky on flavors, which can cause a big problem on the promotion of goat milk. Rational persuasion can hardly win the recognition from teenage consumers. Emotional persuasion can't immediately tell the goat milk from cow milk and other drinks.

At this urgent moment, "the Melamine Incident" had done goat milk a great help. So, the author thinks that teenagers are the best choice as the target group. The following is the analysis on the strategy of advertising.

3. Strategy of advertising

First, I'd like to interrupt with my persuasion to Li Jun.

I am very close to Li Jun, so I would speak my mind to him normally. Therefore, I said to Li Jun like this, "If you can make it in the goat milk market, I'll go sell pigs immediately."

As expected, Li Jun quitted very soon. He was confused and kept asking me the reason.

Actually, the four major combinations of sales, the four marketing methods of personal marketing, publicity, advertisement and improvement on marketing, function like this. The founding of a brand needs advertisements to open the road, which is followed by personal marketing. It is like a tank running in the front to drop booms while the foot soldiers are in the back to gain the battle field. Now, the following are the relative details of advertisement.

(1) The target of the advertisement

Mainly housewives and teenagers.

(2) The purpose of the advertisement

Persuasion and reminding —Safety is the most important thing. Explain from the medication's point of view that melamine can't added in goat milk. And in the meanwhile, analyze that people have been misunderstanding goat milk for so many years because goat milk is the perfect diary source apart from human milk.

Choice of media —TV commercials are the best choice, and roadside board and new paper advertisement can be taken into consideration.

(3) The expression of the topic of the advertisement

Have a person from Xinjiang be the representative because they all grow up drinking goat milk. Once the Xinjiang person shouts out loud on the TV, "I, Maimaiti, grew up drinking goat milk." The advertisement would cause the desire to shop for goat milk among housewives.

(4) The delivery of the advertisement

The advertisements should be delivered densely between short intervals. Only by doing so, could the power be created, and leave no chance for other substitutes (soy bean and syrup drinks).

Of course, these would all cost much. Someone once said, "If you broadcast your commercials on CCTV with the expense lower than 16 million RMB, they would end in vain." So, goat milk is market hard to initiate and Li Jun could consider doing commercials on local TVs.

In addition, why did Li Jun's free hand-outs ended in failure? It was because during the introduction period, advertisements could bring the most obvious effect than improvement on marketing among the four methods.

Chapter Ⅳ   Growth by leaps and bounds

Ⅰ. Where and how to hand them out?

Wang Yong was a technician in a famous foreign cosmetics company, who had been researching on skin-care products. Through 10 years of efforts, he had finally developed a product which could remove freckles.

The documents for cosmetics could be easily applied for. So, after ODM, Wang Yong's freckle-removing product was put on the market. He didn't spend too much money on the advertisements, and he was confident with his product. Therefore, he decided to promote his product by handing out free samples.

Now, if you were his Product Manager, would you agree with his promotion strategy? If you do, where and how would you hand out the free samples?

Answer

Somebody said that during the starting of the entrepreneurship, one would always need moeny. This is quite true. Ji Qi had also said that an entrepreneur should make do with what's available and cook with whatever there is in the basket. So, many entrepreneurs spend one penny like two.

In this case, Wang Yong is a classical case. He used to be a technician, so he didn't worry about the product quality. But he worried about the promotion after production. The precondition was not to have any advertisement, because he had no money for it.

Those who have studied marketing would know that advertisements are needed when launching a new product. Advertisements are like tanks and personal promoters are like soldiers. So, advertisements are the main method in creating the brand. Among the four methods of marketing, apart from advertisements, there are personal marketing, publicity and improvement on marketing. Publicity is a money-burning method just like advertisement.

Therefore, Wang Yong could only choose one method between improvement on marketing and personal marketing.

Wang Yong had decided to use the free hand-outs to open the market because he was confident with product and the customers' choice. For me, this was acceptable because there was no other option. Then, let's discuss where and how to deliver the free hand-outs.

Where should they deliver the free hand-outs? Of course, they should choose the place where their target groups gather. There are two kinds of people whom you could make money from easily-the ones who are afraid of death and the ones who are smug. Therefore, the product manager should present at the places where OLs usually show up. For example, they could deliver the free hand-outs in the office building (off work), super mall (on holidays or festivals) and the best location is the main road next to the building. Thus, the results would be better. They would get thrown out by securities if they hand them out at the gate of malls and office buildings.

How to deliver the free hand-outs? Here are the suggestions. Choose the target first, for example, fashionable ladies who dress themselves well. After handing out the cosmetics to them, explain the reason for the free hand-outs first. Then, ask them if they could leave their contact information. The phone numbers are the best way of contacts, and the product manager should dial the number immediately to check the validity of the number.

Thus, after handing out some practical products, it would be the time to initiate follow-up service, through which you could know the real efficay of your product. Of course, renting a counter in the mall is necessary.

Ⅱ. Which distribution and promotion method to choose?

Chen Qiang was a chief agent in Guangdong of a famous ion bottle brand in the country. This bottle he was selling was amazing-when you pull in some regular drinking water in the bottle, the acid water would change into alkaline water, which could be tested by a PH testing bar on spot. Meanwhile, this bottle was beautifully shaped and looked classical. However, the retail price was a little too high. The cheapest one, a personal set, would cost 499 RMB. The "silver bottle" and "golden bottle" for gifting purpose would cost 1,688 RMB and 2,688 RMB separately.

Chen Qiang dealt this product with 30% of the price. Now that we have known that the manufacturer had already put in a large amount of advertisement on CCTV. Which distribution and promotion method would you choose if you were Chen Qiang? Please express your opinion.

Answer

Ion water was no longer a new thing and people have accepted the idea that the physiques of most common people are slight acid. So, for Chen Qiang, who was selling the ion bottle, it wouldn't take him much effort to explain the effect of ion water.

Besides, there is a powerful sales tool for Chen Qiang's bottle-demonstration on the spot, which could be very convincing. Ordinary tap water is slightly acid, but when the PH testing bar tested water was poured into the bottle, it became alkaline after a while. Such experiment which could be witnessed was more convincing than most logical theories.

So, the current situation was that such bottles weren't cheap, which ordinary consumers wouldn't spend money on. Thus, the choosing of the channel seemed very important. Where to sell it to make it most popular? Could we use direct distribution?

In my opinion, regular supermarkets weren't the first choice. They should consider big shopping malls like Jizhidao, Carrefour and Wall-Mart and rent a room in those stores as a specialty store. Besides, they should consider opening franchise stores in cultural centers like book centers. And they should have their advertising film broadcasted inside the stores. The name of the specialty stores should be × × Customer Experience Center because experience marketing is very popular now.

Chapter V   Listing and Monetizing
Ⅰ. Why wasn't Huawei listed?

Huawei Technology Limited Company is a private technology company with its employees as shareholders which manufactures telecommunication equipments. It was founded in 1988 and headquartered in Longgang district of Shenzhen, Guangdong. Huawei's mainly produced exchange, transfer, wireless and data telecommunication products. They provide Internet applications, services and resolutions to clients all over the world in the telecommunication field. Huaweiwei has set up research institutes in America, India, Sweden, Russia and China' Beijing, Shanghai and Nanjing with more than 80,000 employees, 43% of them are doing research. By the time of June 2008, Huawei had applied for over 29666 patents, being the company with the most patents for many years. . HuaweiHuawei has set up over 100 branches across the globe. Its sales and internet service network covers the world. Now, Huawei's products and resolutions are applied in over 100 countries across the world and in 36 top 50 operators.

In 2008, the company kept growing steadily and healthily. The global sales volume reached 23.3 billion USD and grew 46% over the previous years. The income from the global market took up 75% of it. According to reports from abroad, with such incomes, Huawei could surpass Beidian and become the fifth largest telecommunication equipment seller in 2008.

Seeing such glorious development history, many people couldn't help wondering, "Why didn't such good a company go for listing in all these years?"

Answer

Previously, I have analyzed that there are both advantages and disadvantages in listing. The advantage is that it could solve the capital problem and keep the talents. And if the company is properly managed, it would obtain high reputation. However, after getting listed, it would be dangerous for a company because it will lose all privacy. People would be very clear about the profits by checking the annual reports. This is a disadvantage to the business of the company. In addition, the freedom of the managers is limited and all the major decisions have to go through the board or even all the shareholders by votings. Plus, once a company is listed, it would become a public company and everybody has the right to purchase its shares. As to the reasons why Huawei didn't go for listing, according to Hu Yong, there were three considerations:

First, Ren Zhengfei kept on his wolf spirit to continue his control over Huawei. As the founder of Huawei, Ren Zhengfei had started this business with his bare hands. In the beginning of this business, he had initial capital of 24,000 RMB. To attract and keep talents, he had to apply the management model from Western countries in which core employees held shares of companies which they were working for. Thus, with the development of the company, Ren Zhengfei's shares were diluted. One day in 2007, when Duan Yongji, the headman of Zhongguancun asked about the shares of his, Ren Zhengfei said, "Less than 2%." Duan Yongji was shocked, and he asked urgently, "Aren't you afraid of being laid off?" From here, we could see that Huawei was never going to get listed. If it did, Ren Zhengfei wouldn't be able to control Huawei anymore. In addition, Huawei needed to carry on the wolf spirit-to fight tenaciously under harsh conditions. If Huawei was listed, the Huawei Group would give birth to tens of thousands of billionaires, including the front desk attendants. But, people in Huawei wouldn't be so full of the fighting spirit.

Secondly, the business model of Huawei was not suitable for listing. Huawei was a technology enterprise, which had to spend a large sum of money on research and development of new products. After the new products go in the market, they could make a lot of money. After they retrieve the expenses on research, they put them into further research on new products. But during this time, the followers would swarm in, and the price began to drop. The life circle of the products developed directly from the introduction period to the recession period. The next was a new round of new product research. This was a benign circle, which was also used by most Western listed high technology companies.

This model could be exemplified by the story of Pike's research on ball pens. In those years, Pike Company had researched ball pens that were both convenient and stain-free, which immediately become popular among people. Therefore, Pike Company could sell each ball pen at 5 USD even if it costed only 1 dollar. Later, the Cook Company in the same business saw that Pike counted the money until their hands cramped, so Cook worked overnight on the research of ball pens. When Cook's ball pen entered the market, these two companies began their battle on the price. Cook Company set its price at 4.5 USD per pen, forcing Pike to readjust the price to 4 USD per pen. Cook kept reducing the price to 3.5 USD per pen. Pike followed it and dropped the price to 3.2 USD per pen. The price battle ceased. However, the profits in ball pens had caught attention from other manufacturers, and many of them began to produce ball pens as well. Ever since then, the price of ball pens dropped dramatically to 0.8 dollar per pen, lower than its cost. With no other choices, Pike decided to give up and began to explore new markets.

The model of Pike selling ball pens was not taken by Huawei because Huawei had been famous for its low price. If Huawei were Pike, Ren Zhengfei would have set the price for the ball pen at 0.8 dollar when the new product was first introduced to the market. Even though there was no profit, it cracked down the other company's interest in the market. Gradually the whole market would have been taken by Pike. By then, without any competitor, Pike could gradually increase the price and set the price at 2 USD. By that time, the whole market would have adapted to Pike. It would not be easy for other companies to enter the market. And the ball pens of Pike would have been popular across the globe.

Before entering the market in Brazil, Huawei took such a model, ending in 8-year deficits in its Brazil market. But in the ninth year, Huawei made 100 million profits in a year, which was bigger than the deficit figure in the last year. The second hand of Lenovo Yang Yuanqing had asked Ren Zhengfei for help before he got on his term and said that Lenovo wanted to make researches as well. However, Ren Zhengfei asked, "We have had eight-year experiences of deficits in Brazil and India. Does your company dare to do this?" So, this kind of business model wasn't suitable for listing because listed companies have to be responsible for achievement in every season. Any slight movement could trigger huge influence on the share price.

Thirdly, Huawei had a unique model of financing. In the Western world, the purpose of a company getting listed is to expand production and to integrate the industrial chain. However, the disadvantage was obvious-to buy new production lines with the profits earned from the main business of a company could reduce the competitiveness of the company. Huawei made use of the cheap cost of the Chinese researchers and hired lots of them to develop new products. When the market of the new product had become big enough, he would sell it to others. That's the way of Huawei's financing. Then, he would put the financial investment into the research and market of the core product. And he was responsible for his losses and profits so that he could quickly expand its market share, enhance competitiveness, and finally take control of the overall market. Once, Ren Zhengfei had shouted three times, "The winter is coming!" That was referring to separately 2000, 2004 and 2008. Every time, he was selling new technology and he said that the aim was to obtain a new winter coat to get through the winter.

In conclusion, the concept of Huawei's founder, its business model and its financing model have decided that Huawei wouldn't be listed. (By Hu Yong, *Shenzhen News*, 2008-10-08)

Ⅱ. How to achieve seamless joints?

Li Jun is an Internet constructor with over ten years working experiences and is currently a Internet Technology Supervisor in a famous private company. He is tired of the nine-to-five work and decides to start his own business in the hotel reservation industry. He positions his business at the convenient hotels in the regional markets and plans to connect the single hotels into a virtual chain hotel.

What has made Li Jun's head ache was how to tie his website to the reservation business of the hotels so that it will be both money-saving and convenient for the customers when they make reservations.

Answer

The current situation is that the hotels are very happy when a salesman of a reservation company come and talk about cooperation. After all, it's beneficial promotion for both sides. This wasn't like Ctrip in those years. When a salesman from Ctrip appeared in front of a hotel manager, he wouldn't let him finish his talking and ask him to go out.

Almost all hotels had believed the distribution ability of reservation websites, however, chain hotels were neglectful of them. So, with Li Jun's situation, he would have no advantage to talk to grand chain hotels. After all, his company was still a new one.

Then, how should Li Jun position his market? Personally, I think, first, he should look for some unchained hotels and make them into a virtually grand chain hotel with the power of Internet. Before, Ctrip had similar business. On 28th July 2008, an investor of Ctrip, Ctrip International, had announced to invest and build the Xingcheng Hotel Management (ShangHai) Limited Company. They would charge a certain amount of fee for "brand maintenance" to form an alliance connecting the unchained and low star level hotels in first and second tier cities, helping them to stabilize their feet in the market of economical chain hotels and medium and high class hotels.

Liu Jiajun, the Executive Chief Manager of Xingcheng Hotel Management (Shanghai) Limited Company, promised that most of the "brand maintenance fee" would be used in the promotion of the alliance. He explained that one individual hotel could only use 100,000 on promotion, which would probably end in vain, but things would be different if we collect all the advertisement fees together and deploy the money in the name of the hotel alliance.

Besides, after the reservation companies have made reservations, they would fax them to inform the hotels. If so, the coincidence could happen that after a client has made the reservation, he arrives at his destination only to find that his reservation is unsuccessful. So, with the advantage of Li Jun's technician background, he would develop a hotel room reservation management system and give the system for free to the hotels in a work relationship. The hotels would be happy to work with him if he could offer free software, unless they have already bought it.

In addition, with this soft ware, Li Jun's reservation website can be perfectly jointed with hotel reservation management software. Through the Internet, he could know how many rooms are still available, which, of course, has to be approved by the hotels.

Appendix III Development History of Ctrip (milestones)

The development history of Ctrip. com is colorful, which can't be described in details. Now, I'd like to summarize the big events worth mentioning and let's witness every profoundly meaningful historical moment of Ctrip. com

Octorber 1999 Ctrip. com was official oneline

November 2000 Ctrip purchased the room reservation center of Beijing Modern Yuntong

March 2002 The reservation volume of Ctrip ranked top one in the domestic hotel distribution industry

March 2002 Ctrip purchased Beijing Coast Air Service Company Limited Company

May 2002 Ctrip initiated national central air ticket reservation system

October 2002 The monthly sales volume broke 100 million RMB for the first time

October 2003 Ctrip'S air ticket reservation network had covered 35 cities in the country

December 2003 Ctrip was listed in NASDAQ in America and broke the highest increase rate in three years

February 2004 Ctrip agreed to work with Shanghai Cuiming International Travel Agency holiday tour market.

September 2004 Ctrip and China Merchants Bank promoted together the first double note travel credit card in the country

October 2004 Ctrip had first launched 360 degree holiday tour supermarket and the concept of leisure holiday tour

November 2004 Ctrip founded the first online international ticket reservation platform

November 2004 Ctrip announced to issued dividends, becoming the first Chinese Internet stock to issue dividends

December 2004 Ctrip spent 20 milllion USD to build a modernized online tourist technology service center

January 2005 Ctrip spent one million RMB to set up the natural disaster travel experience insurance

September 2005 The registered members of Ctrip. com surpassed 10 million

March 2006 Ctrip entered market of the business trip management

June 2006 Ctrip set up the Ctrip Sunshine Scholarship in 14 universities in the country

December 2006 Ctrip expanded its starting point of tours to eleven cities

March 2007 Ctrip launched the online business trip management system

May 2007 Ctrip introduced the first business travel elite credit card in the country-Zhonghang Ctrip Card

June 2007 The Ctrip Internet Technology building was officially constructed and put in use

June 2007 Ctrip held the Service 2. 0 Forum

September 2007 Ctrip University was founded

November 2007 The monthly air ticket sales volume surpassed one million

January 2008 Ctrip. com and Travel TV held the Ctrip Global Tour DIY

March 2008 The English version of Ctrip. com was officially online

May 2008 The Ctrip holiday experience centers landed in all major airports

July 2008 Premier Wen Jiabao visited the Shanghai headquarter of Ctrip

July 2008 The Business Travel Intellectual Report was released

Bibliography

I. Biography

1. Li Ruigang. List of heroes of Fortune Life. Shanghai: Shanghai Education Press, 2006

2. Zhu Yingshi, Ma Lei. The Number One Team-Ctrip and Home Inn. Beijing: Zhongxin Press, 2008

3. Yuan Hongsheng, Wang Yu. The Blue Capitalist Shen Nanpeng. Beijing: China Development Press, 2007

4. Fan Jing. A Desperate Hero. Beijing: China Zhigong Press, 2003

5. Wu Xiaobo. A big loss. Reversed Edition. Hangzhou: Zhejiang People Press, 2007

6. Fuye. China Dream: Biography of Tangjun. Nanjing: Jiangsu People Press, 2008

II. Team management

7. Zhang Yiwu. How to Build An Efficient Team. Beijing: Beijing University Press, 2003

8. Fu Zheming. High efficiency Team Organization. Guangzhou: Guangdong Economics Press, 2002

III. Text books

9. Robins Ricky. Trans. Li Yuan, Sun Jianmin. Organizational Behavior. 12th ed.

Beijing: China People University Press, 2008

10. Hill, C. W. L, McShane, S. L. , Li Weian, Zhou Jian. Management. Beijing: Mechanics Industry Press, 2009

11. By McShane, Grillno. Trans. Tang Chaoyin. McShane Organizational Behavior. Beijing: China People University Press, 2008

12. Zhang Yuli. Entrepreneurial Management. Beijing: Mechanics Industry Press, 2008

13. Wan Houfen. Marketing. 2nd ed. Beijing: High Education Press, 2007

14. Yu Wenzhao. A Introductive Theory to Learning Organization. Dalian: Northeastern Finance and Economics University Press, 2008

15. Wu Shengyi. Textbook of Enterprise Culture. Shanhai: Shanghai Finance and Economics University Press, 2008

16. Peng Jianfeng. Introduction to Human Resource Management. Shanghai: Fudan University Press, 2003

17. Chen Chunhua. Organizational Behavior. Beijing: Mechanics Industry Press, 2009

18. Zhou Chunsheng. Financing, Purchase and Company Control. 2nd ed. Beijing: Beijing University Press, 2007

19. Li Ye. Theory of Marketing. Guangzhou: Guangdong High Education Press, 2003

20. Xia Qinghua. Entrepreneurial Management. Wuhan: Wuhan University Press, 2007

Ⅳ. Marketing

21. Fu Yu. Internal Reference of Marketing. Shenzhen: Haitian Press, 2003.

This book is the result of a co-publication agreement between Guangdong Economy Publishing House (China) and Paths International Ltd.

From Start-up to Success: The Xiecheng Management Story
Author: Xiecheng Management Team
ISBN: 978-1-84464-107-9
Ebook ISBN: 978-1-84464-123-9

Paths International Ltd

www.pathsinternational.com

Published in the United Kingdom

CPSIA information can be obtained
at www.ICGtesting.com
Printed in the USA